Walking
Literary London

Walking Literary London

ROGER TAGHOLM

25 ORIGINAL WALKS THROUGH
LONDON'S LITERARY HERITAGE

NEW
HOLLAND

Dedication

For Rosie Katherine Tagholm, born 24 September, 1997

First published in 2001 by
New Holland Publishers (UK) Ltd
London • Cape Town • Sydney • Auckland

86 Edgware Road
London W2 2EA
United Kingdom

80 McKenzie Street
Cape Town 8001
South Africa

14 Aquatic Drive
Frenchs Forest, NSW 2086
Australia

218 Lake Road
Northcote, Auckland
New Zealand

ISBN 1 85974 555 5

Commissioning Editor: Jo Hemmings
Project Editor: Michaella Standen
Copy Editor: Elizabeth Tatham
Cartography: Hardlines
Indexer: Janet Dudley
Production Controller: Joan Woodroffe

Reproduction by Pica Colour Separation Overseas (Pte) Ltd, Singapore
Printed and bound in Singapore by Kyodo Printing Co (Singapore) Pte Ltd

Photographic Acknowledgements
David Paterson: Plates 1, 2, 3, 4, 6, 12, 15, 16, 17, 20, 21, 23, 24, 25, 28, 29, 30, 31, 32, 33;
Life File Photo Library/Andrew Ward: Plate 14; Richard Tames: Plate 18

Front cover: Statue of Peter Pan in Kensington Gardens (David Paterson).
Back cover: No. 29 Fitzroy Square (David Paterson).
Spine: Shakespeare's Globe Theatre (David Paterson).

Contents

Introduction

This book differs from other London walking guides in one important respect. In *Walking Literary London*, it is the sites that dictate the routes, not the other way round. In a book of general walks, a conventionally pretty, scenic route is relatively easy to construct. With a literary guide book – even in a city as rich in literary history as London – it is often not possible to work out a route that is both literary and pretty. Try to bear this in mind when the roar of the traffic gets you down.

That said, there are still plenty of walks in the pages that follow that do take you away from the cars and taxis, even though you are still in the centre of town. The profusion of parks and green spaces is one of the best aspects of the city.

Inevitably, given London's age and the damage wrought by the Blitz, some of the walks are more walks of the imagination than others. But for the very reason that so much literature stems from the imagination, this may be no bad thing. Finally, when the addresses of modern writers are mentioned, they were correct during 1999 when the book was written.

How to Select a Walk

Here are a few general pointers that may help you to decide. If Dickens is your man, you need to concentrate on the Bloomsbury, Wapping to Westferry, Holborn to Chancery Lane, and Southwark walks. He crops up elsewhere, of course, but all these walks take in good Dickens sites.

If you want fresh air, but don't want to leave town, the Kensington and Regent's Park walks are a good bet. If you don't mind making a short journey out, go to Hampstead, where one of the walks crosses the heath. But if you want a real blast of fresh air – and the chance to combine it with a pleasant day trip – then you should choose the Putney to Wimbledon or the Richmond walks. If the river appeals, the Greenwich walk can be combined with a return trip by river instead of by train, while the Wapping to Westferry and the Richmond walks each hug the river along contrasting stretches.

For contemporary, 'happening' London, choose the Soho walk, while for quiet, almost eerie atmosphere and stunning architecture (old and new), choose either of the City walks on a Sunday.

The Putney to Wimbledon, the Richmond, and the Blackheath to Greenwich walks are all good hikes. The others are all of medium length, apart from the Covent Garden walk which can be squeezed into a longish lunch-hour.

A Note on Blue Plaques

The blue plaques that are located on buildings associated with famous people are a familiar feature of London. The Royal Society of Arts erected the first of these at Byron's birthplace (since demolished) in Holles Street near Oxford Circus in 1867. The London County Council took over the scheme in 1901, followed by the

Greater London Council (GLC) in 1965. The GLC was abolished in 1985 by the then Prime Minister, Margaret Thatcher, and since then the scheme has been run by English Heritage. There are now over 700 plaques in existence and in 1998 English Heritage decided to launch the scheme nationally with a pilot project in Merseyside.

To warrant a plaque, a famous person has to meet one of four requirements:

There shall be reasonable grounds for believing that the subjects are regarded as eminent by a majority of members of their own profession or calling. They shall have made some important positive contribution to human welfare or happiness. They shall have had such exceptional and outstanding personalities that the well-informed passer-by immediately recognises their names. They deserve recognition.

In all cases, however, proposals will not be considered unless the subject has been dead for 20 years, or until the centenary of their birth, whichever is the earlier. It is also extremely rare for a plaque to commemorate a fictional character or location, but you will find just such an example in the first Bloomsbury walk. The wording on the plaques is decided by the commemorative plaques panel of English Heritage.

Personal Favourites
Some of the areas that I thought I might least enjoy I have actually found the most interesting. The City walks are a good example. Old Street is a godforsaken place, but well worth the trip to see the pieces of ribbon people still drape over William Blake's gravestone in Bunhill Fields Burial Ground close by on City Road. Southwark may have few blue plaques but it is rich in Dickensian atmosphere. The tiny village of Primrose Hill is a delight, Wapping Underground Station is a wonder (yes, really), Wimbledon Common is invigorating countryside and Lamb's Conduit Street is an example to the rest of London, with its restricted access for cars and its pavement cafés. I could go on. Writing this book has opened the city up to me and made me like it even more than I already did.

One last thought: perhaps it's because I have young children myself, that the story of J. M. Barrie moved me so much. A little bit of me will always be in Kensington Gardens with Peter Pan.

What do we Mean by 'Literary'?

It's a good question. Everyone is familiar with the word and thinks they know a literary writer when they read one. But they would be hard-pressed to define it. The New Oxford Dictionary of English defines 'literary' as 'concerning the writing, study, or content of literature, especially of the kind valued for quality of form…'. 'Literary' language is that 'associated with literary works or other formal writing; having a marked style intended to create a particular emotional effect'.

Few would call Jeffrey Archer a literary writer – and yet his books are widely reviewed in those pages of the newspapers concerned with the 'content of literature' and his books are certainly written in a style 'intended to create a particular emotional effect'. So yes, you will find references to him in the pages that follow – and apologies if that offends anyone (sales of his books do help subsidise publishing books of more literary merit).

It is often the mass market popular authors whom one hesitates to dub 'literary' – the irony being, that in his day that is exactly what Charles Dickens was. He was a mass market popular author whose work was sometimes published in monthly installments waited for by an eager public. Dickens can be seen as performing the same function as today's distinctly non-literary TV soap operas. It is curious to think that in the 19th century few would have thought of his books as something to be studied. Equally, the 'groundlings' who paid a penny to see Shakespeare's plays at the original Globe – the replica of which is on one of the walks in this book - would be puzzled by the bard's rise to academe.

Literary London has existed for hundreds of years. Writers, publishers and book-sellers live and work in the city. The capital is the centre of the UK publishing industry. It has a concentration of superb bookshops staffed by people who love books and who debate their relative merits. London is a highly literate city. The London Review of Books regularly advertises on the Underground (and you'll find literary mentions of Tube stations in this book) and books themselves have increased in importance. 'That woman there looks straight out of Bridget Jones,' someone might say. 'Have you read Harry Potter yet?' people ask. 'Look, there's someone reading *Walking Literary London*.'

Well, hopefully.

Key to Route Maps

Each of the walks in this book is accompanied by a detailed map on which the route of the walk is shown in blue. Places of interest along the walks – such as historic buildings, museums and churches – are clearly identified. Addresses, telephone numbers and opening times for public attractions are given in the Further Information section at the back of the book (see pages 156–160).

The following is a key to symbols and abbreviations used on the maps:

Symbols   *Abbreviations*

route of walk	APP	Approach	PH	Public House
railway line	ARC	Arcade		(Pub)
	AVE	Avenue	PK	Park
major building	BR	Bridge	PL	Place
church	CL	Close	R	River
	CRES	Crescent	RD	Road
public toilets	CT	Court	S	South
park	DR	Drive	ST	Saint
view	E	East	ST	Street
	GDNS	Gardens	TER	Terrace
	HO	House	WK	Walk
	LA	Lane	W	West
	N	North		

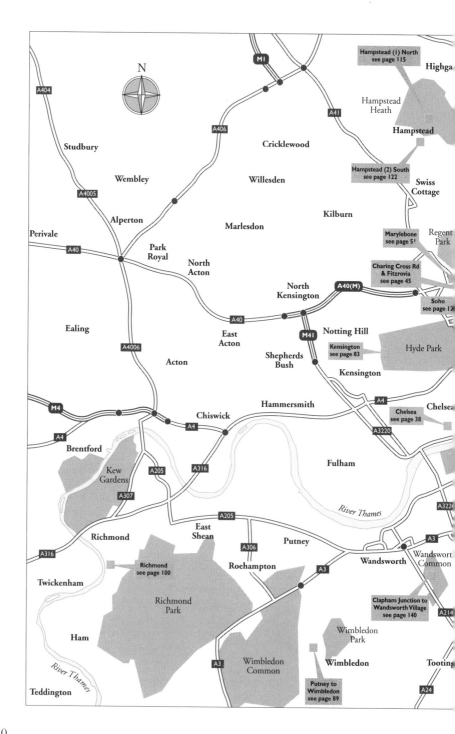

N

Hampstead (1) North
see page 115

Highga

A404

Hampstead
Heath

M1

A41

Hampstead

A406

Studbury

Cricklewood

Wembley

Willesden

Hampstead (2) South
see page 122

Swiss
Cottage

A4005

Kilburn

Alperton

Marlesdon

Perivale

A40

Park
Royal

North
Acton

Marylebone
see page 51

Regent
Park

Charing Cross Rd
& Fitzrovia
see page 45

Ealing

North
Kensington

A40(M)

Soho
see page 12

A40

A4006

East
Acton

M41

Notting Hill

Acton

Shepherds
Bush

Kensington
see page 83

Hyde Park

Kensington

M4

Hammersmith

A4

Chiswick

A4

A4

Chelsea
see page 38

Chelsea

A3220

Brentford

Kew
Gardens

A205

A316

Fulham

A307

River Thames

A322

A205

Richmond

East
Shean

A306

Putney

A3

Wandsworth

Wandsworth
Common

A316

Richmond
see page 100

Roehampton

A3

Twickenham

Clapham Junction to
Wandsworth Village
see page 140

A214

Ham

Richmond
Park

Wimbledon
Park

A3

Wimbledon
Common

Wimbledon

Tooting

River Thames

Putney to
Wimbledon
see page 89

A24

Teddington

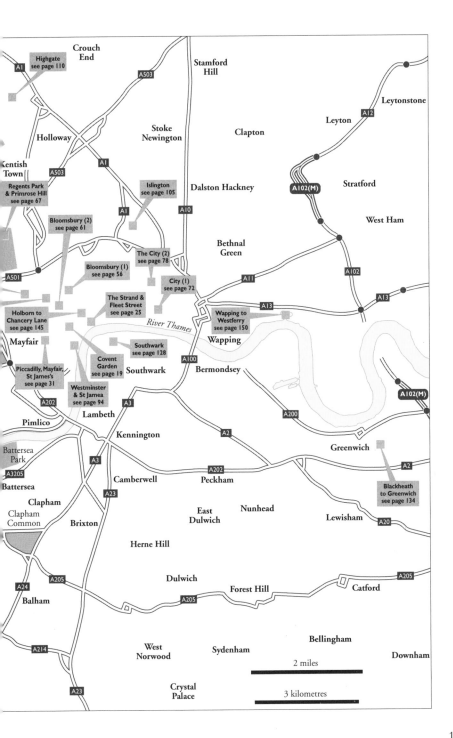

Highgate
see page 110
A1

Crouch
End

Stamford
Hill
A503

Leytonstone

Leyton
A12

Stoke
Newington

Clapton

Holloway

Kentish
Town
A503

A1

Regents Park
& Primrose Hill
see page 67

Islington
see page 105

Dalston Hackney

A102(M)

Stratford

West Ham

Bloomsbury (2)
see page 61

A1

A10

Bethnal
Green

A501

Bloomsbury (1)
see page 56

The City (2)
see page 78

A102

City (1)
see page 72

A11

The Strand &
Fleet Street
see page 25

A13

Holborn to
Chancery Lane
see page 145

Wapping to
Westferry
see page 150

A13

Mayfair

River Thames

Wapping

Piccadilly, Mayfair,
St James's
see page 31

Southwark
see page 128

Covent
Garden
see page 19

Southwark

A100

Bermondsey

A102(M)

Westminster
& St James
see page 94

A202

A3

Lambeth

Pimlico

Kennington

A200

A2

Greenwich

Battersea
Park

A3

A3205

A202

A2

Battersea

Camberwell

Peckham

Blackheath
to Greenwich
see page 134

Clapham

A23

East
Dulwich

Nunhead

Lewisham

A20

Clapham
Common

Brixton

Herne Hill

Dulwich

A205

A24

A205

Forest Hill

Catford

A205

Balham

Bellingham

A214

West
Norwood

Sydenham

Downham

2 miles

A23

Crystal
Palace

3 kilometres

Soho

Summary: This roughly circular walk takes you through one of London's most vibrant districts, passing many of the bars, restaurants and clubs that have fuelled writers in the past and in which today books are frequently launched and discussed. Soho, which takes its name from 'an Anglo-French hunting call, probably of purely exclamatory origin', according to the *Oxford English Dictionary*, has been saved from re-development by the admirable work of the Soho Society. The area is now one of the best preserved in the capital with a low skyline generally little altered since the last century. This walk passes Oscar Wilde's favourite restaurant, the pub in which Dylan Thomas allegedly lost the manuscript to *Under Milk Wood,* and the publishing and media club that takes its name from the most famous member of the Marx Brothers.

Start and Finish:	Tottenham Court Road Underground Station (Central and Northern Lines).
Length:	2.4 kilometres (1½ miles).
Time:	1.5–2 hours.
Refreshments:	The Coach and Horses on Greek Street and The French House on Dean Street are recommended pub stops. The Dog and Duck on Bateman Street has an elegant tiled interior. The Carlisle Snack Bar at 95 Dean Street is very cheap and gives a real taste of Soho in the Fifties. Bar Italia on Greek Street is *the* place to drink cappuccino.

Take Exit 1 (Oxford Street south) from Tottenham Court Road Station and turn right at the top of the stairs. Turn right into Charing Cross Road and take the second right into Sutton Row. This short street leads to Soho Square, which is your first literary site – and one that, appropriately enough for the area, concerns a prostitute and a drug addict. Laid out in the 1680s, this elegant square is where Thomas De Quincey (1785–1859), author of *Confessions of an English Opium Eater,* rested on the steps of a house with his 'noble-minded Ann', a 15-year-old prostitute of whom he had become fond. Poverty stricken and on the point of starvation, De Quincey fainted and Ann ran to Oxford Street for 'port wine and spices'. Perhaps as a result of her actions, De Quincey believed that prostitutes, or 'female peripatetics', as he called them, exhibited the following qualities: 'humanity, disinterested generosity, courage that would not falter in defence of the helpless, and fidelity that would have scorned to take bribes for betraying.'

Turn left on entering the square. On your left is St Patrick's Church (built in 1891), which stands on the site of the assembly rooms run by a failed actress called Theresa Cornelys in the 1760s. It was eventually closed down for being a 'disorderly house'. Laurence Sterne (1713–1768) author of *Tristram Shandy,* and the novelist and diarist Fanny Burney (1752–1840), who was championed by Dr Johnson, were among those to visit the lavish masques and 'entertainments' held here. While there is no evidence that she was running a brothel, Cornelys was eventually prosecuted for allowing 'divers loose, idle, and disorderly persons, as well men as women, to be, and remain, during the whole night, rioting and otherwise misbehaving themselves' – in other words, just the sort of behaviour that has made Soho famous the world over.

Turn left into Greek Street, passing the House of St Barnabas on your left. This was built in 1846 for London's destitute and homeless and is now a hostel for women. It is believed to be the house that Charles Dickens (1812–1870) had in mind for Dr Manette in *A Tale of Two Cities*, hence Manette Street, which you meet shortly after passing the Gay Hussar, a Hungarian restaurant much loved by former Labour leader (and H. G. Wells biographer) Michael Foot and publisher André Deutsch (1917–2000).

Booker Prize Parties

Continuing along Greek Street, you come to The Pillars of Hercules pub on the left, which is almost certainly the Hercules Pillars featured in *A Tale of Two Cities*. The poet and opium addict Francis Thompson (1859–1907), author of *Hound of Heaven*, was a customer here. The unnamed building at No. 50, on your right, houses the Union Club, often used by the publishers Jonathan Cape for their 'win or lose' parties after the Booker Prize. On 27 October 1998, during one such party, a huge cheer from the upstairs room could be heard from the street. Ian McEwan, winner of that year's Booker with *Amsterdam*, had just arrived. Meanwhile, downstairs, his friend Julian Barnes, who had failed to win that year with *England, England*, was having a quiet drink with Michael Ondaatje, author of *The English Patient*. Further down, on your right, is L'Escargot, revamped in 1980 and one of many favoured Soho haunts of those publishing folk able to afford it. Note the snail in the tiles on the steps.

The Italian adventurer Casanova (1725–1798) stayed in Greek Street (his ghost is said to reside in Raymond's Revue Bar, which you pass later in the walk) and Dr Johnson (1649–1703) started one of Soho's first literary clubs, which met every Monday at 7pm, at the Turk's Head (now demolished). The Irish statesman and philosopher Edmund Burke (1729–1797) and the playwright, novelist and poet Oliver Goldsmith (1728–1774) were among the original members. Cross over Old Compton Street and note the delightful frontage of the French patisserie Maison Bertaux on your left. 'Creating daily on the premises' is the boast here – a statement which doubtless amuses Soho's media folk.

Jeffrey Bernard's Local

A little further down Greek Street is The Coach and Horses, one of numerous superb, unspoilt, wood-lined pubs on this walk. It has now become something of a shrine to the writer and drinker Jeffrey Bernard (1932–1997), whose *Spectator* columns, many of them written at the bar here, were famously described by Jonathan Meades as 'a suicide note in weekly instalments'. Keith Waterhouse made him the subject of a West

End play called *Jeffrey Bernard is Unwell* (those words used to appear when his column didn't) and cartoons about him line the wall, many of them from *Private Eye*, which has its fortnightly lunches upstairs here, hosted by its editor Ian Hislop.

A little further on, just before Shaftesbury Avenue, there was a bookshop in the Fifties owned by David Archer, the man whose Parton Press published *18 Poems* by Dylan Thomas (1914–1953) in 1934, when the poet was just 18. It was in this shop too, in 1956, that Soho chronicler Daniel Farson met Colin Wilson, whose study of intellectual alienation, *The Outsider*, had just been published to great acclaim.

Turn right into Romilly Street and pass Kettner's restaurant, founded in 1868. *Kettner's Book of the Table* was once a culinary bible, and Oscar Wilde (1854–1900) described the restaurant as his favourite in London. He dined here in October 1892 with a group that included Lord Alfred Douglas, with whom he was having a relationship and whose father, the Marquis of Queensberry, Wilde attempted to sue for libel in 1895, with disastrous results. Turn right into Frith Street and cross Old Compton Street. One of the capital's most famous cafés is now on your right, easily spotted by its horseshoe-shaped clock. Espresso or cappuccino at the Bar Italia has long been a badge of style in Soho, as you can tell from the self-conscious folk on the pavement (weather permitting). On 27 January 1926, John Logie Baird (1888–1946) gave the first public demonstration of television in a room upstairs. Opposite is Ronnie Scott's world famous jazz club, venue for the launch of Oscar Hijuelos's well-received 1990 novel *The Mambo Kings Play Songs of Love*.

Early this century, long before the days of the Gaggia machine and cappuccino, a small literary group comprising the writer and pacifist John Middleton Murry (1889–1957), the poet-philosopher T. E. Hulme (1883–1917), the translator Sir Edward Marsh (1872–1953) and the sculptor Jacob Epstein (1880–1959) used to meet at a café at No. 67. Mary Russell Mitford (1787–1855), the novelist and dramatist, also completed *Our Life: Sketches of Rural Life* at No. 49 – however unlikely that title might sound in these surroundings today – and the essayist and critic William Hazlitt (1778–1830) died at No. 6. A hotel now commemorates Hazlitt. Beryl Bainbridge's publishers, Duckworth, have offices at No. 61.

Turn left into Bateman Street and left again down Dean Street. Cross over immediately and look back and to your left at the Italian restaurant Quo Vadis. Karl Marx (1818–1883) lived upstairs here from 1851 to 1856 (the plaque has the wrong dates), in a two-roomed flat with his wife, maidservant and three children. It was from here that he walked to the British Museum to work on *Das Kapital*.

A Foul-mouthed Soho Legend

Cross Meard Street and look carefully for a green doorway with three steps at No. 41, on the other side of Dean Street. This is the entrance to the Colony Room, a private club on the first-floor, founded in 1948 by Muriel Belcher, one of Soho's legendary characters, whose use of language seemed to match her surname. Though a refuge more for artists than for writers – Francis Bacon being the most famous – Brendan Behan (1923–1964) and Dylan Thomas occasionally drank here. Or did, until Muriel told them, in no uncertain terms, to take their business to the Caves de France next door (now gone).'They were barred more often than they were allowed

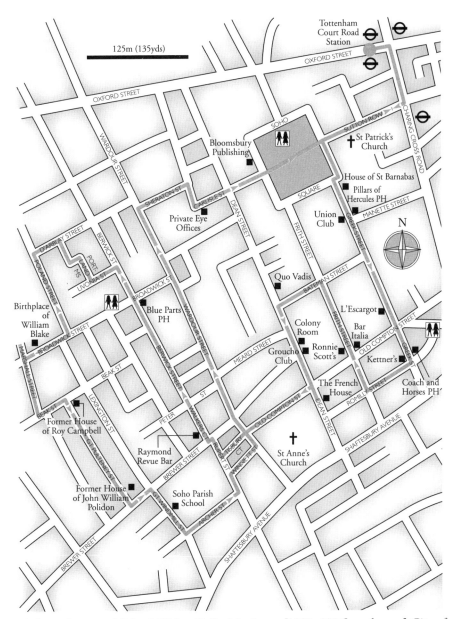

in,' says barman Michael Wojas. Colin MacInnes [1921–1976], author of *City of Spades* and *Absolute Beginners*, and Elizabeth Smart [1913–1986], who wrote *By Grand Central Station I Sat Down and Wept*, also drank here. Kingsley Amis would drop in from time to time too, although in later years he preferred the Garrick. In more recent years the novelist Will Self has been a customer. Daniel Farson, author of *Soho in the Fifties*, was a regular and gave the address at Belcher's funeral in 1979, thanking her for turning life into a 'marvellous party'.

Media London's Watering Hole

The deliberately unnamed building at No. 45 (although if you look carefully you will find a small name plaque) is home to the Groucho Club, founded in 1984 by a number of book folk including publisher Liz Calder (see page 18), then at Cape; Carmen Callil, then at Chatto, and Iris Murdoch's agent, Ed Victor. It takes its name from Groucho Marx (1890–1977), who famously quipped that he'd never join a club that would have him as a member. The Groucho is where media London meets. Countless publishers parties have taken place here and its members include Martin Amis and Salman Rushdie. Oasis singer Liam Gallagher (not the most literary of figures, admittedly) was thrown out in 1996 for smashing a snooker cue, while the novelist David Lodge talks about the 'Groucho stare', which is always over the shoulder of the person one is conversing with to see if someone more important has arrived.

Some Literary Lost Property

At the junction between Dean Street and Old Compton Street, look for The French House, formerly the York Minster, a little further down Dean Street. It usually flies a French flag outside. This is arguably the most famous pub in Soho, whose customers over the years have included the artist and writer Wyndham Lewis (1894–1957), Brendan Behan, Dylan Thomas and Aleister Crowley (1875–1947), as well as more recent names like Auberon Waugh and Anthony Burgess. It was used as a base for the Free French in World War II, and Charles de Gaulle (1890–1970) met with his Resistance colleagues in a room upstairs; and the pub's legendary landlord, the late Gaston Berlemont, apparently rescued Thomas's *Under Milk Wood* manuscript when he left it on a seat. Brendan Behan offended customers by eating his *bouef bourguignon* with both hands, and the painter Augustus John (1878–1961) and the writer and caricaturist Max Beerbohm (1872–1956) drank absinthe together here. It was here too, in February 1960, that the poet Sylvia Plath (1932–1963) signed a contract with Heinemann for the publication of *The Colossus*.

The pub's wooden interior is marvellous, much of it unchanged from its Fifties heyday. Note the little draws marked 'Ten shillings' and 'One pound' behind the bar, remnants of an old cash-system. This pub is also famous for only serving half-pints, a tradition introduced by Berlemont to make it seem more sophisticated and French.

Turn left into Old Compton Street, which is the centre of gay Soho and boasts a constant parade of street life. Pass the famous Algerian Coffee Stores and, if you're feeling tired, breathe in the gorgeous aroma of its myriad blends. At the junction with Wardour Street cross straight over into the narrow Tisbury Court. This is classic Soho, complete with tacky 'Nude Peep Show' sign. Turn right into Rupert Street and you have in front of you probably the most famous view in Soho – Raymond's Revue Bar and the curious bridge in Walkers Court, under which you should now walk. This is the nearest London gets to Amsterdam or the Reeperbahn.

At the end of Walkers Court you can see what Soho might have looked like had not the Soho Society campaigned so hard. They prevented mass demolition and the construction of numerous tower blocks like this one. Go straight on into Berwick Street, home of one of London's famous markets, which dates back to the 18th century. The Blue Posts pub on your right is named after the blue posts that advertised the local sedan chair service outside pubs in the 18th century.

The 'Booker Prize' Street Sign

As you turn left into Livonia Street notice the superb stone street sign that reveals that this was formerly Bentinck Street. The most eccentric member of the Bentinck family, William John Cavendish Bentinck-Scott, 5th Duke of Portland (1800–1879), who built a network of tunnels beneath his home for no apparent reason, was the subject of Mick Jackson's 1997 Booker-shortlisted novel *The Underground Man*. Turn right into Portland Mews which, with a number of stables now converted into offices for film companies, serves as a reminder of London's equestrian past.

Turn left into D'Arblay Street, which is one of the few streets in London named after a female writer. Fanny Burney, the English novelist and diarist whose observations influenced Jane Austen, married the French émigré General D'Arblay and lived at 50 Poland Street, opposite the end of D'Arblay Street. If she were to come back today, she'd be very disappointed: the site on which her house stood is now an enormous car park. Turn left into Poland Street and pass No. 11, where Percy Bysshe Shelley (1792–1822) lodged in 1811 after his expulsion from Oxford. William Blake (1757–1827) lodged at number 28, up towards Oxford Street, but we continue to the end and turn right into Broadwick Street.

Byron's Doctor

Turn right again into Marshall Street and walk a few yards to see the plaque marking Blake's birthplace. Retrace your steps back down Marshall Street, cross Broadwick Street and turn left into Beak Street. On the far corner of Great Poultney Street, where you turn right, is the elegant building in which the poet and Fascist sympathiser Roy Campbell (1902–1957) lived from 1920 to 1922. At No. 37, near the end of Great Poultney Street, is a plaque marking the home of John William Polidori, author of *The Vampyre* (1815). This plaque would not have been here in Daniel Farson's day – a shame, because Farson was distantly related to Bram Stoker, author of *Dracula*, and would have been interested. Polidori was Lord Byron's doctor and accompanied him on the famous Italian holiday during which Mary Shelley, wife of Byron's close friend Percy, wrote *Frankenstein*. Polidori gave his vampire a pale, deathly pallor – rather like that of Byron himself.

Turn left into Brewer Street and right into Great Windmill Street, where you will see one of Soho's most curious sites. Squeezed between two strip clubs is Soho Parish School, a direct descendant of the original St Anne's Church School founded in 1699. The children here receive an education in more than one sense of the word. Turn left into Archer Street, left again into Rupert Street and right into Winnett Street, which brings you out opposite St Anne's Church. Built in the 1670s, it was bombed during the war and only the spire survives. The garden is about

2 metres (6 feet) higher than the road because of the number of bodies buried here, a rather macabre fact that no doubt appealed to former churchwarden Dorothy L. Sayers (1893–1957), whose ashes lie beneath the tower. William Hazlitt also has a commemorative stone at the bottom of the tower.

Leave the churchyard and turn right into Wardour Street, centre of London's film industry. Turn right into Sheraton Street and then right and immediately left into Carlisle Street where, at No. 6, are the offices of *Private Eye*.

A Talking Statue

Cross Dean Street and enter Soho Square; note the offices of Bloomsbury Publishing, founded in 1986, on your left. Their publisher is Liz Calder, who also co-founded the Groucho Club. A former model in Brazil, she published the early work of Salman Rushdie, and at Cape plucked Anita Brookner and Julian Barnes from the slush pile (although *Private Eye* probably doubts whether Brookner can be termed literary – the magazine referred to her most famous novel *Hotel du Lac*, as *Hotel du Lac of Interest*).

Enter the square's gardens but pause at the statue of Charles II to the left of the hut. This should really be a statue of the schoolboy Harry Potter, given the extraordinary success the eponymous hero's publisher, Bloomsbury, have had with J. K. Rowling's Potter novels. But Charles II it is. There is a famous 'morning after' photograph taken here of Jeffrey Bernard with his head in his hands sitting on the statue's plinth. Today, the park-keepers occasionally play a trick on lunch-time strollers. They hide a walkie-talkie behind the little name plaque and then call it up from their fake-Tudor shed. To passers-by it looks as though the statue is talking. Of course many Soho regulars would simply put this down to their having had too much to drink at lunch-time. Assuming that you haven't, now retrace your steps to Tottenham Court Road Station, where the walk ends.

Covent Garden

Summary: This is a circular walk around what is arguably London's most famous tourist district. Covent Garden is certainly one of the most pleasant areas in which to linger, being relatively car-free. The walk passes the site of one of the most famous meetings in literary history and the club that regularly dips its hands into a pot of honey provided by its most famous member. You will also see one of the doorways through which manuscripts from literary hopefuls are regularly delivered.

Start and finish:	Covent Garden Underground Station (Piccadilly Line).
Length:	1.6 kilometres (1 mile).
Time:	1 hour.
Refreshments:	Take your pick from plenty of pubs, cafés and restaurants. The Lamb and Flag pub in Rose Street is a must, however – but mind your head as you enter. The Punch and Judy in the Piazza has a balcony that is a very good place from which to watch the street performers; people occasionally even throw coins from it.

Covent Garden was originally the garden that belonged to Westminster Abbey, or Convent, hence its name. By the 16th century the monks were using the garden as an orchard and probably selling surplus produce, out of which the famous market evolved. The market moved south of the river in 1974, but a successful campaign prevented the demolition of the original buildings. The original shape of the Piazza has not changed a great deal for 300 years – while the proliferation of coffee bars and the like is a modern echo of the area's famous 'coffee houses' of the 17th and 18th centuries.

Begin the walk by turning left out of Covent Garden Station and right into Long Acre, which is named after the long narrow plot of land that lay outside the Convent walls. The tall building in the distance is Freemasons' Hall, on the site of which Samuel Johnson's biographer James Boswell (1740–1795) lived in the 18th century. Turn second right into Bow Street and at the corner of Broad Court on your left is Bow Street Magistrate's Court, formerly a police station, where Oscar Wilde (1854–1900) spent two weeks awaiting trial at the Old Bailey. Most of the time he was groaning and not talking to the other prisoners. In Oliver Twist, the Artful Dodger is also brought here.

In the mid-18th century, before the country had a proper police force, the novelist, barrister and magistrate Henry Fielding (1707–1954) moved into No. 4, on the other side of the road, and established a small group of 'thief-takers', who would eventually become known as the Bow Street Runners. Whilst dispensing justice, Fielding also found time to work on *Tom Jones*, published in 1748. It was a best seller, notching up 10,000 copies in its first year, which is far more than many novels sell today.

London's Oldest Theatre

Continue down Bow Street – so named, incidentally, because of its shape – until you reach Russell Street, undoubtedly one of the most famous literary streets in London. Look to your left and you will see London's oldest theatre, the Theatre Royal Drury Lane; the pillars of its colonnade originally stood in Regent Street. There has been a theatre here since 1663 – Samuel Pepys came to see the very first play – and the present building, the fourth, dates from 1811. All three of its predecessors were destroyed by fire. The third theatre burnt down in 1809 when the Irish dramatist and MP Richard Brinsley Sheridan (1751–1816) had the licence. He heard the news while in the House of Commons, but refused to hurry over, arguing that the public business of the country was more important. Eventually he went to the Great Piazza Coffee House close by – where the market buildings now stand – and ordered a bottle of port, while the flames raged. 'Surely a man may take a glass of wine by his own fireside,' he quipped.

Where the Wits Met

At this point, Bow Street becomes Wellington Street, which is where Charles Dickens (1812–1870) edited *All the Year Round*, the magazine that first serialised Wilkie Collins's *The Moonstone*. The magazine was so popular that crowds would gather, waiting for the next issue. Turn right into Russell Street, in its heyday *the* literary street in London. In the 18th century the phrase 'the chattering classes' did not exist, but this is where they came to exchange views and gossip. There were three famous coffee houses here – Tom's, Button's and Will's. Regulars at Button's at No. 10 included the poet Alexander Pope (1688–1744) and the satirist Jonathan Swift (1667–1745), while at Tom's at No. 17 Fielding and the novelist Tobias Smollett met with the actor and writer David Garrick (1717–1779). Will's at No.1, on the corner with Bow Street and Russell Street, was frequented by Pope, the satirist John Dryden (1631–1700) and the playwright and poet William Congreve (1670– 1729), and was known for a time as the 'Wits' Coffee House'. Samuel Pepys (1633–1703) visited in 1668 and commented on its 'very witty and pleasant discourse'.

Charles and Mary Lamb lived in Russell Street, and there they held regular parties for fellow writers, among them Thomas De Quincey (1785–1859), author of *Confessions of an English Opium Eater*. Charles Lamb (1775–1834) wrote to Dorothy Wordsworth: 'We are in the individual spot I like best in all this great city. The theatres with all their noises. Covent Garden is dearer to me than any Garden of Alcinous, where we are morally sure of the earliest peas and 'sparagus.' Others were less romantic about the produce. In *Humphrey Clinker*, Smollett has his character Matthew Bramble observe that the strawberries available at Covent Garden were a 'pallid, contaminated mash'.

A plaque at No. 8 marks the site of Tom Davies's bookshop where, on 16 May 1763, Davies introduced the Scotsman James Boswell to Samuel Johnson (1649–1703). 'As I knew his mortal antipathy to the Scotch,' wrote Boswell, 'I cried to Davies, "Don't tell where I come from." However, he said, "From Scotland." "Mr Johnson", said I. "Indeed I come from Scotland, but I cannot help it." "Sir," replied he, "that, I find, is what a very great many of your countrymen cannot help".'

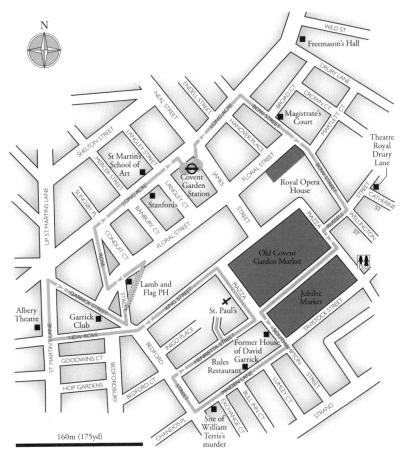

N

Freemason's Hall

WILD ST

DRURY LANE

NEAL STREET

ENDELL STREET

LONG ACRE

HANOVER PLACE

BOW STREET

BROAD CT

CROWN CT

MARTLETT CT

Magistrate's
Court

Theatre
Royal
Drury
Lane

SHELTON STREET

LANGLEY STREET

MERCER STREET

St Martin's
School of
Art

Covent
Garden
Station

JAMES

FLORAL STREET

BOW STREET

Royal Opera
House

CATHERINE
ST

SLINGSBY PL

UP ST MARTINS LANE

LONG ACRE

LANGLEY CT

BANBURY CT

Stanfords

STREET

PIAZZA

RUSSELL ST

WELLINGTON ST

CONDUIT CT

FLORAL STREET

ROSE

Old Covent
Garden Market

Lamb and
Flag PH

STREET

KING STREET

PIAZZA

Jubilee
Market

Albery
Theatre

GARRICK STREET

Garrick
Club

St. Paul's

TAVISTOCK STREET

NEW ROW

ST MARTIN'S LANE

GOODWINS CT

BEDFORD

INIGO PLACE

HENRIETTA STREET

Former House
of David
Garrick

SOUTHAMPTON STREET

BEDFORDBURY

Rules
Restaurant

MAIDEN LANE

LUMLEY CT

STRAND

HOP GARDENS

BEDFORD CT

STREET

BULL INN CT

160m (175yd)

CHANDOS PL

EXCHANGE CT

Site of
William
Terris's
murder

Continue into Covent Garden Piazza, the site of a fruit and vegetable market from 1665 until 1974. Thomas Gray (1716–1771), author of 'Elegy Written in a Country Churchyard', bought flowers for his rooms here, and Dickens would gaze longingly at the pineapples on sale when he had no money. In the 18th century, in addition to the Great Piazza Coffee House frequented by Boswell and Sheridan, there was also the Bedford Coffee House visited by Pope, Collins and Fielding. It described itself as 'the emporium of wit, the seat of criticism and the standard of taste'. With all the talking and showing off to one another, it is a wonder any of these writers got any work done.

Leave the Piazza at the far end via Southampton Street, where Garrick lived at No. 27 (there is an ornate but easily missed plaque) and turn right into Maiden Lane. The poet Andrew Marvell (1621–1678) lived here for a period, as did Voltaire (1694–1778). The Victorian novelist William Thackeray (1811–1863) used to drink at the Cider Cellars, which opened in 1730, while Rules Restaurant on your left is a literary landmark that dates back to 1798. It specialises in English cuisine and numbers Dickens, Thackeray, the novelist and dramatist John Galsworthy

(1867–1933) and H. G. Wells (1866–1946) among its distinguished customers. In 1992, Oxford University Press hosted a party for John Mortimer here, to celebrate the *Oxford Book of Villains*, which he edited.

A little further along on the opposite side, a plaque marks the spot at which the famous Victorian actor William Terriss (1847–1897) was murdered. In the 1950s his ghost was believed to have been sighted at Covent Garden Station. A report sent to London Transport asked: 'Is the statuesque figure wearing white gloves and seen by members of the station staff, the spectre of William Terriss, the actor stabbed to death at the Adelphi Theatre by a maniac…?'

At the end of Maiden Lane, turn right into Bedford Street but look across the road at the large red-brick building on the left, in Chandos Place. This is the site of Warren's Blacking Factory where the 12-year-old Dickens was paid a shilling a day to tie up bottles of blacking and label them. He was there only a few months, but it was a miserable time that haunted him for the rest of his life.

A Street of Publishers

Continue a short way up Bedford Street, passing the Crime in Store bookshop, of which crime writer Minette Walters was one of the co-founders. Turn right into Henrietta Street, home to Dickens's original publishers Chapman & Hall. Victor Gollancz publishers began life at No. 14 in 1927, its list eventually going on to include Dorothy L. Sayers (1893–1957), Daphne du Maurier (1907–1989), Elizabeth Bowen (1899–1973) and Kingsley Amis (1922–1995). Born into an Orthodox Jewish family, the eponymous Gollancz (1893–1967) founded the Left Book Club in the Thirties to protest at the rise of fascism in Europe. A principled man of passionate Socialist beliefs, he would nevertheless walk from these offices to grand establishments like the Waldorf on the Aldwych, or the Savoy Grill on the Strand, for his daily lunch. This was the subject of much publishing gossip, something that hurt him greatly. He pointed out in his defence that his meals consisted of 'a plate of cold beef and mustard pickles eaten in 20 minutes'. His daughter Livia ran the company until its sale to the US publisher Houghton Mifflin in 1989, who in turn sold to Cassell in 1992; Cassell was later bought by the Orion group. The history of Gollancz was repeated over and over by London publishers during the Eighties, as long-established independent houses either merged or were taken over by much larger, often American, companies.

Offely's steak-house, at No. 23, was a favourite resort of Dickens because he always found there 'a fine collection of old boys', while at No. 10 Jane Austen (1775–1817) stayed with her brother from 1813 to 1814, in rooms above the bank of which he was a partner. Look for a gate halfway along on the left, which leads into the courtyard of St Paul's Church (1633, rebuilt 1795), one of London's most delightful hidden gardens. Known as 'the actor's church', it contains numerous plaques commemorating legends of stage and screen, including Sir Noel Coward (1899–1973) and one William Henry Pratt, better known as Boris Karloff (1887–1969). Tom Davies, in whose bookshop Boswell met Johnson, is also buried here.

Retrace your steps to Henrietta Street, turn left, and at the end of the street, where it meets the Piazza, turn left again and continue for a few yards to stand underneath the protruding roof of St Paul's Church. You are now in the spot where Professor Higgins meets Eliza Doolittle in George Bernard Shaw's *Pygmalion*. More likely, you're actually in the middle of some street performer's comedy routine!

From Coffee Houses to Gentlemen's Clubs

Continue past the church and turn left into King Street, where the Garrick Club was founded at No. 35 in 1831, later moving to its more famous home around the corner. The Finish, another club, was also here. Lord Byron (1788–1824) was once seen there and was described thus: 'the rich of the Tuscan grape had diffused an unusual glow over his features, and inspired him with a playful animation.' The Savage Club – which still exists, although elsewhere – was founded at No. 43 in 1857. Named after the poet Richard Savage (1697–1743), its members have included George and Weedon Grossmith (1847–1912; 1852–1919), who together wrote *Diary of a Nobody*, Edgar Wallace (1875–1932), Somerset Maugham (1874–1965) and Dylan Thomas (1914–1953).

Turn right down the pedestrianized New Row, where Johnson dined at the Pineapple. The Albery Theatre is directly opposite the junction with St Martin's Lane. Celebrated runs here include T. S. Eliot's *The Cocktail Party* in 1950 and Dylan Thomas's *Under Milk Wood* in 1956. It was to this theatre that Ted Hughes (1930–1998) came with his publisher Matthew Evans of Faber just a week or so before his death from cancer on 27 October, 1998. They saw Diana Rigg in Hughes's own adaptation of *Phèdre* by Racine. Turn right, noticing the doorway of No. 79, next to a restaurant. This leads to the offices of literary agents A. M. Heath, whose clients include the Booker Prize winner Anita Brookner.

The Garrick's Pot of Honey

At the lights, turn right into Garrick Street and cross over to get a good view of one of the grandest, most imposing, but dirtiest buildings in London. This is the Garrick Club, whose members are easily spotted by their salmon and cucumber ties. One of the most famous clubs amongst literary and publishing folk, it was founded so that 'actors and men of education and refinement might meet on equal terms'. Dickens was a member, as was P. G. Wodehouse (1881–1975), who referred to it as 'The Pesthole'. Another well-known member was A. A. Milne (1882–1956), from whose estate the club annually receives around £2m under the terms of his will. The bar is on the first floor to the right of the flag-pole.

Turn second left into Rose Street, where Dryden was mugged in 1679. It is easy to imagine how dark this street would have been in the 17th century. Dryden was saved only by the swift action of the landlord of the Lamb and Flag, in front of you. The pub is over 300 years old and used to be known as the Bucket of Blood because of the bare-knuckle fist fights it staged. During the Sixties it hosted poetry readings upstairs and on 7 December 1968 some 150 people crammed in to hear Stevie Smith (1902–1971). The diminutive poet was always surprised to find she had an audience at such events, since she 'wouldn't cross the road to hear poetry'.

Take the superb alley to the right, into Floral Street, where you should turn left, then sharp right, back into Rose Street, which brings you back into Long Acre.

In 1847 St Martin's Hall was built at this end of the street, and it was here that Dickens gave three readings from *A Christmas Carol* in 1859.

Turn right and pass Stanfords, the map and travel book specialists that have occupied this site since 1900. The shop is mentioned in Conan Doyle's *The Hound of the Baskervilles* and regular customers include Eric Newby, Redmond O'Hanlon and Rory MacLean. Stanfords prepared the maps for Amy Johnson's record-breaking flight to Australia and, in more recent years, helped Michael Palin plan his hugely successful *Around the World in Eighty Days* trip. Indeed, the former Monty Python member even sent postcards to the manager en route.

Retrace your steps to Covent Garden Station, this time walking on the left-hand side of the road. High up above St Martin's School of Art you can just make out the words 'Carriage Manufacture', a throwback to London's horse-drawn days. In 1668 Pepys bought a secondhand coach in Covent Garden for £53 and spent from three in the afternoon until eight at night watching it being painted yellow. Was it here, perhaps? With that thought, continue to Covent Garden Station, where the walk ends.

Around the Strand and Fleet Street

Summary: Fleet Street and the Strand connect the West End with the City. This walk incorporates some of the noisiest and some of the quietest parts of the capital and takes you through the belly of one of London's most famous hotels and to one of the smallest National Trust sites in the country. You will also pass a highly unusual book launch venue and follow part of the route taken by one of the most valuable pieces of literary furniture in the capital.

Start: Embankment Underground Station (Northern, Bakerloo, District and Circle Lines).

Finish: Blackfriars Underground Station (District and Circle Lines).

Length: 2.8 kilometres (1¾ miles).

Time: 2 hours.

Refreshments: There are numerous pubs, restaurants and coffee bars along the way. Gordon's Wine Bar in Villiers Street is delightfully dark and unspoilt, while the Punch Tavern on Fleet Street has an admirable collection of Punchiana. There is a pleasant café in the Embankment Gardens.

Turn left on exiting the barriers at Embankment Station and walk straight up Villiers Street, a narrow pedestrianized street running parallel to Charing Cross Station. From 1890 to 1891 Rudyard Kipling (1865–1936) lived at No. 43, the first large block on the right. He wrote: 'The Charing Cross trains rumbled through my dreams on one side, the boom of the Strand on the other, while, before my windows, Father Thames under the Shot Tower [since demolished] walked up and down with his traffic.' Gordon's Wine Bar beneath occupies a hugely atmospheric candlelit cellar and is well worth a visit. G. K. Chesterton (1874–1936) and Hillaire Belloc (1870–1953) were customers here too, and the bar looks as though it hasn't altered much since their day.

Turn right by the side of Gordon's into Watergate Walk and take the steps on the left into Buckingham Street, which should really be renamed Pepys Street, since the diarist Samuel Pepys (1633–1703) lived at both Nos 12 and 14, the latter when he was Secretary of the Admiralty. Continue to the end and turn right into John Adam Street, named after the architect. Walk up a slight rise and at the corner of Robert Street notice the Royal Society of the Arts ahead on your left. It was here that HarperCollins launched its 12-volume *Diary of Samuel Pepys*, complete with atmospheric readings of the great man's descriptions of the Fire of

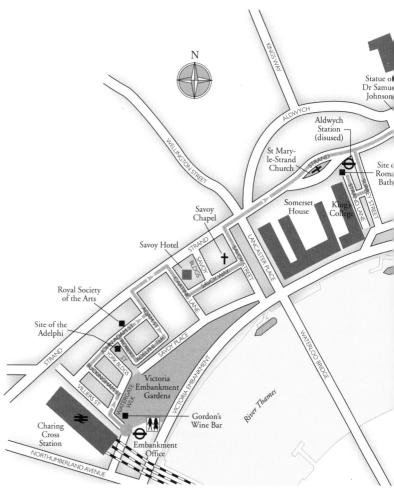

London: 'the poor pigeons I perceive were loath to leave their houses, but hovered about the windows and balconies till they were some of them burned, their wings, and fell down.'

A Curious Roof-top Gathering

Turn right into Robert Street. A plaque on your right notes that Robert Adam (1728–1792), the poet Thomas Hood (1799–1845), the novelist and dramatist John Galsworthy (1867–1933) and the dramatist J. M. Barrie (1860–1937) lived here in the Adelphi – a large, residential block built by Robert Adam and his brothers, whose names are remembered in so many of the streets here. Thomas Hardy (1840–1928) trained as an architect at No. 8 from 1862 to 1867, and used to watch the Embankment being constructed from the office windows. Although the main block was knocked down in 1936, some of its decorative touches have been imi-

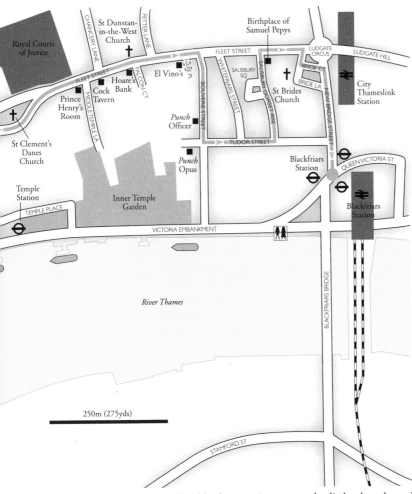

250m (275yds)

tated on the new Adelphi office block opposite – note the little cherubs, a detail that would have appealed to Barrie, creator of *Peter Pan*. Cross over and walk to the end of the street. Look up now at the rooftop flat with the angled window. This is where Barrie lived in his last, sad years, gazing for hours at the seven bridges visible across the Thames. 'Charing Cross Bridge is the ugliest of them all, but I never want to see it pulled down,' he wrote. 'It was across that bridge that the troop trains took our boys to France.' George Llewellyn Davies – one of the so-called 'lost boys' who inspired *Peter Pan* (see pages 45–6) – had been killed in the First World War and Barrie was deeply affected.

In October 1917 George Bernard Shaw (1856–1950), who lived directly across the road and shocked his neighbours with his famous telegraphic address: 'Socialist, London', Hardy, H. G. Wells (1866–1946) and Arnold Bennett (1867–1931), were guests at Barrie's when there was a Zeppelin raid; they all went to the roof to watch.

Fortunately, the Adelphi wasn't hit, but Cleopatra's Needle, just a hundred or so yards away on the Embankment, bears the scars from a similar First World War air-raid.

Around the Savoy

Turn left and walk along Adelphi Terrace, where Samuel Johnson (1649–1703) walked, mourning the death of his friend, the actor and playwright David Garrick (1717–1779), who lived here, then turn left again into Adam Street and continue up to the Strand, where you turn right. The Adelphi Theatre opposite put on lunch-time Shakespeare during the Blitz and the Vaudeville was where Ibsen's *Hedda Gabler* had its premiere in 1897. Walk past the Savoy and turn right into the intriguing passageway called Savoy Buildings. The hotel rises around you now. This passageway is on the site of Fountain Court, where William Blake (1757–1827) took rooms in 1821. Children used to play in the court and Blake once took a friend to the window and pointed to a group of them, saying: 'That is heaven.'

Turn left at the bottom, along Savoy Way, past the Savoy Chapel, where John Donne (1572–1630) secretly married Ann More, with whom he had eloped. Ann was the niece of Lady Egerton, whose son Thomas had employed Donne as his secretary. The chapel dates back to 1505 but was extensively repaired in the 19th century. Turn left into Savoy Street and return to the noise of the Strand, where you turn right, before crossing Lancaster Place. When you see the extraordinary St Mary-le-Strand church, you may be tempted to paraphrase Donne and say, 'No man is a traffic island' – for that is precisely what this church is.

American Visitors

The publisher John Chapman had offices on the Strand at No. 142, where he received many literary figures. The American poet and essayist Ralph Waldo Emerson (1803–1882) visited in 1847 and 1848, and in 1851 Mary Ann Evans, better known as George Eliot (1819–1880), whose works included *The Mill on the Floss*, boarded here. Other American visitors included the nature poet William Cullen Bryant (1794–1878) and the founder of the *New York Tribune* Horace Greeley (1811–1872), who gave us the phrase 'Go West, Young Man!' You, however, should continue east, to the disused Aldwych Station on your right, where Colum McCann's novel *This Side of Brightness* was launched with a torch-lit reading in one of the tunnels in 1998. The station is often used as a location by film companies. Turn right into Surrey Street and halfway down turn right up Surrey Steps, then right again to find the fascinating Roman baths. There is some doubt as to whether these are actually Roman baths, but their literary status is assured: Charles Dickens (1812–1870) knew them as a child and included them in *David Copperfield*. Copperfield talks of 'an old Roman bath...at the bottom of one of the streets out of the Strand – it may still be there – in which I have taken many a cold plunge.'

Return to the Strand, where you turn right. The statue of Samuel Johnson at the front of St Clement Danes (another ecclesiastical traffic island) is famous; easily missed, though, are the figures of his biographer James Boswell (1740–1795) and his friend Mrs Thrale at its base. Continue along Fleet Street until you reach Middle Temple Lane on your right. The small lodge under the gateway was once occupied by the bookseller Benjamin Motte, to whom Jonathan Swift (1667–1745) sold the copyright of *Gulliver's Travels* for £200.

Prince Henry's Room at No. 17 Fleet Street is one of the few houses in the City to survive the Great Fire of London, and has a display of Pepysiana on the first floor. Alfred, Lord Tennyson (1809–1892) was a customer at the Cock Tavern at No. 22, and wrote: 'O plump headwaiter of The Cock/To which I most resort/How goes the time? 'Tis five o'clock/Go fetch a pint of port.' When Tennyson became Poet Laureate, tourists, encouraged by these words, came to see the waiter in question.

Byron's Annoying Hobby

A plaque on the side of Hoare's Bank at No. 37 Fleet Street marks the site of the Mitre Tavern, where Boswell and Johnson used to drink. The words 'Dundee Evening Telegraph' on the side of the building next door to St Dunstan-in-the-West opposite are a reminder of Fleet Street's world-famous newspaper printing past, which ended in the 1980s. The publisher John Murray had offices at No. 33 Fleet Street (there is small plaque on the wall of the tiny Falcon Court), and it was here that Lord Byron (1788–1824) came when Murray published 'Childe Harold', the long poem that caused such a sensation. 'I woke one morning and found myself famous,' Byron wrote later. Murray found some of the visits difficult because Byron, who took fencing lessons, would sometimes use books as his targets, frequently damaging Murray's stock.

Famous Literary Grafitti

El Vino's on the corner of Hare Place was a famous haunt of journalists in Fleet Street's heyday. It was taken to court in 1982 for refusing to serve women at the bar (they could be served only at the tables), and still has a fussy dress code to this day, as a sign on the door testifies. Turn right into Bouverie Street where, at No. 10, *Punch* had its home for most of the 19th century. Among a glittering roll call of writers who have been entertained at the magazine's famous lunches, two giants of humorous writing, both Americans, stand out. Mark Twain (1835–1910) and James Thurber (1894–1961) came to this address in their declining years, both invited by the magazine's editors to become 'members' of the famous *Punch* table – the giant, deal table in the surface of which, since the middle of the 19th century, all the magazine's editors and many of its famous contributors have carved their initials. The table, one of the most important pieces of literary furniture in London, resides in the magazine's current offices opposite Harrods, whose owner Mohamed Al Fayed, bought the magazine in 1996. Among those whose initials can be seen in the table's surface are Anthony Powell (1905–2000), author of *A Dance to the Music of Time*, Keith Waterhouse, who wrote *Billy Liar* and who was one of the El Vino crowd, A. A. Milne (1882–1956) and his *Winnie-the-Pooh* illustrator E. H. Shepard (1879–1976), John Betjeman (1906–1984), and William Makepeace Thackeray (1811–1863). Dickens was a frequent guest, but was never invited to sign. Indeed, his work was rejected by the magazine. An unfortunate footnote is that during the table's last move, to the Harrods offices, one of the contractors carved the name Jesus in its surface. A specialist from the Victoria & Albert Museum was called in to remove it.

A Surprise in the Cupboard

Mark Twain came to Bourverie Street in 1907, at the end of his last visit to England, for a special lunch in his honour. He was invited to carve his initials in the table, but seeing those of W. M. Thackeray, he famously quipped, 'Two-thirds of Thackeray will do for me.' Once lunch had been served, the editor's eight-year-old daughter emerged from a cupboard in which she had been hiding and recited a special poem for the writer, presenting him with an original cartoon depicting Twain with Mr Punch. Thurber was honoured in 1958, and though he was by then nearly blind he managed to carve the 'Th' with which he used to sign his cartoons.

Walk down Bouverie Street and turn left into Tudor Street. *Punch* and its famous table moved to No. 23, beneath the lions' mouths, in 1969, and it was here that Alan Coren was Editor during the period many consider the magazine's finest. Turn left up Dorset Rise and notice the 'wedding cake' steeple of St Bride's rising on your right. Salisbury Square, which soon appears on your left, is where Samuel Richardson (1689–1761) lived at No. 1 and wrote *Pamela*, considered to be the first modern English novel. Further up on your right a plaque marks Pepys's birthplace. The site of his house is now occupied by Reuters and the Press Association, which is entirely appropriate, since Pepys's diaries can be read as 17th-century reportage.

On rejoining Fleet Street, notice the magnificent listed frontages of the former *Daily Telegraph* and *Daily Express* buildings. The latter was used in a television dramatization of Evelyn Waugh's classic Fleet Street novel *Scoop*. Turn right and, after Reuters, right again, into Bride Lane, which leads to St Bride's, the so-called journalists' church. Pepys was baptized here and John Milton (1608–1674) lived for a time in the churchyard.

Turn right immediately on leaving the churchyard, cross Bride Lane and walk straight over into the pretty Bride Court. This comes out on busy New Bridge Street, which leads to Blackfriars Bridge, one of the seven bridges J. M. Barrie could see from his apartment. Turn right and continue to Blackfriars Station, where the walk ends.

Piccadilly, Mayfair and St James's

Summary: This is a longish circular walk through some of the smartest parts of London. You will see where the Royal Family buy their books – or rather, has them bought for them – and where former Conservative Prime Ministers like to curl up with theirs. You will see where there was a book-burning long before the days of Salman Rushdie, and where Penguin paperbacks were first planned. The walk also passes one of the most distinguished addresses in London, as well as two of the most sharply contrasting bookshops, each with its own literary history. St James's is home to numerous gentlemen's clubs – including Evelyn Waugh's favourite – while the quiet, elegant residential streets of Mayfair provide a welcome relief from the unceasing traffic of Piccadilly.

Start and finish:	Piccadilly Underground Station (Bakerloo and Piccadilly Lines).
Length:	4 kilometres (2½ miles).
Time:	2–3 hours.
Refreshments:	Shepherd Market off Curzon Street, roughly at the halfway point, has plenty of pubs and cafés and is an interesting part of London in its own right. The Punch Bowl pub, in Farm Street, has plenty of character. The middle section of the walk has fewer cafés and pubs than the first and last sections.

Take Exit 3 (Piccadilly south side) from Piccadilly Underground Station and bear left at the top of the stairs. Almost immediately you will see the Waterstone's awning over the pavement. This branch is not only the chain's largest, it is also the biggest bookshop in Europe (see page 60). The shop occupies the former Simpson clothes store that was the inspiration for the Seventies sitcom *Are You Being Served?* Waterstone's bought it from Simpson's Japanese owners in 1998 and on 14 September 1999 the bookshop was officially opened with a party attended by numerous authors, including Doris Lessing, A. S. Byatt and her sister Margaret Drabble (they don't get on), Beryl Bainbridge and the ubiquitous Salman Rushdie. Bainbridge was particularly pleased with one aspect of the store: 'It's got a bar where you can buy alcohol and smoke', she said.

St James's Church, on your left after Waterstone's, was built by Christopher Wren (1632–1723) in 1684, but looks more American than English. It would not be out of place in New England. William Blake (1757–1827) was baptized here, and in 1918 Robert Graves (1895–1985), author of the classic First World War memoir *Goodbye to All That,* married his first wife Nancy, with Max Beerbohm (1872–1956)

31

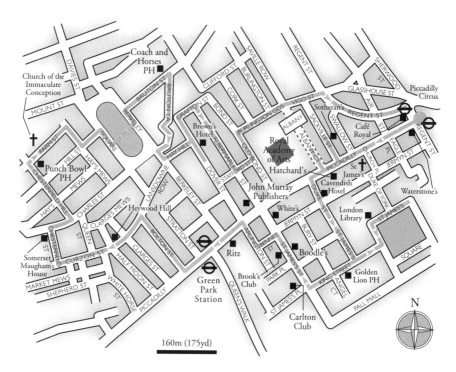

160m (175yd)

and Wilfred Owen (1893–1918) in the congregation. Owen had fought on the Somme in 1916 and recovered from 'trench-fever' in hospital in Edinburgh (he had been thrown into the air by a blast from a shell and had spent several days sheltering from gunfire in a trench in which a fellow officer's remains lay scattered around him). Soon after the wedding he returned to France and was killed in November 1918, a week before the Armistice.

Cross Piccadilly at the lights; then turn right off Piccadilly into Sackville Street. A few yards up on your right is the antiquarian bookdealer's Sotheran's, a splendid wood-lined emporium well worth a visit. In particular, it usually has good selections of travel and English literature. Interestingly, like St James's Church, it also has a First World War connection. After its founder was knocked down by a bus on Piccadilly, the shop was owned briefly in the Twenties by Siegfried Sassoon (1886–1967), the writer and poet who suffered from shell shock during the First World War. Sassoon met Owen in hospital and encouraged his writing. In recent times the shop's customers have included John Betjeman (1906–1984), Bob Hope, Lady Thatcher, Alastair Cooke and Tom Stoppard. Its Chairman is the amiable Martyn Goff, who since 1970 has been Administrator of the UK's most prestigious literary award, the Booker Prize.

A Highly Distinguished Address

Returning to Piccadilly, turn right and continue a few yards until you reach Albany Court on your right. The elegant building at the end of this small courtyard is one

Plate 1: *Soho Square, where Thomas De Quincey fainted and Jeffrey Bernard was photographed looking hung over (which he probably was). The park-keeper's hut dates from the 1870s (see pages 12 and 13).*

Plate 2: *The splendid Pillars of Hercules pub in Greek Street is almost certainly the Hercules Pillars featured in Charles Dickens's* A Tale of Two Cities *(see page 13).*

Plate 3: *The magnificent interior of Rules restaurant in Covent Garden where Dickens, Thackeray, Galsworthy and H. G. Wells dined. The restaurant dates back to 1798 (see page 21).*

Plate 4: The fourth Theatre Royal, Drury Lane, built in 1811. Lord Byron wrote the address to celebrate its opening. He called it 'the Drama's tower of pride' (see page 20).

Plate 5: Bernard Partridge's cartoon of Mr Punch toasting Mark Twain at the magazine's offices in Bouverie Street in 1907 (see page 29).

Plate 6: The famous statue of Dr Samuel Johnson outside the church he attended – St Clement Danes on the Strand (see page 28).

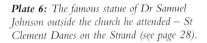

Plate 7: *Brown's Hotel on Dover Street where Kipling and his wife stayed after their marriage and where Stephen King wrote some of* Misery *(see page 35).*

Plate 8: *Hatchard's book-shop on Piccadilly. Laurie Lee said that a heart attack here would be a pleasant way to die (see page 33).*

of the most distinguished addresses in London and has a rich literary history. This is Albany – not 'the Albany', just 'Albany' – built in 1802–3. Writers who have lived in its 69 exclusive 'bachelor' apartments include Byron (1788–1824), Aldous Huxley (1894–1963), Graham Greene (1904–1991), J. B. Priestly (1894–1984), Evelyn Waugh (1903–1966), Sir Harold Nicolson (1886–1968) and Terrence Rattigan (1911–1977). It was here, in 1955, that Greene smoked opium in a nostalgic attempt to re-create the 'fumeries' of Vietnam. He wrote: 'what pleasure it was to recapture the smell and the quiet and the serenity, however crudely, just off Piccadilly. The quiet of Albany was very similar to the quiet of a fumerie where no one interrupts the repose of another.'

Waugh stayed at Albany in 1932, while working on a film script. He wrote to a friend: 'Well, I am living like a swell, in Albany, as it might be Lord Byron, Lord Macaulay, Lord Lytton, or any real slap up writer!' J. B. Priestly moved to Albany in 1943, to apartment B4, the same address as John Worthington's in *The Importance of Being Earnest*. Priestly lived at Albany until the late Seventies, by which time, he complained, the traffic was ruining his afternoon walks.

'The Top People's Bookshop'
Return to Piccadilly where, directly opposite, is Hatchard's bookshop, frequented by so many of Albany's distinguished residents. Long known as 'the top people's bookshop', it was founded in 1797 and in its early years used to have benches outside for the customers' servants. Byron, Oscar Wilde (1854–1900), Bernard Shaw (1856–1950) and Somerset Maugham (1874–1965) all shopped here, and today it is still possible to bump into authors or politicians on practically any day. It became part of the Waterstone's group in 1998 and hosts a grand Authors of the Year party every year, which used to include a liveried toastmaster barking out the names of the arriving writers. Laurie Lee (1914–1997) was a regular at these occasions, right up to his death. In fact, he once said that a heart attack in Hatchard's would be his favourite way to die. At the Authors of the Year party in 1996 he was reunited with the 96-year-old member of the Bloomsbury Group, Frances Partridge. 'We used to play Bach's Double Violin Concerto together 30 years ago', he said, adding: 'Well, we weren't always together when we played it, if you see what I mean.' The shop also holds two Royal warrants and supplies the Queen's 'holiday reading'.

Cross at the lights by Fortnum and Mason to visit Hatchard's, and then continue along the south side of Piccadilly and turn left into Duke Street St James's. Cross Jermyn Street, where Albany folk buy their shirts, and you'll pass the rebuilt Cavendish Hotel, where Waugh used to stay. Turn left into King Street and, when you reach St James's Square, turn left to find the London Library tucked away in the corner. For the best view of the library, walk away from it until you reach No. 10, the former home of Prime Ministers Pitt and Gladstone. Now you can see the library's grand first-floor windows. Writers who have gazed out from here across the trees of the square include Virginia Woolf (1882–1941), George Eliot (1819–1880) and H. G. Wells (1866–1946). Evelyn Waugh used the library, too, and during the Blitz wrote to his second wife Laura, 'the biographies in the London Library are buried in plaster.'

Club-land

Return to King Street which, further along, was home to the St James's Theatre until its demolition in 1957. Wilde's *The Importance of Being Earnest* was premiered here and during his trial for 'acts of gross indecency with other male persons', black strips were placed over his name on the theatre's hoardings to spare the audience's embarrassment. The Golden Lion pub on your left contains memorabilia of the theatre, while in Angel Court to its side you can see the four tableaux that decorated the theatre's balconies. Wilde's face is in the middle one.

Now cross King Street and continue left towards St James's Street. The pillared building you can see ahead of you is the Carlton Club, the Conservative Party's home away from the House. Note the security cameras on the roof and the walls, introduced when Lady Thatcher was in power and the IRA's campaign in London was at its peak. At the junction with St James's Street turn right. You are now in the heart of London club-land. Cross the road and continue up the slope, crossing Park Place to find Brook's Club on your left. Brook's has been here since 1778 and is chiefly a political club, although the actor and writer David Garrick (1717–1779) was an early member. The grand white building opposite with the white weather vane is Boodle's, founded in 1762. Ian Fleming (1908–1965) was a devoted member and used it as the model for Blade's in the James Bond stories.

A Venue for 'Gamblers, Lords and Heroes'

On the corner of Bennet Street, pause. The last but one building on St James's Street – the one with four figures on its frontage and two lamps at the entrance – is White's, the oldest gentlemen's club in London. It began life as White's Chocolate House in 1693 and moved here in 1753. Evelyn Waugh loved it. Many of his letters were written here and he referred to it as 'this glorious place'. He revelled in its rakish, lordly atmosphere and disapproved when other professional, middle-class men such as himself sought to join. When he learnt that Nancy Mitford's publisher, Hamish Hamilton, a businessman, had become a member, he wrote to her: '[White's] should be a club for gamblers, lords and heroes.'

Turn left into Bennet Street, where Bryon lodged at No. 4 (since demolished) in 1813–14. Turn right into Arlington Street and rejoin Piccadilly, into which you turn left, passing the Ritz. The latter was popular with Waugh, who referred to it as 'marble halls'. Walk past Green Park Station and cross at the lights to walk straight up Bolton Street. Henry James (1843–1916) took lodgings at No. 3 in 1876. The house has now gone but it would have been similar to that occupied by the novelist Fanny Burney (1752–1840), who lived at No. 10. James took long walks in the fog and spoke of London's 'agglomerated immensity'. He thought the city 'the most complete compendium of the world'.

Turn left into Curzon Street and look for the bookshop Heywood Hill on the right, opposite Half Moon Street. A small, ramshackle affair, 'HH', as Waugh called it, has been providing a personal service to the upper classes and literary great since 1936. Nancy Mitford (1904–1973) worked here during the war and once left the door open all night. The Sitwells were regular customers, and in more recent years Muriel Spark, Gore Vidal and A. S. Byatt have all enjoyed its unique atmosphere, one that is a world away from the chains and their computerised stock-ordering. Visit it to see the way many bookshops used to be run before bookselling became global big business.

Continue along Curzon Street and then turn right into Chesterfield Street, where you should walk on the left pavement to see Somerset Maugham's house at No. 6, on the other side. Assessing his work at the end of his life, Maugham felt that he stood 'in the very first row of the second-raters'. Still, he has a blue plaque to make up for it now.

Turn right down Charles Street and then left up Chesterfield Hill, a quiet, elegant residential street. Cross Hay's Mews, where bookseller Tim Waterstone had an office in the first days of his fledgling eponymous chain, and then turn right into Farm Street, passing the Punch Bowl, which is indeed 'an inn of distinction'. The Church of the Immaculate Conception, beneath the row of London plane trees, is where Waugh was received into the Roman Catholic church on 29 September 1939, his only witness being his friend Tom Driberg (1905–1976), who would later write a biography of the newspaper proprietor Baron Beaverbrook (1879–1964), whom Waugh had already satirised in *Scoop*, published in 1938.

A Literary Hotel

Follow Farm Street around to the right, down to Hill Street, where you turn left. On entering Berkeley Square turn right, cross at the zebra and then walk straight across the square, noting the London plane trees, planted in 1789 and reputedly the oldest in the city. Turn left at the far exit and cross the zebra to go into Bruton Street where Richard Sheridan (1751–1816), author of the plays *The School for Scandal* and *The Rivals*, lived in 1868. At the Coach and Horses (note its 'model' sign), turn right down the nondescript Bruton Lane, which brings you out at the bottom of Berkeley Square.

Turn left, and immediately left again into Hay Hill, which leads to Dover Street. Turn right and look for the Union Jack that marks the entrance of Browns Hotel. Founded in 1837 by James Brown, whose wife was a maid to Lady Byron, it was here that Rudyard Kipling (1865–1936) and Caroline Balestier stayed after their marriage in All Souls, Langham Place, on 18 January 1892. When they left the hotel on 26 January, Brown sent them their bill of £22, cancelled, as his wedding present, with a note begging them 'to allow him the privilege as a slight repayment for the pleasure Rud has given him'. Nearly a century later, a writer of a very different style stayed in Kipling's room at the hotel, working at another of his international best sellers. Stephen King told the *Observer* in 1998, 'I wrote most of *Misery* by hand, sitting at Kipling's desk in Brown's Hotel in London. Then I found out he died at the desk. That spooked me, so I quit the hotel.'

A fellow American writer – of a different genre yet again – was also a Brown's regular. In 1953 the celebrated *New Yorker* contributor (and Marx Brothers scriptwriter) S. J. Perelman (1904–1979) wrote to his wife Laura: 'The hotel is very old-fashioned (but rigidly kept up), full of brass trim and mahogany and decrepit wealth. On the lobby floor there's the usual series of depressing public rooms, dimly lit and dotted about with corpses breathing gently. Gentility hangs over the place like a pall, also servility...' But these somewhat sour words did not stop him from returning.

A Book-burning that Still Upsets

Retrace your steps to the end of Dover Street, noting the three pairs of black cones at the entrances to Nos 8–10 on the left. Before the advent of street lighting, 'link boys' used to walk in front of sedan chairs with torches to light the way. On arrival at their destination the torches would be placed inside these cones to extinguish the flames. Turn right into Grafton Street and right again into Albemarle Street. Walk to the far end to find No. 50, home to one of London's few remaining independent publishers, John Murray, the house that has published Byron since the early 19th century. The eponymous Murray hosted numerous dinner parties for Byron and his circle in the first-floor dining-room, behind the railings. When it published the first two cantos of Byron's *Don Juan* in 1824, so great was the crush of booksellers' messengers besieging the building that Charles Lamb dubbed the street 'John Murray Street'. It was in this room, too, that Murray burned Byron's memoirs in 1824 because of concern over its supposed immorality. Today, the publisher receives visits from a number of 'Byronphiles', who stare wistfully at the grate in which the memoirs were burnt, thinking about the words of this controversial and handsome figure – the first 'literary superstar', as he has been called – which have been lost for ever. There was also the emotional lady who planted a kiss on a valuable bust of the author, which then had to be sent away for cleaning!

The Most Famous Bird in Publishing

Turn left into Stafford Street and right into Old Bond Street where, at No. 41, Lawrence Sterne, author of *Tristram Shandy* died in 1768. Retrace your steps and continue up this street of fashion flagship shops (among them DKNY and Chanel) and turn right into Burlington Gardens. Walk past the British Museum's handsome Department of Ethnography and, on your right, look for the black, shuttered, back entrance to Albany, the exclusive apartments seen at the beginning of the walk. This is now Vigo Street and next door at No. 8 a plaque records that Sir Allen Lane (1902–1970) published the first Penguin paperbacks here in 1935. But this building had been occupied by a publisher since long before that. It was here that in 1887 Lane's uncle, John Lane, had established Bodley Head, whose first authors included Aubrey Beardsley (1872–1898) and Oscar Wilde. As Ian Norrie observes in *Mumby's Publishing and Bookselling in the Twentieth Century*, Beardsley apparently tried John Lane's patience by slipping into his drawings for *The Yellow Book* minute indecencies, some of which could be discovered only with the aid of a magnifying glass. John Lane's nephew Allen joined the firm, and in the Thirties, after being unable to find anything to read at Exeter railway station for the journey back to London, became convinced that there was a need for cheap editions of good quality contemporary writing. He started to approach London publishers for the rights to reprint their leading authors' works in a new series of books to sell at the price of ten cigarettes – sixpence each. Lane wanted a 'dignified but flippant' name for his new series, suggesting an animal or a bird. His secretary Joan Coles came up with idea of a penguin, and Edward Young of the production department went off to London Zoo to sketch the new symbol. Initial orders for the first ten titles were poor – just 7,000 copies – and ironically it was Woolworths, not especially known for sales of Penguins today, who saved the day by placing an order for 63,500. A world-famous logo was launched.

Turn right into Regent Street and, after the arch that marks Air Street, pass, on the far side, the Café Royal, where Wilde had lunch every day at precisely 1pm. It was not his favourite London restaurant, though. To see that, you will have to try the Soho walk. It was at the Café Royal, too, that at the 1972 Booker Prize dinner John Berger, who had won the prize with his novel G, famously denounced Booker's 'colonialist' treatment of West Indian sugar workers and gave half his prize money to the Black Panthers. Weidenfeld & Nicolson MD Ion Trewin recalls: 'Rebecca West, a guest, was so shocked – as much by what she considered Berger's bad manners as anything else – that she rose to her feet and protested volubly.'

But you can calmly continue down Regent Street to Piccadilly Circus Station, where the walk ends.

Chelsea

Summary: This is a longish walk that encompasses both this famous area's fashion-conscious present and its pretty, village-like past. Punks no longer roam King's Road – you'll see them only on the postcard racks now – and mobile phones rather than safety pins are the order of the day. Along the way, you will pass the homes of P. G. Wodehouse, A. A. Milne, Henry James and T. S. Eliot – and also see where Dirk Bogarde liked to buy his books.

Start and finish:	Sloane Square Underground Station (District and Circle Lines).
Length:	5.8 kilometres (3½ miles).
Time:	3–3.5 hours.
Refreshments:	This is quite a long walk, so you need to pace yourself. There are more cafés in the first half of the walk, while you are on the King's Road, than there are in the second, although one of Dylan Thomas's favourite pubs, The King's Head and Eight Bells, is on this latter section of the walk.

Sloane Square Station will for ever be tragically linked with the dramatist J. M. Barrie (1860–1937) and his most famous work, *Peter Pan*. It was here, on 5 April 1960, that the eponymous Peter Davies, a publisher, threw himself under an oncoming train. Peter Llewelyn Davies was one of the five boys Barrie took under his wing after their parents died, and on whom he based his most famous creation (see pages 83–4). But the media never let any of the five forget it. When Davies began Peter Davies Ltd, the headlines ran 'Peter Pan Becomes Publisher'. Davies came to loathe what he called 'that terrible masterpiece', and after his death the Coroner's Jury returned a verdict of 'suicide while the balance of his mind was disturbed'.

Where Dirk Bogarde Bought his Books
Cross at the lights outside the station and continue along Sloane Square, past WH Smith. Look back to see the handsome brick frontage of the Royal Court Theatre, completed in 1888 and refurbished with an £18m National Lottery grant in 1998/9. Famous first nights here include *Look Back in Anger* (1956) and *The Entertainer* (1957), both by John Osborne (1929–1994). Continue straight ahead into King's Road – the king in question being Charles II – until you reach Blacklands Terrace on your right. A short way down, on the left, is John Sandoe Books, founded in 1958 and favourite bookshop of long-time Chelsea resident Dirk Bogarde (1921–1999). He referred to it as 'those squashed little cottages' and wrote in *The Bookseller*: 'The absolute love of books which this shop engenders is hugely joyous.'

Return to King's Road and turn right. At the corner of Bywater Street, look across the road at the white houses in Wellington Square. The fourth house on the right, No. 32, is where Thomas Wolfe (1900–1938) lodged in 1926 while writing *Look Homeward Angel*. Drunken brawls alternated with spasms of writing, and his rent was paid by his 45-year-old mistress, Aline Bernstein, a stage designer who lived in New York. During the afternoons he went for 'enormous promenades through the East End of London', returning for a bath, after which he would go out for the evening and then come back to write until midnight. He was famous for writing his huge novels standing up, and died at 38, the same age as the century, after an infection following pneumonia.

George Smiley's House

Bywater Street itself is full of very pretty houses, whose colours give the impression of a long, Battenberg cake. John le Carré's George Smiley lives here, at No. 9. 'I think I may have put him there,' Le Carré wrote, 'because a cul-de-sac is very difficult to keep under surveillance and No. 9 is well up at the blind end of Bywater Street.' Next on the right along King's Road is the attractive, tree-lined Markham Square, where P. G. Wodehouse (1881–1975) lodged in 1900, and from where he used to walk – and sometimes run – to his depressing job at the Hong Kong and Shanghai Bank in the City.

Just past Markham Square, on the right, with an ornate portico, is the Pheasantry, so called because pheasants used to live in the garden of the house that stood here in the 19th century. At the time of writing the building is a Pizza Express, but in 1916 the 'Russian Dancing Academy' was opened here by Princess Serafina Astafieva, a great niece of Leo Tolstoy. One wonders if she knew that in 1861, years before he achieved fame with *War and Peace*, her great uncle had walked the streets of Chelsea while visiting St Mark's Practising School at the far end of King's Road. Tolstoy was interested in education and had with him a letter of recommendation from the poet Matthew Arnold (1822–1888), then a senior official at the Department of Education. 'Count Leo Tolstoy', wrote Arnold, 'is particularly anxious to make himself acquainted with the mode of teaching Natural Science, in those schools where it is taught.'

Turn right into Burnsall Street, with Dutch-looking houses on the left. Follow it round to the left, turn right into Astell Street and then left into Britten Street. Soon you will see St Luke's Church on your right, built out of Bath stone between 1820 and 1824. Charles Dickens (1812–1870) married Catherine Hogarth here in April 1836, rather quietly and with a special licence, since his 20-year-old bride was under age. To visit the church, turn right into Sydney Street. Retrace your steps, turning right and following Britten Street to Doveshouse Street. Turn left back to King's Road, where you should turn right.

A little further down, on the right, is Manresa Road, where Dylan (1914–1953) and Caitlin Thomas lived in 1942, and where their second child, Aeron, was born. Shortly afterwards you meet Carlyle Square, on the right, where Sir Osbert Sitwell (1892–1969) lived at No. 2, the first house on the right, with its grand first-floor living-room. He produced many volumes of poetry, fiction, autobiography and travel

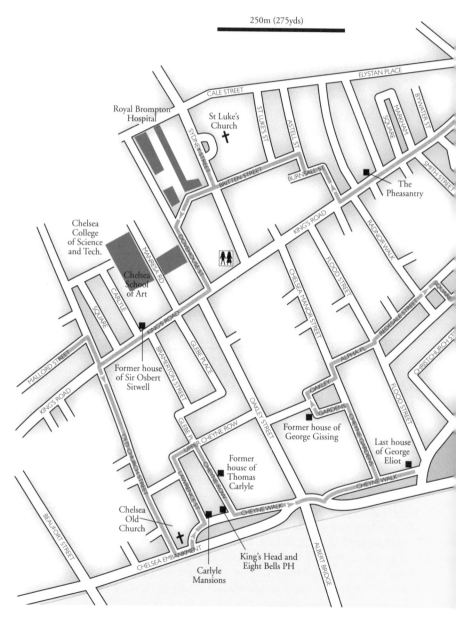

250m (275yds)

ELYSTAN PLACE

CALE STREET

Royal Brompton
Hospital

St Luke's
Church

ST LUKES ST

ASTELL ST

MARKHAM
SQUARE

BYWATER ST

SYDNEY STREET

SMITH STREET

BRITTEN STREET

BURNSALL ST

The
Pheasantry

Chelsea
College
of Science
and Tech.

KING'S ROAD

RADNOR WALK

MANRESA RD

DOVEHOUSE ST

Chelsea
School
of Art

CARLYLE

CHELSEA MANOR STREET

FLOOD STREET

REDESDALE STREET

CHRISTCHURCH ST

SQUARE

KING'S ROAD

ALPHA PL

FLOOD STREET

MALLORD STREET

BRAMERTON STREET

GLEBE PLACE

Former house
of Sir Osbert
Sitwell

KING'S ROAD

OAKLEY

GARDENS

CHEYNE GARDENS

GLEBE PL

OAKLEY STREET

UPPER CHEYNE ROW

Former house of
George Gissing

Last house
of George
Eliot

OLD CHURCH STREET

LAWRENCE ST

CHEYNE ROW

Former
house of
Thomas
Carlyle

CHEYNE WALK

BEAUFORT STREET

Chelsea
Old
Church

CHEYNE WALK

King's Head and
Eight Bells PH

ALBERT BRIDGE

CHELSEA EMBANKMENT

Carlyle
Mansions

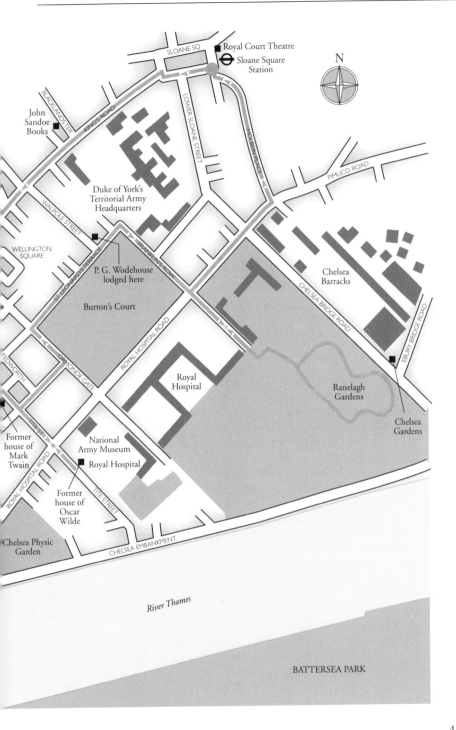

writing, and was a great supporter of Ezra Pound, T. S. Eliot and Wyndham Lewis. He also had a famously aristocratic disposition and today would doubtless vehemently object to the traffic on the King's Road, just yards from his windows.

Winnie-the-Pooh's House

Leave the square and continue along King's Road until Old Church Street, where you turn right, then first left, into Mallord Street, where A. A. Milne (1882–1956) wrote *Winnie-the-Pooh* at No. 11 (now No. 13). Milne's inspiration was his son Christopher Robin, who was born in the house in August 1920. His night and day nurseries were on the top floor, and the teddy bear that became Pooh was a present from Harrods. Milne's American publisher, John Mcrea, remembered seeing the author and the artist Ernest H. Shepard (1879–1976), whose drawings contributed so much to the success of the books, at work in 1926, 'Milne sitting on the sofa reading the story, Christopher Robin sitting on the floor playing with the characters which are now famous in *Winnie-the-Pooh*, and, by his side, on the floor, sat E. H. Shepard making sketches for the illustrations which finally went into the book.'

Retrace your steps to King's Road, cross over, and go directly down Old Church Street. It is easy to spot the elegant, shuttered Georgian house on the right at No. 53, where John Betjeman (1906–1984) lived when he was 11. 'Yes, the slummy end', he admits in his autobiography *Summoned by Bells* – which just shows how the passage of the years can alter property values. Note the house's delightful walled garden.

Writers' Block

Continue to the bottom of the street to find Chelsea Old Church, where Henry James (1843–1916) often worshipped and where his funeral was held in 1916. Rudyard Kipling (1865–1936) and Edmund Gosse (1849–1928), author of the autobiographical masterpiece *Father and Son*, were among the mourners. Gosse wrote: 'As we stood round the shell of that incomparable brain, of that noble and tender heart, it flashed across me that to generations yet unawakened to a knowledge of his value the Old Chelsea Church must forever be the Altar of the Dead.'

Turn left alongside the church, into Cheyne Walk, and pause on the corner of Lawrence Street. The grand apartment block opposite, with the carvings of the birds up the side, is Carlyle Mansions; Henry James lived and died at No. 21. He moved there in 1913 and wrote: 'This Chelsea perch, the haunt of the sage and the seagull proves, even after a brief experiment, just the thing for me.' It is an imposing building, and worthy of the phrase 'writers' block' since later in the century T. S. Eliot (1888–1965) took a flat on the third floor, No. 19, beneath James's apartment. In 1950, four years after the writer of *The Waste Land* moved in, Ian Fleming (1908–1965), creator of James Bond, also took a flat here. It would be hard to find two more contrasting literary neighbours.

Eliot shared a flat with John Hayward, his disabled editor, whom he would often push in his wheelchair across Albert Bridge to Battersea Park. Eliot lived in monastic austerity. His bedroom resembled a monk's cell, with a bare light bulb and crucifix over the bed, and he often ate his meals off a tray on his knees. Hayward was gregarious; Eliot was solitary, often retiring to his room early for study or contemplation. Fleming, meanwhile, was bashing out *Casino Royale* on a gold typewriter, bought especially for the project.

Turn left up Lawrence Street, passing the Cross Keys, which Dylan Thomas visited. The very last cottage at the top on the left was the home of novelist Tobias Smollett (1721–1771) for a while. Turn right into the equally pretty Upper Cheyne Row, crossing Glebe Place, where the writer Vera Brittain (1894–1970) used to live. Before turning right into Cheyne Row, note No. 22 Upper Cheyne Row, where the poet and essayist Leigh Hunt (1784–1859) lived. Walk down Cheyne Row, past the home of the historian and essayist Thomas Carlyle (1799–1881) at No. 24, now restored and opened as a museum. Dickens, Tennyson (1809–1892) and William Thackeray (1811–1863) all visited him here. The King's Head and Eight Bells at the end of the street is where Dylan Thomas played shove-halfpenny and darts, and is also featured in John le Carré's spy stories.

A Literary Menagerie – And an Animal One, Too
Turn left and continue along Cheyne Walk. Cross at the lights and notice the green taxi driver's shelter on the Embankment. Tudor House at No. 16, the home of Dante Gabriel Rosetti (1828–1882), was the meeting place of writers and artists in the 1860s. Visitors included Oscar Wilde (1854–1900), Lewis Carroll (1832–1898) and Charles Algernon Swinburne (1837–1909); the latter also lived here for a time amidst Rosetti's famous animal menagerie, which included armadillos, a kangaroo and a racoon – some of which could be seen in the front garden. There was a collection of curiosities of another sort in Don Saltero's Tavern, to the left at No. 18. Assembled from the travels of Sir Hans Sloane's head valet, the collection included 'a starved cat found between the walls of Westminster Abbey when repairing, and a Staffordshire almanac in use when the Danes were in England'. It was popular with writers including Jonathan Swift (1667–1745) and was visited by Benjamin Franklin (1706–1790).

Cross Cheyne Gardens and continue a short way to find George Eliot's last home, where she lived for just a few weeks before her death in 1880. Return to Cheyne Gardens and turn right, then left into Oakley Gardens where, on the corner at No. 33, lived George Gissing, author of *The Nether World*, a graphic account of Victorian poverty. Continue around the square and turn left into Chelsea Manor Street and right into Alpha Place. Continue into Flood Street and into Redburn Street where, at the time of writing, William Boyd was living. His debut novel *A Good Man in Africa* won the Somerset Maugham Award in 1982 and his follow-up, *An Ice Cream War* was shortlisted for the Booker Prize in the same year.

Huck Finn in SW3
Continue into Tedworth Square and turn right. At No. 23, on the corner of Tite Street, Mark Twain (1835–1910) lived during 1896–97. He wasn't happy. He was in debt and was mourning the death of his daughter Susy. However, from the second-floor bay windows he could watch 'young men and maids' hugging and kissing in the square, and was relieved not be the target of curious attention when he walked up to King's Road. What he wrote in his notebooks over a hundred years ago is still partly true today: '[London] is a collection of villages. When you live in one of them

with its quiet back streets and its one street of stores and shops, little bits of stores and shops like those of any other village, it is not possible for you to realize that you are in the heart of the greatest city in the world.'

Turn down Tite Street, where Christopher Robin was taunted on his way to school, and cross Royal Hospital Road to find No. 34, where Oscar Wilde lived from 1885 to 1893. W. B. Yeats (1865–1939) came to Christmas dinner in 1888 and annoyed Wilde by telling a frightening story about giants to Wilde's son Cyril – Wilde's giants were always amiable – and incurred Wilde's aesthetic disapproval by wearing yellow shoes, a botched attempt at the vogue of undyed leather.

Retrace your steps, noting Shelley Court on your right, home to the explorer and writer Wilfred Thesiger. Turn right into Christchurch Street and left into Smith Street, with the Royal Hospital grounds to one side. Turn right along St Leonard's Terrace and if you have any garlic about your person, clasp it now as you pass No. 18, the former home of Bram Stoker of *Dracula* fame.

The Homes of Two Great Humorists

Continue to Walpole Street where, in 1902, P. G. Wodehouse lodged at the top of No. 23. A friend called one cold evening to find him writing by the light of an oil lamp, his feet wrapped in a woollen sweater to keep warm. Note the gateway next door, which says '6½' – that would have amused Wodehouse. Retrace your steps and turn left, then right down Franklin's Row. Cross at the zebra to enter the grounds of the Royal Hospital, which was commissioned by Charles II as a retirement home for old or wounded soldiers, the 'Chelsea pensioners', whose distinctive caps are a common and much-loved sight. Thomas Hardy (1840–1928) came here in the 1870s to talk to the veterans of Waterloo and the Napoleonic Wars. He was gathering material he would later use in his long verse drama *The Dynasts*.

Continue past the museum and through the Garden Gate, then turn left into Ranelagh Gardens. Today, apart from the annual Chelsea Flower Show held here, these are among the least-visited gardens in the capital. Take the right-hand path to the small pavilion, which tells the history of the gardens as a Georgian pleasure resort, visited by Samuel Johnson (1649–1703) and Tobias Smollett (1721–1771), who wrote of its 'thousand golden lamps that emulate the noon-day sun'. Walk through the pavilion and take the path that slopes away to the left. At the railings by the road, walk along until you see a tall, dark brick apartment block called Chelsea Gardens on the other side. There is a blue plaque at street level for Jerome K. Jerome (1859–1927), who wrote *Three Men in a Boat*, published in 1889, when he was living here. You can spot his flat from his description of his 'little circular drawing-room' on the top floor, '...nearly all windows, suggestive of a lighthouse', and looked down upon the Thames and over Battersea Park to the Surrey hills beyond.

Take the path away from the railings and follow it round to exit the gardens. Retrace your steps out of the Royal Hospital and turn right into Royal Hospital Road. Continue and cross at the lights into Pimlico Road, then take the first left into Holbein Place. The large brick building with the grey turrets at the far end is the former head office of WH Smith. Continue to the end of the road and turn right to find Sloane Square Station, where the walk ends.

Charing Cross Road and Fitzrovia

Summary: Charing Cross Road is still the most famous bookselling street in the world. This walk tells the story of some its best-known names, including that of the bookseller who corresponded with Adolf Hitler. You will pass the former teashop frequented by some of the War poets, and a literary club that actually overlooks this busy street yet is little-known. Fitzrovia, north of Oxford Street, has kept its literary and artistic reputation intact, with numerous restaurants popular with publishing folk and many small art galleries. Finally, you will see some of the favourite drinking haunts of Dylan Thomas, George Orwell and Anthony Burgess – and discover why one particular pub proved more popular than the others towards the end of the evening.

Start:	Charing Cross Station (Overground trains, and Northern, Bakerloo and Jubilee Underground Lines).
Finish:	Goodge Street Station (Northern Underground Line).
Length:	2.25 kilometres (1⅓ miles).
Time:	1 hour.
Refreshments:	There are plenty of pubs and cafés. All Bar One on Charing Cross Road occupies the site of the famous bookshop at 84 Charing Cross Road. The Wheatsheaf and the Fitzroy Tavern, both on the walk, have interesting literary displays.

Follow the signs from Charing Cross Station to Trafalgar Square and make your way to the right-hand side of the square, where there is often a mobile pigeon-food shop! Laid out in the 1830s, Trafalgar Square did not endear itself to Charles Dickens (1812–1870), who complained about its 'abortive ugliness'. In August 1931, just as the square reached its centenary, George Orwell (1903–1950) slept rough here during one of his periodic 'tramps'. Recalling these uncompromising expeditions to the bottom of society in *The Road to Wigan Pier*, the Eton-educated writer wrote: 'I knew nothing about working class conditions. I had read the unemployment figures but I had no notion of what they implied… What I profoundly wanted, at that time, was to find some way of getting out of the respectable world altogether.'

Orwell barely slept during his night in the square, but observed: 'Some of the people I met…had been there without a break for six weeks, and did not seem much the worse, except that they are all fantastically dirty.' In the morning he shaved in the fountains and left London for Kent.

Nearly 60 years later, in 1988, a writer with a similar political conscience, although not in the same league in literary terms, scaled Nelson's Column in protest about acid rain. Joe Simpson, a Greenpeace activist, had just written *Touching the Void*, a critically acclaimed account of survival in the Peruvian Andes described by George Steiner as 'one of the absolute classics of mountaineering'. The book went on to win a number of awards and become a worldwide best seller.

Where Kipling Dined
Over to the west of Trafalgar Square is Admiralty Arch, beneath which some scenes from the film version of E. M. Forster's *Howards End* were filmed, but you should leave the square up the sloping pavement on your right, crossing the road (still keeping to the left-hand pavement) to pass St Martin-in-the-Fields.

Continue past the National Portrait Gallery into Charing Cross Road. Opposite the Garrick Theatre, and to the left of a modern, white building, is an old building with tall, leaded windows on the first floor. This is No. 9 Irving Street, home to the Beefsteak Club since 1896. Founded in Covent Garden in 1735, the original club had just 24 members, who dined on beefsteaks, followed by toasted cheese and washed down with port, porter, punch and whisky toddy. Members of the club have included Rudyard Kipling (1865–1936), the diplomat, writer and critic Sir Harold Nicolson (1886–1968), the cartoonist, writer and theatrical designer Osbert Lancaster (1908–1986) and John Betjeman (1906–1984). One new member, not recognising his neighbour at the long table just the other side of the windows you are looking at, lectured him on how to write short stories. The neighbour in question turned out to be Kipling. This anecdote is often told as a warning to new members.

Tearooms, Bookshops and an Exclusive Restaurant
The Garrick Theatre, opposite, opened in 1889. Plays staged here include adaptations of Walter Greenwood's *Love on the Dole* (1935), Graham Greene's *Brighton Rock* in the Forties, and J. B. Priestly's enduring classic *An Inspector Calls*, which opened in October 1995 and at the time of writing was booked until January 2001. Turn right into Cecil Court, a small walk-through that is full of character. The antiquarian book- and map-sellers Alan Brett, immediately on your left at No. 24, was a tearoom before the First World War, and the poets Edward Thomas (1878–1917), Walter de la Mare (1873–1956) and Rupert Brooke (1887–1915) visited it. Its tiny wooden balcony dates from this period. Further along, also on your left at No. 4, is the first-edition specialists Bell, Book and Radmall, which has a distinguished visitor's book that includes the signatures of Tom Stoppard, Philip Roth, S. J. Perelman, Paul Theroux, William Boyd, V. S. Naipaul, John le Carré and David Lodge. Continue to the end and turn left and left again into St Martin's Court, which brings you back out on Charing Cross Road, where you should turn right.

The curtain at Wyndham's Theatre first rose in 1899. Joe Orton's *Entertaining Mr Sloane* (1964) opened here, as did an adaptation of Muriel Spark's *The Prime of Miss Jean Brodie* (1966). After crossing Cranbourn and Great Newport Streets, you now pass a long and famous run of secondhand and new bookshops, including the feminist specialists Silver Moon and the art and design specialists Zwemmer.

Silver Moon at No. 66 occupies the site of the left-wing booksellers Collets. In 1937 Penguin installed a curious machine – called the 'Penguincubator' – on the pavement outside. This Penguin paperback vending machine was operated by putting sixpence in the slot and pressing the appropriate key for your book. Unfortunately, it was soon discovered that you could get *more* than one book for sixpence and the experiment was abandoned. Turn right into Litchfield Street, passing another branch of Zwemmer, the chain founded by the art patron and publisher Anton Zwemmer in the twenties. It was in this shop at No. 24 that some of the first exhibitions of Dali and Miro were held in the UK. On the corner at the end of the street is the Ivy, an upmarket restaurant much favoured by agents and publishers. Here, Keith Waterhouse once declared, 'Billy Liar will never die!', Ray Bradbury celebrated his 70th birthday, Arthur Miller his 80th, and Random House held a reception for A. S. Byatt when she became a Dame of the British Empire in 1999. Turn sharp left into West Street and cross at the lights to return to Charing Cross Road.

Thanks to the book and film of the same name, the next address, 84 Charing Cross Road, is one of the most famous in bookselling. The former premises of the bookdealers Marks & Co. have now been merged with the café next door. Helene Hanff's correspondence with manager Frank Dole is well known. What is less well-known is that Marks's son, Leo, worked in Intelligence for the Special Operations Executive in the Second World War and wrote 'code poems', the most famous of which begins, 'The life that I have/Is all that I have/And the life that I have/Is yours.'

Notice Blackwell's on your right. The chain was founded in 1879. Its current chairman, Toby Blackwell, famously lists 'chopping firewood' as his recreation in *Who's Who*. Cross at the lights further up to visit Foyles, arguably the world's most famous bookshop. It is chaotic, has an arcane payment system, and never answers the phone. But the books! No other bookshop has its selection. The shop is really a series of specialist shops under one roof and invariably has titles you won't find in its smarter, more fashionable neighbours, like the US-owned Borders opposite (although the latter serves fine coffee and is good for imported titles from the States).

Hitler and Charing Cross Road
Founded by the brothers William and Gilbert Foyle in 1904, Foyles opened in Charing Cross Road in 1907. During the Second World War a bomb narrowly missed the shop, creating a huge crater in the road, right outside the doors, and the Royal Engineers built a wooden bridge across it. The bridge was nicknamed the 'Foyle bridge' and William Foyle cut the tape when it opened.

Coincidentally, a year or two earlier, William's daughter Christina, who died in 1999, had been receiving letters from Hitler. She had written to the Führer after she learnt that he intended to burn books and told him that Foyles would buy them! Apparently, he wrote back saying that he was very grateful for the suggestion, but he would no sooner corrupt the morals of the British than those of the Germans.

Christina began the famous Foyles literary lunches in 1931. These are rather old-fashioned affairs, at which members of the public pay to hear authors speak after lunch at the Grosvenor Hotel on Park Lane. Evelyn Waugh (1903–1966) cut quite a sight at one in 1957. He was going deaf and arrived with a tin Edwardian ear

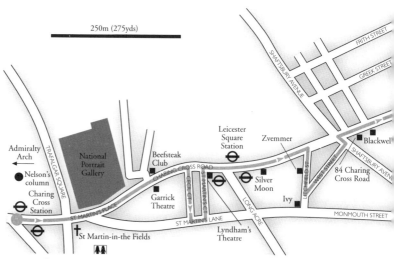

trumpet that was nearly two feet long. 'My ear trumpets are a great convenience and a great success socially,' he boasted to his friend, Lady Diana Cooper.

Right on Foyles's doorstep is Waterstone's, the country's premier bookselling chain, which also has branches in the States and Amsterdam. Ray Monk, who wrote an acclaimed biography of Wittgenstein, used to work in this branch.

The Story of the Country's Premier Bookselling Chain

The story of Waterstone's eponymous owner and his chain's rise to prominence is the stuff of popular fiction itself. Tim Waterstone was born in Glasgow in 1949, the son of an East India merchant. After Cambridge and Harvard Business School, he joined Allied Breweries and became marketing director of its wine and spirits division. In 1973 he joined WH Smith, who sent him to the States to establish a book sales and distribution business. It failed spectacularly in 1981, losing the company over $20m. Waterstone was sacked, but borrowed £10,000 from his father-in-law the following year and opened the first branch of Waterstone's in Old Brompton Road. This new-style bookshop opened late, played music, stocked heavily, and encouraged browsing – all commonplace today, but then quite revolutionary.

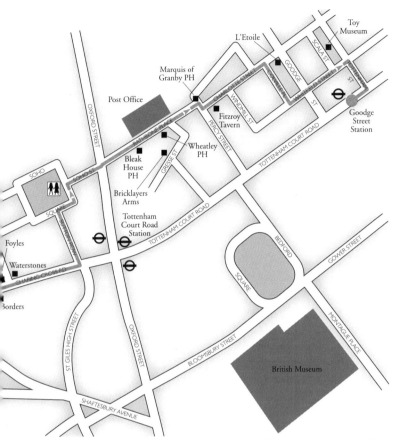

The chain grew rapidly until, in 1989, with a delicious irony, Waterstone sold it to the people who had sacked him for £49m, rather more than the £70,000 pay-off Smiths had originally given him. It gets better. In 1997 he tried to buy WH Smith itself. He failed, but when Smiths decided to de-merge Waterstone's, he joined forces with EMI (who already owned Dillons) and in January 1998 succeeded in buying back his old company – along with the HMV chain. Then, in spring 2000, he was attempting to separate Waterstone's from the HMV media group. Along the way he has also managed to write a handful of reasonably well-received novels.

Bohemian Pubs
Turn left into Sutton Row, then right into Soho Square, exiting along Soho Street and crossing straight over Oxford Street into Rathbone Place. You are now entering Fitzrovia, a fashionable bohemian area in the Thirties and Forties.

Anthony Burgess (1917–1993) recalls pub crawls here in his memoirs *Little Wilson and Big God*. The Black Horse on your right he described as being 'too funereal to be convivial', while the Bricklayers Arms along Gresse Street, also on the right, was 'quiet, small and a good place for assignations'. The Wheatsheaf is inextricably linked with Dylan Thomas (1914–1953), who drank here and met his wife Caitlin here in 1936.

Stand opposite the Wheatsheaf and you can see two other pubs – The Marquis of Granby, and beyond it, around the corner to the right, The Fitzroy Tavern. These three pubs formed a kind of Bohemian triangle. The Marquis is slightly to the west of the other two, and in the Thirties was in the borough of Marylebone, as opposed to that of Holborn, which meant that it closed half-an-hour later than its neighbours. So for George Orwell and others, the Marquis was always the last pub of the night.

Continue along Rathbone Place, bearing to the right into Charlotte Street and passing Percy Street, where Wyndham Lewis (1894–1957) and Ezra Pound (1885–1972) celebrated the launch of their 'Vorticist' magazine *Blast* at a small hotel in 1914. The Vorticists attacked the sentimentality of 19th-century art and celebrated violence, energy and the machine. Continue into Charlotte Street to find the Fitzroy Tavern, on your right, where the artist Augustus John (1878–1961) first met Dylan Thomas, recognizing 'the somewhat blurred but no less authoritative accents of South Wales'.

A little further up on the right is T. S. Eliot's favourite restaurant, L'Etoile, which was just a short walk from Faber's offices in Russell Square, where he worked. Turn right into the pretty Colville Place, where the 19th-century writer George Gissing (1857–1903) lived at No. 22 in 1878. Turn left into Whitfield Street, where Jerome K. Jerome used to share a cramped bed-sit with George Wingrave, the future bank manager with whom he made the trip that was to become *Three Men in a Boat*. Jerome didn't do much writing in his room, apparently. He preferred the street, particularly Portland Place, about half-a-mile away. He would walk along at night, trying out sentences and phrases, then scribbling them down beneath each lamp-post.

The 'Ugliest Street in London'

On the corner of Scala Street is Pollock's Toy Museum, which moved here in 1969. Robert Louis Stevenson loved its original shop in Hoxton Street in Hackney and J. B. Priestly (1894–1984) even wrote a play for the museum. Turn right into Tottenham Street, which soon joins Tottenham Court Road, described by V. S. Pritchett as 'the ugliest and most ludicrous street in London'. Turn right to find Goodge Street Station. The following evocative memory of war-time London from John Mortimer's *Clinging to the Wreckage* is rather appropriate, given the route you have just taken: 'It seemed a perpetual adventure to buy second-hand books in the Charing Cross Road…or stand outside Goodge Street Underground Station in that long silence, filled with infinite possibilities, between the moment when the buzz-bombs cut off and the thud as they fell somewhere else.' The walk ends at the station.

Marylebone

Summary: Marylebone takes its name from the old church of St Mary (now gone) near which the river Tyburn passed. The river's name was originally 'Tybourne' and the church was known as 'St Mary-by-the-Bourne'. This walk tells the story of the great love affair between Robert Browning and Elizabeth Barrett, and reveals why a building society and a fictional detective are so inextricably linked. You will also see where H. G. Wells played his radio much too loudly.

Start:	Bond Street Underground Station (Central and Jubilee Lines).
Finish:	Baker Street Underground Station (Jubilee, Bakerloo, Hammersmith & City and Circle Lines).
Length:	2 kilometres (1¼ miles).
Time:	1–2 hours.
Refreshments:	Marylebone High Street is good for pubs and cafés. The café at Daunt Books, which you pass, is particularly recommended. There is also a café/restaurant in Regent's Park, just a few yards from the walk.

Turn sharp left after the barriers at Bond Street Station and exit via the stairs. Turn right into Oxford Street, immortalized by Thomas Hardy (1840–1928) in his poem 'Coming up Oxford Street, Evening'. Cross at the traffic lights into Marylebone Lane, by Debenhams, then turn right into Henrietta Place and immediately left into Welbeck Street. Second on the left is Bentinck Street where, at No. 7, Edward Gibbon (1737–1794) worked on his masterpiece *The Decline and Fall of the Roman Empire*, which he came to describe as an 'old and agreeable companion'.

Return to Welbeck Street and turn left. As you pass Queen Anne Street on the right, note the elegant iron balconies of the houses. James Boswell (1740–1795) lived in what was then Queen Anne Street West and worked on his *Life of Samuel Johnson*. At No. 33 Welbeck Street the publishers J. M. Dent had their home in their last years as an independent. The house was founded in the 1880s by Joseph Malaby Dent, an apprentice bookbinder from Darlington. His wife died just as he began publishing his first books and he lost two sons in the First World War.

A Correspondence of Love

Turn right into New Cavendish Street, where the Telecom Tower looms on the horizon. Browning Mews, on your left, with its elegant lamps, is an indication that you are nearing one of London's most famous literary sites. To find it, turn left into Wimpole Street where, at No. 50, the poet Elizabeth Barrett (1806–1861) lived with her family and tyrannical father, who would not allow Elizabeth or her sisters to marry. The original house has been demolished, but its replacement is not hugely

51

dissimilar. Indeed, the whole line of the street is not much different from how it would have looked in the middle of the 19th century.

Elizabeth Barrett was a housebound invalid. As a teenager, she had developed a tubercular complaint that had damaged her spine, although doctors were unable to diagnose her condition at the time. Her room was on the second floor and had an inter-connecting door to that of her father. At night he would take her hand and they would pray. She would occasionally be carried to the street in a wheelchair, but her room was really her world. It was crowded with a sofa, a bed, a washstand, and crimson bookcases overflowing with books and lined with busts of poets. She loved flowers and greenery but had trouble keeping them alive because the room was dark and there was also an open fire.

On 10 January 1845 her fellow poet Robert Browning (1812–1889) sent her a letter beginning, 'I love your verses with all my heart, Dear Miss Barrett.' Thus began an extraordinary correspondence. Although he had never met the woman to whom he was writing, Browning seemed to cast Victorian caution aside and dared to express his feelings towards the end of that first letter: 'I do, as I say, love these verses with all my heart – and I love you too.'

The very next day Barrett answered, 'I thank you, dear Mr Browning, from the bottom of my heart.' It was to be another five months before the couple met. Browning would note down on the back of Elizabeth's letters the number of each letter and the date, time and duration of his last visit. The pair exchanged lockets of hair and over a 20-month period wrote 574 letters. The story of their affair was told in a very successful 1930 stage play *The Barretts of Wimpole Street*. Today, Elizabeth Barrett Browning is best remembered for a single line of love poetry: 'How do I love thee? Let me count the ways.' You will meet them again later in the walk.

Sherlock Holmes and a Literary Bus-driver

Continue along Wimpole Street and cross into Upper Wimpole Street, where at No. 2, with its elegant fan-tail window above the door, Sir Arthur Conan Doyle (1859–1930) set up an ophthalmic practice, having studied medicine at Edinburgh University. The complete lack of patients allowed him to spend the days writing short stories, a craft he had begun some years previously, and Upper Wimpole Street was quiet and provided an ideal location for writing. Among these short stories were the early Sherlock Holmes tales. It was their success that allowed Conan Doyle to give up medicine altogether. 'I should at last be my own master', he recalled later. 'No longer would I have to conform to professional dress or try to please any one else. I would be free to live how I liked. It was one of the great moments of exultation in my life.'

Retrace your steps to Weymouth Street and turn right. Continue to Marylebone High Street, turn right and cross at the zebra to find Daunt Books and café at No. 83. Founded in 1990 by James Daunt, a former City banker and Arabia enthusiast, this is one of the most elegant bookshops in London. It specialises in travel and has a distinguished list of customers, among them Wilfred Thesiger, Thomas Pakenham and William Dalrymple. It is also where *The Restraint of Beasts* by the 'Booker bus-driver' Magnus Mills was launched in 1998. Mills was driving a No. 137 out of Streatham Hill Bus Garage in south London when his book was shortlisted for the Booker Prize.

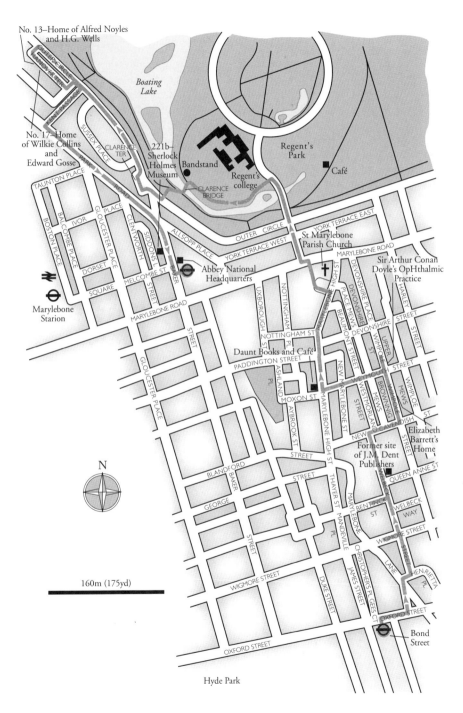

No. 13–Home of Alfred Noyles and H.G. Wells

Boating Lake

No. 17–Home of Wilkie Collins and Edward Gosse

CLARENCE TER

221b–Sherlock Holmes Museum

Bandstand

Regent's college

Regent's Park

Café

SUSSEX PLACE

PARK ROAD

CLENTWORTH

SIDDONS LANE

ALLSOPP PLACE

OUTER CIRCLE

YORK TERRACE EAST

St Marylebone Parish Church

YORK TERRACE WEST

CLARENCE BRIDGE

TAUNTON PLACE

BOSTON PLACE

BALCOMBE PLACE

IVOR PLACE

GLOUCESTER PLACE

DORSET SQUARE

MELCOMBE STREET

BAKER STREET

Abbey National Headquarters

MARYLEBONE ROAD

Sir Arthur Conan Doyle's OpHthalmic Practice

UXBOROUGH PLACE

NOTTINGHAM STREET

DEVONSHIRE MEWS

DEVONSHIRE STREET

BEAUMONT STREET

NEW CAVENDISH STREET

HARLEY STREET

WIMPOLE STREET

UPPER WIMPOLE STREET

Marylebone Starion

MARYLEBONE ROAD

GLOUCESTER PLACE

NOTTINGHAM ST

Daunt Books and Café

PADDINGTON STREET

MOXON ST

ASHLAND PL

AYBROOK ST

MARYLEBONE HIGH ST

NEW MARYLEBONE ST

WESTMORLAND STREET

BROWNING MEWS

WIMPOLE MEWS

WIMPOLE ST

WEYMOUTH STREET

N

160m (175yd)

BLANDFORD STREET

GEORGE STREET

BAKER STREET

Former site of J.M. Dent Publishers

THAYER ST

MARYLEBONE LANE

BENTINCK ST

Elizabeth Barrett's Home

QUEEN ANNE ST

WELBECK WAY

WIGMORE STREET

MANDEVILLE PL

DUKE STREET

JAMES STREET

CHRISTOPHER'S PL

GEES CT

HENRIETTA PL

WIGMORE STREET

OXFORD STREET

Bond Street

OXFORD STREET

Hyde Park

53

A Literary Church

A small Memorial Garden of Rest on the left, just before the end of the street, marks the site of the 15th Marylebone Parish Church, in which Byron (1788–1824) was baptized in 1788. A few yards further on, turn left into the grounds of St Marylebone Parish Church where, on 12 September 1846, Robert Browning and Elizabeth Barrett were married in secret. They left for Italy on 18 September, Elizabeth stealing out of the house in Wimpole Street without saying goodbye to her sisters and taking with her all Robert's letters. Her health had improved and was to do so even more in Italy, where they settled. She died in her husband's arms in 1861 after 15 happy years of marriage.

Just before the main doors into the church, a doorway on the left leads into the Browning Chapel. You will probably have to ask for it to be unlocked. Inside, a stained glass window commemorates their wedding and there are various items of Browning memorabilia and old editions of their works. Copies of the marriage certificate are sold inside the main church, and every year, on 12 September, Browning aficionados come from around the world to mark the anniversary.

Turn left on leaving the church and cross at the lights into York Gate, where William Macready, manager of the Drury Lane Theatre, lived at No. 1. He was reported to have lost £10,000 while living here, and recalled in his diary in January 1840: 'Dear Dickens called to shake hands with me. My heart was quite full; it is much for me to lose the presence of a friend who really loves me.' It was in that year that Charles Dickens went to America on a lecture tour. Frances Palgrave, compiler of his famous *Golden Treasury* verse anthology, lived at No. 5.

A Poet's Park

Continue into Regent's Park, crossing the water over a little bridge (or you can take the right-hand path, which leads to a café, and then retrace your steps) and follow the path by the side of the lake. Just under a year after Robert Browning's first visit to Elizabeth Barrett, she sent him a flower that she had picked from this park with her sister Arabel and her dog Flush. 'Look what is inside of this letter – look!' wrote Elizabeth, whose health had improved a little during her months of correspondence with Browning. 'I gathered it for you to-day when I was walking in the Regent's Park... Dearest, we shall walk together under the trees some day!' As you come to the iron Clarence Bridge on your left, you will see the bandstand away to your right. Cross the bridge over the lake. The concrete tower you can see ahead, above the rooftops, is Abbey National's headquarters and has its own literary connection, which you will discover shortly.

Cross at the lights and then turn right to find Clarence Terrace, with its six cream pillars. Elizabeth Bowen (1899–1973), author of the war-time classic *The Heat of the Day*, lived at No. 2. The essayist and critic Cyril Connolly (1903–1974) lived in the next terrace along, at No. 25 Sussex Place, beneath its ten oriental domes. Continue along and turn left into the third terrace, Hanover Terrace, with its rooftop figures and blue friezes. Wilkie Collins (1824–1889) lived at No. 17 and apparently received the inspiration for his most famous novel, *The Woman in White*, while walking close to the park one warm, moonlit night, probably in 1854, with his brother Charles and the artist John Millais. The story is a good one. Collins and his companions were startled by a piercing scream, and the figure of a young and beautiful woman dressed in flowing white robes rushed past them. Collins followed her, and the next day explained to the others that he had rescued her from a brutal captor in a nearby villa. Kate Dickens, Charles Dickens's daughter, added another chapter to the story in the 1930s by confirming that Collins had had a 'mistress called Caroline, a young woman of gentle birth and the original of The Woman in White'. Collins would share the rest of his life with Caroline – the woman he had met near Regent's Park in such dramatic circumstances – and with the much younger Martha Rudd, whom he met ten years later. It was a highly unusual arrangement that seemed to work for all parties.

'Mr Grumpy' at No. 13

Edward Gosse (1849–1928), author of *Father and Son*, later lived at No. 17 Hanover Terrace too, while further along, two more writers occupied No. 13 at different times. The poet Alfred Noyes (1880–1958) lived here before the Second World War, and then, more famously, H. G. Wells (1866–1946). The previous occupant had called it 12A, but Wells firmly restored it to 13. When the war came, and with it the Blitz, he had the 13 painted even larger. The war drove most of the inhabitants of Hanover Terrace away but, with his cook and Margaret the maid, Wells stayed on, a defiant, tetchy, visionary old gentleman. The solid walls of the terrace withstood the bombs, but were no match for the blast of Wells's radio. As he grew deafer the radio grew louder; when neighbours finally complained, he wrote back saying he would consider doing something about his radio if they would 'de-bark' their dog. He died here in his four-poster bed in August 1946 – on the 13th.

Leave Hanover Terrace and turn right into Outer Circle, then right into the narrow Kent Passage. Turn left into Park Road and eventually cross at the lights to reach Baker Street. On the right, at No. '221b' (the real number is 239) is the Sherlock Holmes Museum. Opened in 1990, this clever tourist attraction looks like a little film set; indeed, Dustin Hoffman and family have been among its celebrity visitors. The offices of Holmes and Dr Watson have been lovingly recreated, based on the stories. In the first-floor study you can sit beside the fire, try on Holmes's famous hat and hold his pipe.

Further down Baker Street is the real '221b', occupied by the enormous headquarters of Abbey National, whose tower you saw from Regent's Park. The building society receives up to 100 letters a week from Holmes's admirers around the world and those who call at the building in person receive a free Sherlock Holmes booklet and postcard.

The huge apartment block above Baker Street Station is Chiltern Court, where Arnold Bennett (1867–1931) lived for the last few months of his life. He didn't like it much: he strained his back moving his library and was annoyed by the rumble of the Underground trains beneath the building. He died here in 1931.

The walk ends at Baker Street Station, which is itself a little shrine to Sherlock Holmes, featuring his silhouette on its tiles.

Bloomsbury (1):
Tottenham Court Road
to Holborn

Summary: Bloomsbury takes its name from 'Blemund's bury' – 'Blemund' being William de Blemund, a 13th-century landowner, and 'bury' being a manor house. So 'Bloomsbury' really means 'Blemund's house'. And talking of houses, every one here seems to cry 'Woolf!' One can trace the movements of the intellectual pack known as the Bloomsbury Group from house to house and square to square (and often from bed to bed). But countless books already exist on that famous artistic clan, so this walk concentrates as much on some of the other literary giants who have lived and worked in this well-preserved quarter of London, among them the 20th century's greatest poet.

Start:	Tottenham Court Road Underground Station (Central and Northern Lines).
Finish:	Holborn Underground Station (Central and Piccadilly Lines).
Length:	4.2 kilometres (2⅗ miles).
Time:	2 hours.
Refreshments:	There are plenty of cafés and pubs along the first two-thirds of the route; not so many when you reach Dickens House. If you take coffee in the café in Russell Square you will, broadly speaking, be looking at the view that would have greeted T. S. Eliot when he walked to work from Russell Square Station.

Take Exit 3 (New Oxford Street north) from Tottenham Court Road Station and turn first right into Great Russell Street. A plaque at Nos 13 & 14, above the Cinema Bookshop, notes that Charles Kitterbell lived here in 'The Bloomsbury Christening', one of the stories in Dickens's *Sketches by Boz*. The plaque is unusual in that it commemorates a fictional character, rather than its creator. At the traffic lights at the end of the street turn left into Bloomsbury Street and walk up to Bedford Square, which you enter on your left. This is generally regarded as the most perfectly preserved Georgian square in the capital and was, until the late 1980s, the centre of British publishing.

The poet Robert Bridges (1844–1930) lived with his mother at No. 52, immediately on your left, and wrote his lovely poem 'London Snow' here. Hodder &

Plate 9: *The elegant frontage of No. 4 Cheyne Walk in Chelsea, the final home of George Eliot, whose novel* Middlemarch *is considered to be her masterpiece. She died here in 1880 (see page 43).*

Plate 10: *This should be called Writers' Block. Henry James, T. S. Eliot and Ian Fleming, creator of James Bond, all made Carlyle Mansions on the Chelsea Embankment their home (see page 42).*

Plate 11: *L'Etoile on Charlotte Street, T. S. Eliot's favourite restaurant (see page 50).*

Plate 12: *Rare books and theatre ephemera in quaint Cecil Court (see page 46).*

PENGUINCUBATOR

Plate 13: *Penguin's book vending machine, the Penguincubator (see page 47).*

Plate 14: *Dickens's house at 49 Doughty Street, where he worked on Oliver Twist (see page 60).*

Plate 15: *Bedford Square in Bloomsbury, famous for its beautifully preserved Georgian buildings, was the home of British publishing for much of the 20th century (see page 64).*

Plate 16: *The plaques on No. 29 Fitzroy Square state that it was home to both George Bernard Shaw and Virginia Woolf. Surprisingly, Shaw called it 'a most repulsive house' (see page 66).*

Stoughton had their offices at No. 47 and the distinguished houses of Chatto & Windus, Jonathan Cape and Bodley Head shared Nos 31 and 32. Chatto had bought Leonard and Virginia Woolf's Hogarth Press in 1945. Cape's list included the likes of Hemingway, T. E. Lawrence and Sinclair Lewis. Bodley Head's history was no less literary, since they had originally published Wilde and the celebrated *Yellow Book* of Aubrey Bearsdley, although not from these premises. The original Jonathan Cape was formerly the London rep for the eponymous Gerald Duckworth. Duckworth refused to make him a partner because he didn't consider him a gentleman – somewhat ironic, since Duckworth famously made sexual advances towards his own half-sister, Virginia Woolf.

A gloom descended on the square in 1991, when some 120 jobs were lost at Hodder as the recession bit. In 1987 Chatto, Cape and Bodley Head had been bought by the American Random House conglomerate, and Hodder & Stoughton later departed too, to an anonymous tower block on the Euston Road a mile or so to the north, where they were merged with Headline. It was the end of a publishing era and, although some of the snobbish divide between editorial and sales vanished with it, many lamented the fact that the muse had now surely been replaced by Mammon.

Literary Soirées

Bedford Square's gardens were used in the Seventies for the 'Bedford Square Book Bang', a mini book festival held beneath the glorious plane trees. The former Temple barrister Anthony Hope (1863–1933), author of *The Prisoner of Zenda*, lived at No. 41, and the society hostess Lady Ottoline Morrell (1873–1938) lived at No. 44. Lady Ottoline's taste leant towards the rebellious and unconventional in music, painting and books and she had the wealth to patronize those she favoured. She met Virginia Woolf in 1908, and the writer became a frequent visitor to the parties Lady Ottoline hosted in Bedford Square, alongside many of the leading artistic and political figures of the day. Henry James (1843–1916) was among the guests in May 1912 and remarked on Lady Ottoline's eccentric 'window-curtaining clothes'.

Continue around the square and turn left into Gower Street. Shortly you come to No. 10, on the right, where Lady Ottoline lived from 1927, after a period in the country. Her parties resumed, including one in June 1932 at which T. S. Eliot (1888–1965) met a young Italian novelist called Alberto Moravia (1907–1990), who would later reach fame with *The Conformist*, filmed by Bertolucci in 1970.

The 'Ministry of Truth'

Store Street, on the left at the traffic lights, is where Mary Wollstonecraft (1759–1797) wrote *A Vindication of the Rights of Woman*. Turn right into Keppel Street, where one of the most prolific of 19th-century writers, Anthony Trollope, was born in 1815. At the end of this short street, cross at the zebra and carry straight on through the gates of London University's imposing Senate House (if the gates are locked, turn right, then left into Montague Place and left again into Russell Square, where you will rejoin the route). This concrete monolith, built in the 1930s, was home to an unlikely triumvirate of writers during the Second World War, when it was occupied by the Ministry of Information. Its staff included Evelyn Waugh

(1903–1966), George Orwell (1903–1950) and the crime writer Dorothy L. Sayers (1893–1957), who were all employed to help boost the nation's morale. In *Put Out More Flags*, Waugh describes the building as 'that great mass of masonry', while Orwell almost certainly based his 'Ministry of Truth' on it in *1984*: 'It was an enormous pyramidal structure of glittering white concrete, soaring up, terrace after terrace, 300 metres into the air.' Sayers remarked, '[Since] the place is packed with everybody's wives and nephews and all the real jobs seem to have been handed over to other departments, it's as good a spot as any to intern the nation's troublemakers.'

Continue on to Russell Square, where you turn left. The curious green shed on the traffic island is one of London's 13 taxi shelters, established by various Victorian philanthropists at the end of the 19th century to provide cabbies with a place to eat and drink away from the temptations of the public house.

T. S. Eliot's Office

The building with the orange frontage on the corner of Russell Square is the former offices of Faber & Faber. A plaque on its side records that Faber & Faber's most famous employee, T. S. Eliot, had an office here from 1925 to 1965. There was also a top-floor flat that he would occasionally use. His office was at the back of the building, on the second-floor, with a view over the trees of Woburn Square (which you will visit shortly). It was reached in a small and creaking lift, although Eliot himself was often seen bounding up the stairs. There were photographs on his mantelpiece of Virginia Woolf and the French poet Paul Valery, and the floor was piled with books. Many writers visited him here, including Eliot's fellow poet George Barker (1913–1991), who recalls him standing looking out of the window in 1939, shortly before war was declared: 'And, after a while, in a tired voice, he said, "We have so very little time…".' The building itself was hit in June 1944, although fortunately Eliot was not staying in the flat at the time.

Eliot has a reputation as having been a melancholy man, but there are accounts that describe him doing things like putting firecrackers in the coal scuttles at Faber on the Fourth of July. Life was difficult for him, though, after he separated from his first wife, Vivien. She would sometimes appear unannounced at Faber, demanding to see him. His secretary would detain her in the waiting-room while Eliot slipped out of the building. Vivien was later admitted to a mental hospital. It was in this building, too, that in 1956 Eliot proposed to his secretary Valerie Fletcher, the woman who would become his second wife. They married the following year. He was 68; she was 30.

Continue to the left of the Faber building, past the modern buildings of London University into, first, Woburn Square and then Gordon Square. Virginia Stephen (later Woolf) moved to No. 46 Gordon Square with her brother and sister in 1904. The elegant gardens in front of this terrace are little changed. In a memoir of Old Bloomsbury, Woolf (1882–1941) wrote: 'It was astonishing to stand at the drawing-room window and look into all those trees; the tree which shoots its branches up into the air and lets them fall in a shower; the tree which glistens after rain like the body of a seal.'

The cream and brick building opposite No. 46, on the other side of the gardens, is Dr Williams's Library, chiefly a theological library that also has the original manuscripts of the 17th-century poet George Herbert (1593–1633). Enter the gardens

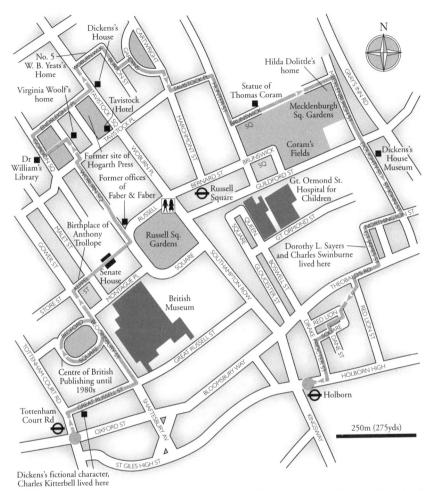

Dickens's fictional character,
Charles Kitterbell lived here

through a gate, walk straight across, then turn right and right again into Endsleigh Place. Continue into Tavistock Square, where Virginia Woolf (1882–1941) and her husband, Leonard (1880–1969), later lived and ran their Hogarth Press. The building was destroyed during the war. At the far end, to your right, you can see the Tavistock Hotel. Wilfred Owen (1893–1918) had lodgings in a building on this site from October to November 1915. Carry straight on to the busy main road and cross over to find a plaque commemorating Charles Dickens (1812–1870), who lived in a house on the site now occupied by the British Medical Association from 1851 to 1860. Turn left and walk a short way to find the pretty Woburn Walk on your right.

The 'Most Interesting Room in London'

This tiny, paved walk-through of secondhand bookshops and cafes hides one of London's best-kept literary secrets. Few Londoners know that W. B. Yeats

(1865–1939) lived at No. 5 from 1895 to 1919 (it was then known as 18 Woburn Buildings). There is a plaque, but it is too high and too hidden by the trees to be noticed. Yeats used to be 'at home' to friends on Monday evenings from 8pm into the early hours of Tuesday morning. Ezra Pound (1885–1972) was a frequent visitor and would dominate proceedings, freely handing round Yeats's cigarettes and Chianti. John Masefield (1878–1967), another visitor, called Yeats's sitting-room 'the most interesting room in London', and recalls a 'big, dark blue lectern, on which his Kelmscott Chaucer stood, between enormous candles in big blue wooden sconces'.

Continue to the end of Woburn Walk and bear right into Burton Street. Turn left into Burton Place and right into Cartwright Gardens. Turn right into Marchmont Street and left into Tavistock Place. These are quiet, somewhat bohemian streets, with secondhand bookshops tempting the students at nearby London University. Turn right into Hunter Street and then second left into Brunswick Square (there is a sign to the Thomas Coram Foundation), with the School of Pharmacy on your left. Virginia Woolf lived briefly in this square too, after her marriage.

Continue straight ahead until you find both the statue of Thomas Coram (1668–1751) and, next to it, the current offices of the children's welfare organization that he founded in the 18th century (see page 61). Take the path to the right by the playing fields. This comes out in Mecklenburgh Square, where the American 'Imagist' poet Hilda Doolittle (1886–1961), who wrote as 'HD', lived at No. 44 from 1917 to 1918. The Imagists favoured short poems, composed of short lines of musical cadence rather than metrical regularity.

Follow the square around to the right and into Doughty Street. Cross over the busy Guildford Street to find the Dickens House Museum on your left at No. 48. Dickens only lived here from 1837 to 1839, but these were among his most productive years. Much of *The Pickwick Papers*, *Oliver Twist* and *Nicholas Nickleby* was written here. Among many interesting exhibits, the house has some of Dickens's own annotated 'reading' copies of his novels, which he used for his celebrated public performances. No. 58, a little further up, is where the writers Vera Brittain (1894–1970) and Winnifred Holtby (1898–1935) lived.

A Scientific Best Seller

Turn right into Northington Street, passing Cockpit Yard on your left, an echo of how Londoners amused themselves in the days when cock fighting was commonplace (it was banned in 1849). Follow it around into Great James Street, where Dorothy L. Sayers and the poet Charles Swinburne (1837–1909) lived at different times. Turn right on to the busy Theobalds Road and left into Red Lion Street. Immediately on your right take the tiny Lamb's Conduit Passage to Red Lion Square. Turn left and enter the gardens. Take the left-hand path and exit opposite Dane Street. A plaque on the right here commemorates John Harrison (1693–1776), inventor of the marine chronometer, who lived in a house on this site. The American writer Dava Sobel gave a literary treatment to this scientific story in her book *Longitude*, one of the most phenomenal best sellers of the 1990s, later made into a television film starring Jeremy Irons and Michael Gambon. Continue to the end of the square and turn left into Procter Street. At the lights turn right and follow High Holborn to Holborn Station, where the walk ends.

Bloomsbury (2): Russell Square to Warren Street

Summary: The second Bloomsbury walk is a longish one that takes you into Fitzrovia. You will see where Ted Hughes and Sylvia Plath got married and where they spent their wedding night. You will pass two houses lived in by Charles Dickens and visit a rather spooky bookshop. The walk ends in one of London's finest squares and one that is rich in literary history.

Start:	Russell Square Underground Station (Piccadilly Line).
Finish:	Warren Street Underground Station (Northern and Victoria Lines).
Length:	4 kilometres (2½ miles).
Time:	2.5 hours.
Refreshments:	Lamb's Conduit Street, Cosmo Place and Charlotte Street all have attractive bars, cafés and restaurants.

Turn right out of Russell Square Station along Bernard Street and then first right into Grenville Street. Turn left into Guildford Street and cross Lansdowne Terrace to find Coram's Fields on your left. This small recreation ground is named after Captain Thomas Coram (1668–1751), the philanthropist and sea captain who was shocked by the numbers of abandoned babies and children on London's streets. This was a social problem that concerned Charles Dickens (1812–1870) too, and when Coram established the Foundling Hospital here, Dickens supported it with an article in his own magazine *Household Words*. The hospital also appears in Dickens's story 'No Thoroughfare', which he wrote with Wilkie Collins (1824–1889). As you pass, look at the roof of the white buildings in the corner – if you are lucky you will see some of the park's resident peacocks.

Ted Hughes and Sylvia Plath's Wedding Night
Directly opposite, cross into Guildford Place, which leads up into Lamb's Conduit Street, a fashionable, attractive street of cafes and restaurants. After a short way turn left into Rugby Street to find No. 18 on your left. This is where Ted Hughes (1930–1998) and Sylvia Plath (1932–1963) spent their wedding night, at the home of Hughes's friend from Cambridge, Daniel Huws. Plath was not fond of the house and referred to it as a 'slum'.

Retrace your steps back down Lamb's Conduit Street and turn left into Great Ormond Street, passing the famous Great Ormond Street Hospital for Children on your right. Dickens supported this hospital, raising money for it at talks and public readings of his works, especially *A Christmas Carol*. He described the hospital in *Our*

61

Mutual Friend as 'a place where are none but children; a place set up on purpose for children; where the good doctors and nurses pass their lives with children, talk to none but children, touch none but children, comfort and cure none but children'. All royalties from J. M. Barrie's *Peter Pan* go to support the hospital too, in accordance with the express wishes of its author, for whom childhood was an obsession.

A Literary Marriage

Continue into the pretty, tree-lined, faintly French-looking Queen's Square. Cross to the railings in front of you and look across the gardens to the modern building opposite, the one with the balcony running along its top floor. This is No. 3 Queen's Square, head office of the publisher's Faber & Faber since the early Seventies. Some years before the publisher moved here, the two writers who would become among its most famous authors were married just a few yards away in the Church of St George the Martyr. It was here, in pouring rain, at 1.30pm on 16 June 1956 – Bloomsday, the date chosen for its literary associations – that Ted Hughes and Sylvia Plath took their vows. It was an odd wedding, arranged in a great hurry. Aurelia Plath, Sylvia's mother, was present, but Hughes's parents did not even know about the wedding until the following day. The couple had to prevail upon the curate to delay a trip to the zoo with some local children in order to be a witness. Hughes remembered the children sitting on the bus outside until the ceremony was over. Given the tragic nature of what was to follow, it is odd to think that in all those subsequent visits to his publishers here, Hughes must have passed this scene of early happiness.

Continue across the square and into the pretty, cobbled Cosmo Place, which runs along the side of the church. Turn left into the busy Southampton Row and go over at the zebra crossing into Bloomsbury Place. Enter Bloomsbury Square Gardens on your left and take the right-hand path. Leave the gardens by the right-hand exit at the far corner and turn right into Bloomsbury Way. Continue until you come to St George's Church, in all its carbon monoxide-and-pigeon-splattered grandeur. Built by Nicholas Hawksmoor (1661–1736) and completed in 1731, it survived the Blitz, but the thundering traffic outside has taken its toll. Much of the building is peeling away, something that would delight Horace Walpole, the 18th-century man of letters and author of the supernatural romance *Castle of Otranto*. He dismissed the church as 'a masterpiece of absurdity'. A board outside notes that Anthony Trollope (1815–1882) was baptized here and that the church features in Hogarth's famous 'Gin Lane', and in Charles Dickens's story 'The Bloomsbury Christening' in *Sketches by Boz*.

Turn right into Museum Street to find one of the capital's more unusual bookshops, on the right at No. 49a. The Atlantis Bookshop is an occult bookshop that was founded in 1922 by Michael Houghton, a Jew who escaped the pogroms in his native Hungary. Houghton, whose real name was Horowitz, was a poet who wrote under the pen name Michael Juste. The shop has been visited by many occult writers over the years, among them Aleister Crowley and Dion Fortune, while the traveller and mystic Paul Brunton apparently used to doss down here between trips. You'd need a firm resolve to do that today. A large, rather unsettling statue of the Egyptian God Anubis greets customers.

Continue up this attractive street of rare book dealers and cafés, noting the ornate frontages of the block at the far end. Soon you pass on your right Ulysses, the book dealers who specialise in first editions of modern fiction.

The 'Valley of the Shadow of Books'

Cross at the end of Museum Street to visit the British Museum. This venerable institution has undergone many changes, largely as a result of the British Library's move to Euston. However, for literary tourists this is good news, since the famous Reading Room – straight ahead of you when you enter – is now open to the general public for the first time. Hitherto seen only by academics and specialist researchers and writers, who each required a reader's ticket, the original desks at which the likes of Marx, Shaw, Hardy, George Eliot, Browning and Kipling studied, and the splendid, restored ceiling, are now available for all to see. However, finding the exact desks at which they sat is rather more difficult – Marx (1818–1883) apparently liked to be seated next to the old reference shelves, which would mean rows K to P.

Novelist George Gissing (1857–1903) called the Reading Room 'the Valley of the Shadow of Books', and George Bernard Shaw (1856–1950) educated himself here, working through the entire *Encyclopaedia Britannica*. 'My debt to that great institution…is inestimable,' he wrote. The Reading Room also houses the Paul Hamlyn Reference Library: 25,000 books relevant to the collections in the museum and named after the publisher (and Shaw's fellow Socialist), who made it possible.

Some Literary Urns and Marbles

The entire museum has of course been an inspiration to writers for years. Benjamin Robert Haydon (1786–1846), the English painter and friend of Keats (1795–1821), described how he 'loved to take him to the British Museum and [hear him] expatiate…on the glories of the antique'. The poet particularly admired the Greek spirit, calling it the 'religion of Joy'. After Haydon took him to see the Elgin Marbles on Sunday, 2 March 1817, Keats responded with a sonnet. The Greek collections also inspired one of his most famous poems, 'Ode on a Grecian Urn', with its closing couplet: 'Beauty is Truth, Truth Beauty – That is all/Ye know on Earth, and all ye need to know.' To visit the Elgin Marbles – and pass a few urns on the way – turn left on entering the museum and walk past the shop, following the signs for the restaurant. Turn right into Room 2, and go straight through into Room 4. Pass through a dogleg into Room 7 and then go left into Room 8.

After leaving the museum, turn right into Great Russell Street, noting the home of the artist and book illustrator Randolph Caldecott (1846–1886) at No. 46 opposite. The Caldecott Medal has been awarded annually since 1938 to the best American artist-illustrator of children's books. The building is now home to the antiquarian booksellers Jarndyce, a name taken from Dickens's *Bleak House*, which sells lots of 'Dickensiana'. Souvenir Press, on the corner of Coptic Street, is one of the last independent publishers in London. Founded by Ernest Hecht, an Arsenal-loving Czechoslovak Jew with an impish sense of humour who fled his country in 1939, its motto is 'Milia librorum toto qui vendidit orbe iudicis adversi temnere verba potest', which translates loosely as 'Best sellers are the best revenge'!

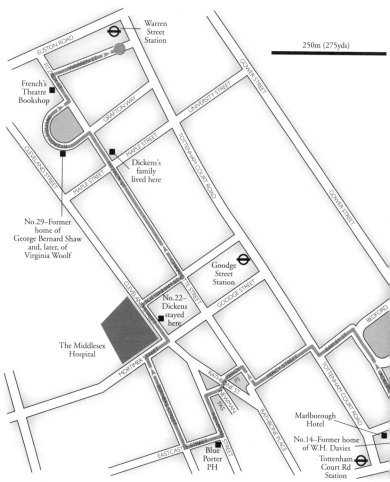

On the corner of Willoughby Street, at No. 38, was the home of the long-departed Poetry Bookshop, in which W. H. Davies (1871–1940), author of *The Autobiography of a Supertramp*, was introduced to the shop's founder, fellow poet Harold Monro (1879–1932). Opposite, at No. 91, lived the French-born artist, cartoonist and novelist George du Maurier (1834–1896). Straight ahead, the Marlborough Hotel, with the domed roof, features briefly in the film of Willie Russell's play *Shirley Valentine*.

Iris Murdoch's 'Laundry Bags'
Cross over to continue along Great Russell Street. W. H. Davies lived for a time at No. 14, the first house of the block at the far end on the left. Turn right, opposite, into Adeline Place, which leads up into Bedford Square. Keep to the left-hand pavement and walk to the far corner of the square, then turn left into Bayley Street. Just before you turn, look for No. 6 Bayley Street. This is the office of the Armani-

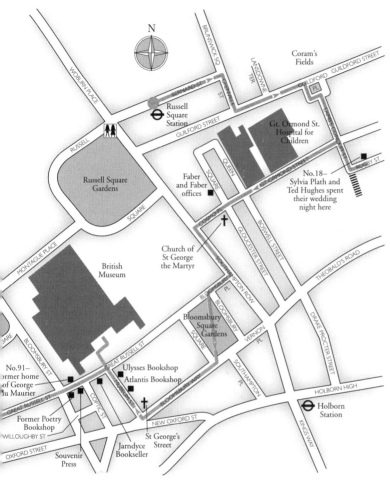

wearing, image-conscious, American literary agent Ed Victor. His most literary client remains Iris Murdoch (1919–1999), who was a frequent visitor here. After her death, he recalled: 'She would arrive at my office, always alarmingly early for her appointment, carrying a bunch of blue plastic laundry bags, stuffed full of notebooks in which she had handwritten her novel... I would despatch one of our staff to the photocopying shop with instructions to guard the new-born novel with her very life until it was safely copied.'

Cross Tottenham Court Road, going straight into Percy Street, where the English poet (and assistant librarian at the British Museum) Coventy Patmore (1823–1896) lived at No. 15. The novelist, painter and critic Wyndham Lewis (1894–1957) lived in this short street too. Turn right into Charlotte Street, then left after a few yards, down a little alley called Percy Passage. Cross the next street and go into Newman Passage, which brings you out on Newman Street. The poets Algernon Charles Swinburne (1837–1909) and Dante Gabriel Rosetti (1828–1882) both lived here.

Turn left and then right into Eastcastle Street at The Blue Posts pub. Turn right into Berners Street, where Samuel Taylor Coleridge (1772–1834) lived briefly between 1812 and 1813. Bombing and the passage of the years have considerably altered the street, but one building that has remained unscathed despite the Blitz is the great red-brick monolith of The Middlesex Hospital. Re-built in 1935, it has in imposing frontage, redolent of Empire. It was here that Rudyard Kipling (1865–1936), a writer for whom the idea of Empire meant much, died. T. H. White, author of *The Once and Future King* and *The Goshawk*, stood outside the hospital on the night Kipling died and looked at 'the great barrack of a wall half resentfully, also blankly, confusedly, self-consciously'.

Turn right into Mortimer Street, pass the hospital, then turn left into Cleveland Street where, during 1829–30, Dickens stayed with his family above a greengrocer's shop at No. 22. The building, with its pretty fan-tail window, still exists and is one of the locations Peter Ackroyd visited when writing his mammoth biography of Dickens. Turn right into Tottenham Street, passing the attractive, cobbled Goodge Place on your right.

A Literary Square and its Cheeky Dog

Turn left into Charlotte Street, which at this end is full of advertising agencies and film production companies. Charlotte Street soon runs into Fitzroy Street. After you cross Maple Street, go over to the right-hand pavement to get a better view of No. 25 Fitzroy Street on your left. Dickens's family lived here when he was 20. Glorious plane trees at the end of the road mark Fitzroy Square, another splendid Georgian square and, like Bedford Square, rich in literary history. Turn left and follow the square until you come to No. 29, on the left-hand side, one of the few houses in London to have more than one plaque. George Bernard Shaw and his mother took lodgings on the third and fourth floors here in 1887. He wasn't keen on the house at first. 'Depressing hall' was one of his first reactions; he also called it 'a most repulsive house' – a remark that may seem strange when one looks at the grandeur of this square today. Still, he bought the lease for his mother and was to stay here for the following 11 years. He wrote his first seven plays in a chaotic, top-floor study here; his bedroom was one of the big rooms overlooking the square.

From 1907 to 1911 Virginia Stephen, who later became Virginia Woolf, lived here with her brother Adrian. They revived the 'Thursday evenings' that their brother Thoby had begun elsewhere, which had been interrupted by his untimely death the year before. Numerous literary and artistic figures came to these gatherings in the first-floor reception room where, according to the art and literary critic (and Bloomsbury Group member) Clive Bell, Woolf's dog Hans 'delighted in extinguishing visitors' matches with its paws'. Before you move on, notice the boot-scrapers in the doorway and wonder which distinguished names have made use of them.

The dramatist and dramatic critic William Archer (1856–1924), the chief force in introducing Ibsen to England, lived at No. 27.

Continue around the square and turn left into the continuation of Fitzroy Street, passing French's Theatre Bookshop. Turn right into Warren Street to find Warren Street Station at the end, where the walk ends.

Regent's Park and Primrose Hill

Summary: A walk which combines the very best that London offers – a beautiful park, an impressive view and one lovely street that has a continental atmosphere being full of cafés and interesting shops. You will also get a free glimpse of the elephants in London Zoo and discover where Kingsley Amis used to enjoy his whisky. The walk also includes the tragic story of Sylvia Plath.

Start:	Regent's Park Underground Station (Bakerloo Line).
Finish:	Camden Town Underground Station (Northern Line).
Length:	5.25 kilometres (3¼ miles).
Time:	2–2.5 hours.
Refreshments:	There is good café in Regent's Park, and further cafés, pubs and restaurants on Regent's Park Road.

Turn right on leaving Regent's Park Station and cross at the lights to visit the sandstone coloured church a short distance away. This is Holy Trinity Church, built in the 1820s, the crypt of which – bizarre though it sounds – was home to Penguin Books for the first 18 months of its life in 1936. Before this time the crypt was a storeroom of the publishers Bodley Head, whose MD, Allen Lane, went on to begin the world's most famous paperback imprint (see page 36). Some 10 million Penguins were distributed from here, the noise having to be kept to a minimum when services were being conducted upstairs. Staff were given a penny a day to use the lavatories in Great Portland Street Station opposite. The church's association with books continues today – Holy Trinity is now the headquarters of the publishers SPCK (Society for the Propagation of Christian Knowledge) and the main body of the church houses an attractive bookshop. There are probably even a good few Penguins on the shelves.

Walk round the outside of the church by going left up Osnaburgh Street, where George Bernard Shaw (1856–1950) lived at No. 36, and left into Osnaburgh Terrace. The Fabian Society was founded in 1884 on the site of the White House Hotel, on your right, and Shaw was a prominent early member.

Writers and the Zoo

Turn left into the busy Albany Street and return to Marylebone Road, where you turn right. The artist and writer Edward Lear (1812–1888) lived at No. 61 Albany Street so that he could walk to London Zoo, where he was employed sketching the parrots and other animals. You are walking to the zoo too, but by another, quieter route. Walk along Marylebone Road and turn right into Park Square East, which has gates at its entrance. At the top, cross over and enter Regent's Park through St Andrew's Gate at the corner. The publisher André Deutsch (1917–2000) used to play tennis here with his fellow Hungarian George Mikes, author of *How to be an Alien*, in which he summed up the English character thus: 'Continental people have a sex life; the English people have hot-water bottles.' Take the middle path straight ahead and note the traffic noise begin to fade away. This path soon meets the main, tree-lined Broad Walk, where you turn right. Carry straight on, crossing over one road and soon coming to a pleasant, mock-Tudor café on your left. When you come to an ornate fountain, bear left to walk along the perimeter wall of the zoo.

London Zoo, opened in 1828, has a number of literary connections. Soon after it opened, the 18-year-old Edward Lear worked here, drawing the animals, and some of his work was used in early guides. The artist who would become one of the Victorian era's greatest eccentrics did not restrict himself to the animals: he also drew very funny caricatures of the public who watched him.

The novelist William Makepeace Thackeray (1811–1863) was a visitor, too, and wrote an account of a visit for *Punch* in 1846. '[We] were then driven to the Zoological Gardens, a place which I often like to visit (keeping away from the larger beasts, such as the bears, who I often fancy may jump from their poles upon certain unoffending Christians; and the howling tigers and lions, who are continually biting the keepers' heads off), and where I like to look at the monkeys in the cages (the little rascals!) and the birds of various plumage.'

London Zoo inspired – and disturbed – many writers. Stevie Smith's poem, 'The Zoo', begins: 'The lion sits within his cage,/Weeping tears of ruby rage,/He licks his snout, the tears fall down/And water dusty London town.' As you walk next to the wall, if you look carefully between the buildings you will see the crisp, clean, curved white lines of the Grade One listed Penguin Pool (1934). Like Holy Trinity Church, it too played a part in the birth of Penguin paperbacks (see page 36).

Leave Regent's Park via the appropriately named Monkey Gate and cross Regent's Canal on Primrose Hill Bridge, with views of the Snowdon aviary on your right. Turn right into Prince Albert Road and cross at the zebra to enter Primrose Hill itself. Take the left-hand path and, halfway up, bear right to reach the viewpoint at the summit. Standing here, only 63 metres (206 ft) above sea level, you have a splendid view of London. Here too, you are able to enter the lives of Sylvia Plath (1932–1963) and Ted Hughes (1930–1998), who lived close by. After the collapse of their marriage, Plath and her young children Frieda and Nicholas moved to Fitzroy Road, away to your left (the walk passes the house shortly).

Kingsley and Martin Amis

Take the path away to the far side, which slopes down to the coloured façades of Regent's Park Road. Exit to Primrose Hill Road, turning right, and then turn left into Regent's Park Road by the Queen's pub on the corner. This was the local of the novelist and poet Kingsley Amis (1922–1995) from 1985 until his death; its recent, trendy make over would not have appealed to him at all. Much of Amis's later life can be traced in the short, pretty and very expensive stretch of street you now walk along. He would come to the Queen's *en route* to the Garrick and would stay

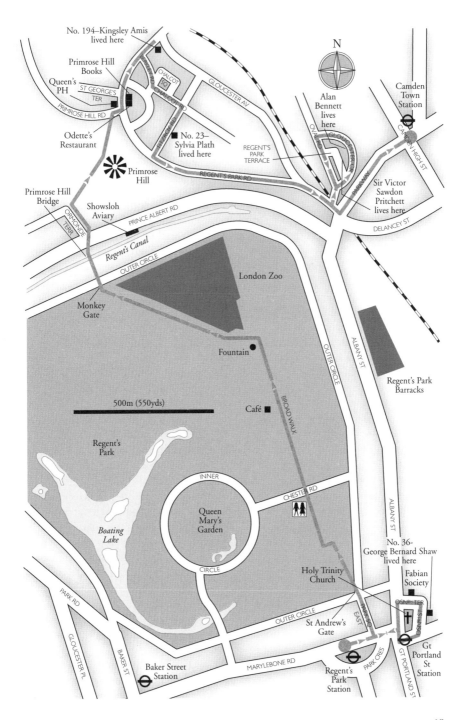

No. 194–Kingsley Amis
lived here

Primrose Hill
Books

Queen's
PH

ST GEORGE'S
TER

CHALCOT RD

CHALCOT
SQ

GLOUCESTER AV

N

Camden
Town
Station

Alan
Bennett
lives
here

CAMDEN HIGH ST

PRIMROSE HILL RD

FITZROY RD

REGENT'S
PARK
TERRACE

GLOUCESTER CR

PARKWAY

Odette's
Restaurant

No. 23–
Sylvia Plath
lived here

Primrose
Hill

Primrose Hill
Bridge

REGENT'S PARK RD

Sir Victor
Sawdon
Pritchett
lives here

DELANCEY ST

Showsloh
Aviary

PRINCE ALBERT RD

ORMONDE
TERR

Regent's Canal

OUTER CIRCLE

London Zoo

ALBANY ST

Monkey
Gate

Fountain

OUTER CIRCLE

Regent's Park
Barracks

500m (550yds)

Café

BROAD WALK

Regent's
Park

INNER

ALBANY ST

CHESTER RD

Queen
Mary's
Garden

*Boating
Lake*

No. 36–
George Bernard Shaw
lived here

Fabian
Society

CIRCLE

Holy Trinity
Church

OSN TER

PARK RD

PARK RD EAST

St Andrew's
Gate

GLOUCESTER PL

BAKER ST

Baker Street
Station

OUTER CIRCLE

MARYLEBONE RD

PARK CRES

GT PORTLAND ST

Regent's
Park
Station

Gt
Portland
St
Station

longer on Saturdays, when the Garrick was closed. He was also fond of eating at Odette's restaurant opposite. Next to Odette's is Primrose Hill Books, where Amis's son, Martin, can sometimes be seen browsing in the secondhand selection outside (staff at the shop say that this is because smoking is not permitted inside, and Martin always has a cigarette in his mouth). Amis *fils* was also living on Regent's Park Road at the time of writing, although at the opposite end to that at which his father lived. Other writers who live in this upmarket and artistic area and frequent the bookshop include Alan Bennett, Tobias Hill, Ian McEwan and Claire Tomlin.

Continue along Regent's Park Road, passing St George's Terrace on your left, where Plath and Hughes were able to share a study in the house of the American poet W. S. Merwin while he was away. Just before the road ends look for No. 194 on your right, near the end of an elegant terrace of substantial white houses. Kingsley Amis moved here in July 1985, in an unusual arrangement that saw his first wife, Hilly, living in the basement with her third husband, Lord Kilmarnock, while Amis had separate quarters upstairs. Martin Amis would bring his children here at weekends, and the two writers would try not to discuss their work. Of one of his son's novels, Kingsley wrote to a friend: '[it is] too boring. Little sod said on TV you had to read it twice. Well then HE'S FAILED hasn't he?'

The Tragic Story of Sylvia Plath

Retrace your steps and turn left into Berkley Road, which leads into Chalcot Square. Ted Hughes and Sylvia Plath moved into a third-floor flat at No. 3 in February 1960, when the area was quite down-at-heel. Plath told her mother that according to the woman living in the flat above her, the sounds of lions, seals and exotic birds at Regent's Park Zoo were quite audible when the building's windows were open in summer.

Two years later, after the marriage had ended, Plath moved with her children to a house just a few hundred yards away, at No. 23 Fitzroy Road. To find the house, which was to be Plath's last home, continue past Chalcot Square and turn right at the junction. The house is on the left and has a blue plaque recording that W. B. Yeats also lived here (until he was nine), a fact that greatly excited Plath.

Plath had a history of psychological problems and had tried suicide once before. Her fragile psychological condition at the time was exacerbated by a recurring sinus problem, the freezing weather (the winter of 1962–3 was one of the century's worst) and the strains of being a single mother with two very young children. At about 6am on Monday 11 February 1963 she took a plate of bread and butter and two beakers of milk up to Frieda and Nicholas's room. She left the bread and milk by their cots, opened the window wide and then closed the door behind her. She put tape along the edges of the door and stuffed towels and cloth underneath.

She went downstairs to the kitchen and did the same on the inside of the kitchen door. She then opened the oven door, placed a small folded cloth inside, turned the gas taps full on and placed her head on the cloth.

Plath had been seeing her local doctor, Dr Horder, and a nurse sent by him arrived at the house at 9am. Unable to get any reply at the door, she eventually broke into the flat with a local builder. They dragged Plath to the sitting-room and the nurse attempted artificial respiration. It was too late. Plath had also taken a fatal overdose of sleeping tablets. A note was pinned to the pram in the hall saying: 'Please call Dr. Horder.' The builder went upstairs to the children, who were both crying. They were cold, but otherwise unharmed.

Today, Frieda Hughes, who was then nearly three, is an artist and poet herself, while her brother Nicholas, then 13 months old, is a scientist working in Canada and Alaska. A cult has grown around their parents, feminists blaming Hughes for the affair he had with Assia Wevill, who also killed herself and their daughter Shura. Hughes himself always kept silent, speaking only through *Birthday Letters*, published nine months before his death. He lived quietly in Devon with his third wife, and turned his back on the literary life of interviews and parties.

Continue up Fitzroy Road to Regent's Park Road, where you turn left. At the traffic lights turn left to cross the railway bridge into Oval Road, and then immediately right into Gloucester Crescent. At the time of writing Alan Bennett was living in this very select road – you may even spot him on his bicycle. Follow the road round and turn left to walk past Regent's Park Terrace on Oval Road, where the writer and critic Sir V[ictor] S[awdon] Pritchett (1900–1997) lived in the last years of his life. Retrace your steps to the lights, then turn left and left again down Parkway, which eventually brings you out at Camden Town Station, where the walk ends.

The City (1): St Paul's to the Tower

Summary: The City is a paradox. In many respects the least literary part of London – you will find few publishers and agents lunching authors here – it has nevertheless been host for many years to the country's most prestigious literary award, the Booker Prize. Although it is strange to think that poets like Keats once lived in what is now the heart of the financial district, the City does in fact have a rich literary history. This walk passes places where such contrasting writers as T. S. Eliot and Kenneth Grahame worked. You will also see some stunning architecture – some very old and some very new.

Start:	St Paul's Underground Station (Central Line).
Finish:	Tower Hill Underground Station (District and Circle Lines).
Length:	4 kilometres (2½ miles).
Time:	2.5–3 hours.
Refreshments:	There are many bars, pubs and cafés to choose from during the week, but of these very few are open on Sundays, when the area is eerily quiet. The alleys visited off Cornhill have some atmospheric bars, like the Jamaica Wine House. The George and Vulture Inn in St Michael's Alley has associations with Dickens.

Take Exit 2 (St Paul's Cathedral) from St Paul's Station and turn left at the top of the stairs. Cross Paternoster Row, now an ugly modern development, but famous for its booksellers and publishers until its destruction in the Second World War. Close by stood the Chapter Coffee House, where the poet Thomas Chatterton (1752–1770) stayed in 1770, writing to his mother, 'I am staying at the Chapter Coffee House and know all the geniuses there.'

Turn right into St Paul's Churchyard and follow it round to the front to visit the cathedral. The poet John Donne (1572–1630) was Dean here from 1621 to 1631, and it is worth visiting his tomb at the far end on the right in the south choir aisle. This white marble statue was one of the few items to survive the Great Fire of London in 1666, falling through the floor and into the crypt, where it was later discovered in one piece. Scorch marks can be seen around its base.

Betjeman's Church

Turn left on leaving the cathedral and keep to the path that hugs the building. Enter the churchyard on your left and leave it by Paternoster Row, opposite the tall, statue of St Paul, with his golden halo. Head for the grey church opposite in Foster Lane, on the other side of the traffic lights. This is St Vedast's, destroyed in the Great Fire, rebuilt by Wren, and restored in 1962. The poet Sir John Betjeman (1906–1984) was once a churchwarden here and wrote about the bells of City churches on a Sunday: 'Sunday Silence! with every street a dead street,/Alley and courtyard empty and cobbled mews,/… Till all were drowned as the sailing clouds went singing/On the roaring flood of a twelve-voiced peal from St Paul's.' If you look back from the church you have a splendid view of St Paul's, the view that Betjeman would have had on leaving the church.

Walk up Foster Lane, past Goldsmiths' Hall on your right where the diminutive Indian writer Vikram Seth won the £10,000 WH Smith Literary Award in 1994 for his giant novel *A Suitable Boy*. It was here, too, that in 1961 the poet Sylvia Plath (1932–1963) collected a rather smaller cheque – for £75 – when she won a prize in an annual award sponsored by Guinness.

Turn right into Gresham Street (look out for wall plaques to churches lost in the Great Fire in these streets) and left into Wood Street, where the single surviving tower of St Alban's looks surreal amid the modern architecture that surrounds it. The church was destroyed during the Blitz, but Betjeman remembered its 'gas mantles and sparse congregation'. As a young boy he loved to visit City churches, 'especially on a Sunday evening when single bells beat from moon-lit steeples down gas-lit alleys.' Today, the moon shines off steel and glass.

The Home of the Country's Most Famous Literary Prize

Turn right into Love Lane, passing a little garden that includes a bust of Shakespeare, who is believed to have lived close by, and then right into Aldermanbury. An entrance on the left soon leads into the grand piazza of the Guildhall, where the annual dinner for the Booker Prize for fiction is held. The Booker Prize is the most important event on the literary calendar and if you stand here on 'Booker night' in early October you will see literary London arriving *en masse*. The men are all in dinner jackets, the women in evening dress, and Faber publisher Joanna Mackle invariably wears one of her huge hats. Walk into the centre of the piazza. Until 1999 guests used to file along the glass corridor to your left. Now they enter through the new building straight ahead, the refurbished Guildhall Art Gallery. The actual hall in which the dinner is held – the Guildhall – is to your left, behind the entrance with the carved dragons. It dates back to the 15th century and is the seat of the City of London Corporation.

It was in this hall that Kingsley Amis famously declared that he would spend his £20,000 prize money on 'booze, of course' when he won the Booker in 1986 for *The Old Devils*, and here that Roddy Doyle declared, 'Jesus, I don't know if this is good, bad or indifferent. But it makes my friends smile,' when he won in 1993 with *Paddy Clarke Ha Ha Ha*. There have been many controversies since the Booker was established in 1969, and all of them have boosted its status. In 1977, Philip Larkin (1922–1985), Chair of the judges, threatened to jump out of the window if Paul Scott's *Staying On* didn't win (it did); and in 1983, the year Salman Rushdie didn't win with *Shame*, the author was rude to Booker Prize administrator Martyn Goff as the pair passed outside the toilets, Rushdie incorrectly believing Goff to be a judge.

Leave the piazza at the back of St Lawrence Jewry Church, opposite the Guildhall, and cross into King Street. Turn left into the narrow Prudential Passage and right into Ironmonger Lane, which brings you out onto Cheapside. The poet John Keats (1795–1821) lived with his brothers at No. 76 (long since demolished) in 1816, when he was still working as a dresser at Guy's Hospital. The church of St Mary-le-Bow, away to your right, existed in Keats's day, and his lodgings were on the same side of the road, just a hundred or so yards this side of the church. St Mary's contains the famous 'Bow bells', which tolled the curfew during the 14th century and probably gave rise to the idea that every true Cockney is born within hearing distance of them. It was to these Cheapside lodgings that Keats returned from the poet Leigh Hunt's house in Hampstead, walking the cold miles one November morning before dawn and feeling 'brimfull of the friendliness/That in a little cottage I have found.'

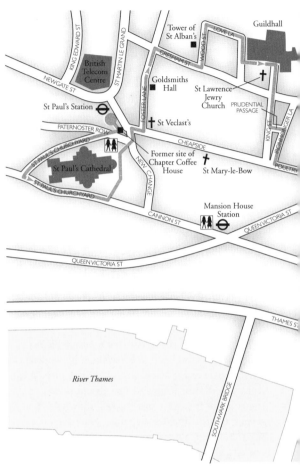

Literary Bankers

Turn left and follow Cheapside into Poultry (there is little so wonderful as London street names), where the poet Thomas Hood was born in 1799. Keeping to the left, pause at the mighty junction known simply as 'Bank'. Who would imagine that this busy thoroughfare, entirely given over to money, would have a literary heritage? Yet it does and it can be seen or, more accurately, imagined, if you stand by the steps to Bank Station. The long, concrete monolith to your left is the Bank of England, where the writers Kenneth Grahame (1859–1932) and P. G. Wodehouse (1881–1975) worked. The future author of *The Wind in the Willows* joined the bank in 1879 as a 'gentleman clerk' and became its youngest ever Secretary in 1898. A

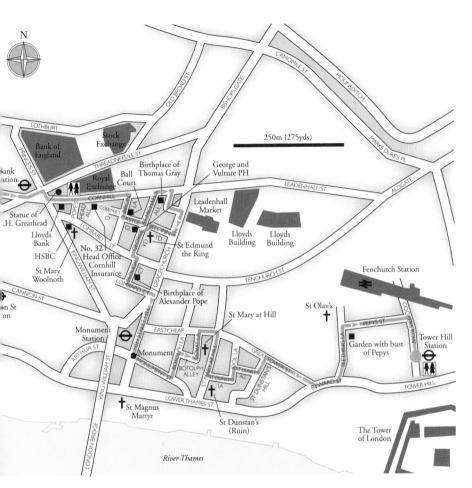

few years later, on 21 November 1903, a respectable looking visitor arrived, demanding to see the Governor of the Bank. Grahame informed him that he was not on the premises. The man pulled out a revolver. Three shots were fired, but Grahame was not injured and was able to stop one of the directors from entering the room. The man was eventually arrested and charged with 'Wandering in Threadneedle Street: deemed to be a lunatic'.

The incident could almost come straight from Wodehouse. From 1900 to 1902 Pelham Grenville Wodehouse worked (though he might dispute that choice of verb) in the London branch of the Hong Kong and Shanghai Bank in Lombard Street, which is to the left of the church with the twin towers and protruding hexagonal clock opposite. Wodehouse once opened a new ledger, wrote a short story on the first page, then tore it out. The head cashier discovered the ledger and accused the bank's stationer of supplying defective goods. Wodehouse recalled the incident thus: 'Somebody must have cut out the page', he said. 'Absurd!', said the head cashier.

'Nobody but an imbecile would cut out the front page of a ledger.' 'Then', said the stationer, coming right back at him, 'you must have an imbecile in your department. Have you?' The head cashier started. This opened up a new line of thought. 'Why, yes,' he admitted, for he was a fair-minded man, 'there is P. G. Wodehouse...' The writer's banking career ended soon after this.

An Elegy for Commuters

The twin-towered church is St Marry Woolnoth, remembered by T. S. Eliot, who worked for Lloyds Bank in Cornhill, two streets to its left, from 1919 to 1922. He joined the Colonial and Foreign Department on a salary of £270 per annum, and his job was to tabulate and interpret the balance sheets of foreign banks so that their development could be charted. In *The Waste Land,* he described the journey of the commuters walking over London Bridge, and down King William Street to Saint Mary Woolnoth. The same journey is still made today.

Cross Princes Street to your left, then Threadneedle Street, and walk up the left-hand pavement of Cornhill until you reach the statue of the civil engineer J. H. Greathead (1844–1896). Lloyds Bank is on the other side of the road. This building replaced the one in which Eliot worked. The critic I. A. Richards (1893–1979) visited the poet in his office at the time and recalled 'a figure stooping, very like a dark bird in a feeder, over a big table covered with all sorts and sizes of foreign correspondence. The big table almost entirely filled a little room under the street. Within a foot of our heads when we stood were the thick, green glass squares of the pavement on which hammered all but incessantly the heels of the passers-by...' If you cross the road now you can easily see the pavement lights outside the bank and imagine Eliot at work beneath your feet.

A short detour can be made along Pope's Head Alley to visit St Mary Woolnoth; otherwise, continue up Cornhill, pausing to note the wooden door of No. 32, the head offices of Cornhill Insurance. The bottom right-hand panel records the meeting between William Thackeray and the Brontë sisters at the publishers Smith, Elder & Co, which used to be on this site

City Alleys and a Big Climb

Turn right into Birchin Lane and find Cowper's Court on your right, where Eliot used to visit a wine shop. Retrace your steps back up Birchin Lane and turn right into Castle Court, noting Ball Court on your left – these are delightfully atmospheric City alley-ways. Mr Pickwick stays at the George and Vulture, on your right, in *The Pickwick Papers.* Turn left in to St Michael's Alley and return to Cornhill, where you turn right. A plaque on the building adjacent to the alley records the fact that the poet Thomas Gray, author of 'Elegy Written in a Country Churchyard', was born on this site in 1716.

At the pink building topped by the gargoyle, turn right into St Peter's Alley (the church features in Dickens's *Our Mutual Friend*) and right again into Gracechurch Street. Turn right into Bell Inn Yard and follow it round to the left, to come out by the church of St Edmund the King at the bottom of George Yard. Cross over into Plough Court, where the poet Alexander Pope (1688–1744) was born. Turn left into

Lombard Court, which brings you out onto Gracechurch Street again, where you turn right. Now head for the gold-topped Monument in the distance, completed in 1677 to commemorate the Great Fire of London. James Boswell (1740–1795), biographer of Dr Johnson, climbed its 311 steps in 1762 and found it 'horrid to be so monstrous a way up in the air, so far above London and all its spires'. At the top of the cobbled Fish Street Hill, just before you descend to the Monument, note the church of St Magnus Martyr beyond. This church is also mentioned in Eliot's *The Waste Land*, where he notes its 'Inexplicable splendour of Ionian white and gold'. He described the church as 'one of the finest among Wren's interiors'.

Pepys's Adventures

Turn left at the Monument into Monument Street, then left into Botolph Lane and right into Botolph Alley, which comes out on Lovat Lane, opposite another Wren church, St Mary at Hill, much loved by Betjeman. Continue up Lovat Hill to Eastcheap, where you turn right and right again into St Mary at Hill. Just past the back of the church, turn into St Dunstan's Lane, which has a classic 'old against new' view at the end, as a modern City building can be seen through the shell of St Dunstan's in the east. Another Wren church, St Dunstan's was damaged in the Great Fire, rebuilt, and all but destroyed in the Second World War. It now houses one of London's secret gardens and is well worth visiting. On 23 April 1668 the diarist Samuel Pepys (1633–1703) was nearly mugged near the church after an evening's merrymaking with a Mrs Knipp: 'It being now 10 at night, and so got a link; and walking towards home, just at my entrance into the ruines at St Dunstan's, I was met by two rogues with clubs, who came towards us; so I went back and walked home quite round by the Wall and got well home.' A 'link' was a 'linkman' or 'linkboy' who, in the years before street lighting, would light the way with a flaming torch for a small charge.

Walk along St Dunstan's Alley and then left into St Dunstan's Hill, with views of modern City Gothic architecture ahead. Turn right into Great Tower Street and follow it until you reach Seething Lane on your left. This is where Pepys was living in 1666 and where, still wearing a nightgown, he loaded all his possessions on to a cart at 4am on 3 September to escape the flames of the Great Fire. Actually, he didn't take all his possessions. He buried his wine and Parmesan cheese in a pit in the garden.

The Navy Office, where Pepys worked, was also in Seething Lane. At the top of the street is St Olav's Church, where the diarist was buried in 1703. Pepys was very fond of the church, referring to it affectionately in his diaries as 'our own church'. In 1660 he had an outside stairway and small gallery built from the Navy Office to the church so that he could attend services without getting wet. It was later removed, but the garden you passed on your right, which has a bust of Pepys, marks the site where the gallery stood. Now turn right into Pepys Street and right again into Coopers Row, which leads to Tower Hill Station, where the walk ends.

The City (2): Mansion House to Old Street

Summary: This walk includes London's oldest church, in the grounds of which John Milton once hid from the forces of Charles II; it has also been used by film-makers in two of the most popular films of the last ten years. For much of the way you will be walking in the footsteps of John Betjeman, who loved the City's alleys and passageways. The walk ends with a visit to one of London's least-known but most interesting 'literary' graveyards.

Start:	Mansion House Underground Station (District and Circle Lines).
Finish:	Old Street Station (Northern Line; overground trains to Moorgate).
Length:	3.6 kilometres (2¼ miles).
Time:	2.5–3 hours.
Refreshments:	There are plenty of cafés, bars and restaurants to visit during the week, but very little is open at weekends. Betjeman's wine bar, beneath the poet's apartment, is of interest (although its clientele of businessmen look nothing like poets), as is the 'John Keats at the Moorgate' pub.

Take Exit One (Queen Victoria Street) from Mansion House Station and turn immediately left at the top of the steps, taking the subway across the street. Leave the subway at Exit Four (Queen Victoria Street east), turn right at the top of the steps and right again into Canon Street. Walk along a short way and when St Paul's comes into view turn right into Bread Street. Here, in a house in a court on the west side of the street, the poet John Milton (1608–1674) was born. In those days the houses did not have numbers; the custom was to name houses after a sign hanging above the entrance, as pubs do today. So Milton's house was known as the Spread Eagle and his father had a seal made with a double-headed, stretch-winged eagle on it, which his son cherished.

Poetic Trees

Walk past dull office buildings and at Cheapside look to your right to see St Mary-le-Bow, which the poet John Keats (1795–1821) would have walked past when he lodged in Cheapside in 1816. The magnificent, single plane tree above L&R Wooderson Shirtmakers, opposite and to your left, has poetic associations too. William Wordsworth's poem 'The Reverie of Poor Susan' concerns a girl walking along Cheapside who hears a thrush singing in this tree and feels her country childhood tugging at her heart. You now cross over to walk up Wood Street, past the tree in the scruffy garden where the church of St Peter in Chepe once stood. The railings date from 1712. Note Milk Street on your right. The name 'Cheapside' is derived from ceap, the Old English word for 'market', and many of the streets here take their name from the goods sold in years gone by.

A Park that Made the West End Stage

Turn left into Gresham Street, noting the exposed tower of St Alban, and at St Martin-le-Grand turn left to cross at the lights and then right to continue up to the Museum of London. Another isolated plane tree marks the entrance to Postman's Park, one of London's most curious gardens. So called because of its proximity to the General Post Office, it was opened in 1880 and features at its back a 'national memorial to heroic men and women'. This wall, with its plaques commemorating noble deeds by ordinary men and women (such as Thomas Simpson, who 'died of exhaustion after saving many lives from the breaking ice at Highgate Ponds, January 25 1885') was re-created on the West End stage in 1998 in the play *Closer*, by Patrick Marber, one of the country's most acclaimed young playwrights. A character in the play takes her identity from one of the people mentioned in the plaques.

Leave the park and turn left. Immediately you notice the residential towers of the Barbican, seeming to protrude like two enormous jaws from the brick bagel of the Museum of London plonked in the middle of the road. Pass St Botolph's Church, a favourite of John Betjeman's with its splendid wooden galleries, and turn left into Little Britain. Cross at the top and follow the road round to the right, past St Bartholomew's Hospital. Keep to the left, pass the quaint Nurses' Gate, and shortly you walk down a pedestrian precinct that brings you out into West Smithfield, with the splendid market buildings opposite and the entrance to the priory church of St Bartholomew the Great on your right.

From Betjeman to Hugh Grant

St Bartholomew the Great is London's oldest church, the only surviving part of an Augustinian priory founded in 1123. For Betjeman it was one of only two churches that brought back Medieval London; he knew it well because for a period he lived close by, in Cloth Fair, which you pass shortly. Visiting the church is a must. An arch in Bartholomew Close provided refuge for John Milton, whose head was wanted by Charles II because of his anti-royal writings, in 1660.

The Lady Chapel was once a printer's office and in 1725 the American statesman and scientist Benjamin Franklin came here to work as an apprentice. In more recent years, the main body of the church featured in the films *Four Weddings and a Funeral* and Tom Stoppard's *Shakespeare in Love*.

Retrace your steps and, on leaving the churchyard, turn right. Turn right again into the narrow Cloth Fair. The second passageway on the left is Cloth Court, where you will find a plaque records the fact that Betjeman lived on the first floor. Downstairs there is a wine bar that bears his name. In 1977 the Poet Laureate wrote of his home here:

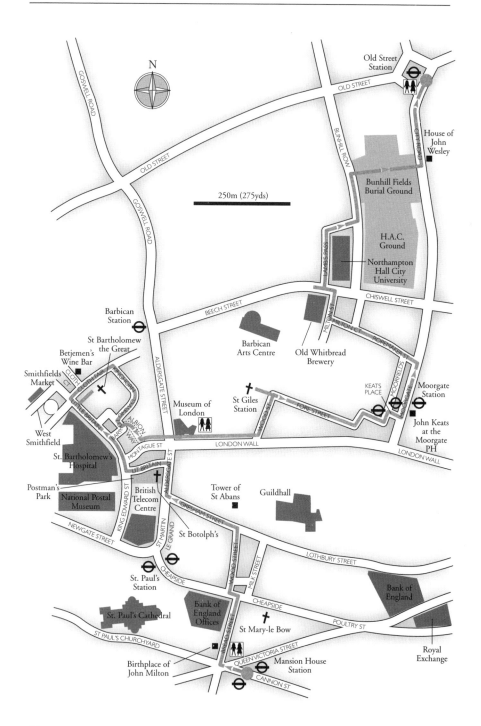

N

250m (275yds)

Old Street
Station

House of
John
Wesley

Bunhill Fields
Burial Ground

H.A.C.
Ground

Northampton
Hall City
University

OLD STREET

GOSWELL ROAD

BUNHILL ROW

CITY ROAD

JAMES PASS

CHISWELL STREET

MILTON ST

MILTON CT

ROPEMAKER ST

Barbican
Station

St Bartholomew
the Great

Betjemen's
Wine Bar

Smithfields
Market

West
Smithfield

St. Bartholomew's
Hospital

Postman's
Park

National Postal
Museum

BEECH STREET

Barbican
Arts Centre

Old Whitbread
Brewery

KEATS
PLACE

Moorgate
Station

MOORFIELDS

MOORGATE

John Keats
at the
Moorgate
PH

Museum of
London

St Giles
Station

FORE STREET

WOOD ST

LONDON WALL

LONDON WALL

ALDERSGATE STREET

MONTAGUE ST

LIT BRITAIN

ALBION WAY

BARTH WAY

LITTLE BRITAIN

CLOTH FAIR

CLOTH CT

KINGHORN ST

British
Telecom
Centre

Tower of
St Abans

Guildhall

St Botolph's

KING EDWARD ST

ST MARTIN

LE GRAND

ALDERSGATE ST

GRESHAM STREET

WOOD STREET

LOTHBURY STREET

NEWGATE STREET

St. Paul's
Station

St. Paul's Cathedral

ST PAUL'S CHURCHYARD

CHEAPSIDE

Bank of
England
Offices

St Mary-le Bow

CHEAPSIDE

MILK STREET

Bank of
England

POULTRY ST

Royal
Exchange

Birthplace of
John Milton

Mansion House
Station

QUEEN VICTORIA STREET

CANNON ST

This was the nicest place in London to live in because everything could be reached on foot, down alleys and passages. Like all county towns it had a bit of every trade. I was lucky enough to live in Cloth Fair where there was still a shop which sold cloth. On some weekly nights there was bell-ringing from the Tower of St Bartholomew's the Great, just such bells as the walled city must have heard when there were 108 churches in its square mile. Behind me was Smithfield meat market with its cheerful Chaucerian characters and Medieval-looking hand barrows.

The Museum of London to Grub Street

This is still an attractive area of alleys and passageways. When Bartholomew Close opens out into a courtyard on your right, turn into it, take the alley-way on your left and follow your nose. Turn sharp left on leaving the alley and walk past the trees in the middle of the road to turn left into Albion Way. Turn right, cross over and take the steps up to the Museum of London. At the first London Festival of Literature in 1999, the black American author Walter Mosley – Bill Clinton's favourite writer – gave a reading here that was splendidly atmospheric, if poorly attended.

Walk over the road on the footbridge and turn right, following the Wallside signs. You are now on the 21st-century equivalent of the old city walls, some remains of which you soon pass on your left. Walk underneath one of the City's new and glinting towers, then turn left. Take the Wallside exit to Wood Street on your left and enjoy the view of St Giles without Cripplegate as you descend the stairs. Turn left at the bottom of the stairs to visit the church. It was in this church that the writer Daniel Defoe (1660?–1731) was baptized, and Milton was buried here in 1674. Milton's grave was opened in 1793. An account of this ghoulish act records that the corpse's teeth were loosened by a blow with a stone and that, 'a rib bone was also taken and the hair from the head which was long and smooth was torn out by the handful.'

Leave the church and continue straight along Fore Street, with the steel corduroy of the International Finance Centre rising ahead of you. Follow Fore Street round to the left and right, coming out in Moorfield, site of the original Grub Street, described by Samuel Johnson in his famous *A Dictionary of the English Language* in 1754 as, 'a street near Moorfields, much inhabited by writers of small histories, dictionaries, and temporary poems; whence any mean production is called Grub Street.' Note the John Keats at the Moorgate pub opposite and walk past it, then turn left, and left again, to come out in Moorgate in front of the pub. The plaque above records that John Keats was born in a house on this site in 1795.

A Literary Brewery

Continue up Moorgate, past the station, and turn left into Ropemaker Street, where Defoe died in April 1731. Pass into Milton Court and turn right into Milton Street, with the walls of the old Whitbread Brewery on your left. Turn left into Chiswell Street to find the entrance to the Brewery. This is where the annual Whitbread Book Awards dinner is held. The awards began life in 1970 and one of the most emotional dinners took place in January 1999, when Ted Hughes's *Birthday Letters*, which deals movingly with Hughes's relationship with Plath, won the Whitbread Book of the Year. The poet (1930–1998) had died three months previously, but his daughter,

Frieda – whose mother was the poet Sylvia Plath (1932–1963) – collected the award on his behalf. At the 1999 dinner, a hush came over the audience as Frieda read out a private letter from her father to a friend:

I think those letters do release the story that everything I have written since the early 1960s has been evading. It was a kind of desperation that I finally did publish them – I had always thought them unpublishably raw and unguarded, simply too vulnerable. But then I just could not endure being blocked any longer. How strange that we have to make these public declarations of our secrets. But we do. If only I had done the equivalent 30 years ago, I might have had a more fruitful career – certainly a freer psychological life...

Retrace your steps and cross over into Lamb's Passage on the left, which comes out on Bunhill Row, where you turn left. Milton lived at No. 125 (now gone) from 1662 until his death in 1674, finishing 'Paradise Lost' and writing 'Paradise Regained'. He was totally blind, and one early biographer recalls him being 'read to and written for by friends, daughters, hired men or other assistants of varying degrees of usefulness.'

The Cult of William Blake
You will soon find Bunhill Fields Burial Ground on your right. The writers William Blake (1757–1827), Daniel Defoe and John Bunyan (1628–1688) are all buried here. To find their graves, follow the path until you see the brick park-keeper's hut. Bunyan's tomb, with its cross-carrying pilgrim, is away to your right; Blake's and Defoe's are opposite a fig tree growing by the fence. Defoe's tomb originally said 'Dubowe' and was not corrected until 1870, when the *Christian Monitor* newspaper collected funds for the present monument. No one knows the exact position of the bodies of Blake and his wife Catherine Sophia. As befits the mystical, visionary nature of his work, Blake's tomb is still something of a pilgrimage point. On a cold, windy day in March 1999 the following words were laid out in different coloured strips of Plasticine in front of the tombstone: 'Did He who made the lamb make thee?'

Leave the cemetery by a gate in the opposite fence, which brings you out on City Road, opposite the preacher John Wesley's house. Turn left to continue up to Old Street Station, where the walk ends.

Kensington

Summary: This is a walk that shows some of the best that London can offer, taking in an attractive park and pretty residential streets. It tells the little-known story of a famous literary statue, passes the homes of two giant literary neighbours and explains why a publisher took some fridges to the Royal College of Art for a party.

Start:	Lancaster Gate Underground Station (Central Line).
Finish:	Notting Hill Gate Underground Station (Central, District & Circle Lines).
Length:	4.8 kilometres (3 miles).
Time:	2.5–3 hours.
Refreshments:	There are some attractive cafés in the village-like Thackeray Street (approximately halfway) and there are also some quiet pubs along Albans Grove. In Notting Hill there is plenty of everything.

Turn right on leaving Lancaster Gate Station and cross at the lights to enter Kensington Gardens. Originally the grounds of Kensington Palace, these gardens did not become a public park until 1841. Take the path to the right of the fountains and follow it along the side of the Long Water. It was here that Harriet Shelley, the deserted first wife of the poet Percy Bysshe Shelley (1792–1822), drowned herself in December 1816.

The Secret History of Peter Pan
Shortly you reach the statue of Peter Pan – one of London's most unusual literary monuments, since it commemorates a fictional character rather than its creator. It was erected in great secrecy, under cover of darkness, on the night of 30 April 1912. The idea was that early May morning strollers would think that 'the boy who never grew up' had arrived by magic and a fairytale atmosphere would pervade the spring air. The workers had been hired by Peter Pan's creator, J. M. Barrie (1860–1937) himself, and he also commissioned and paid for the statue. So many children have touched the statue's bronze animals that their tops have become polished and smooth.

It was in Kensington Gardens that Barrie had met the Llewellyn Davies boys – pretty, upper-class Edwardian children who often wore 'blue blouses and bright red tam o'shanters' and were accompanied on their 'constitutionals' by their nurse. Barrie, whose marriage was childless, befriended them and when their own father died became a surrogate father, inventing games for them, arranging exciting holidays and taking an intense, extremely affectionate interest in their development – an affection that some deemed inappropriate. When their mother died he became guardian to all five.

Barrie had an idyllic view of childhood, once writing, 'Nothing that happens after we are twelve matters very much.' In his biography of Barrie, *JM Barrie and the Lost Boys*, Andrew Birkin quotes Nico Llewellyn Davies, the youngest of the brothers, on the difficult subject of Barrie's sexuality: 'All I can say for certain is that I…never heard or saw one glimmer of anything approaching homosexuality or paedophilia: had he had either of these leanings in however slight a symptom I would have been aware. He was an innocent – which is why he could write *Peter Pan*.'

The Llewellyn Davies boys became the models for Peter Pan – the 'lost boys' who headed for the enchanted Neverland through the nursery window and never grew up. Tragically, two of them did achieve a youthful immortality: Michael drowned in the Thames at the age of 20, and George was killed in the First World War aged 21. In 1960 their brother Peter Llewellyn Davies committed suicide (see page 38). It is curious that one of the most enduring children's classics should have such sad associations.

Take the right fork after Peter Pan to the Serpentine Gallery. Follow the path to the right of the gallery and then the right-hand fork towards the Albert Memorial, whose gold cross you can see peeking out above the trees. The memorial soon appears on your left, with the Royal Albert Hall – 'round in the middle and not much above', according to Wodehouse – behind it.

Writing on the Fridge

Turn towards the memorial and take the Flower Walk on your right, going through the gates and between the lines of trees and shrubs. Turn left at the first junction to leave the gardens via Queen's Gate. The dark, rather boring-looking office building on the other side of the road to your left is the Royal College of Art, where Stephen King's novel *Misery* was launched in 1998. Guests mingled next to giant fridges that had been specially bought for the party and covered with magnetic letters to echo the messages that are written by telekinesis in the story. Later, King played the guitar – he is a passable rock musician and plays in the States with a band called The Rock Bottom Remainders.

Literary Neighbours

Cross at the lights and turn right. Many of the grand homes in the roads to your left are now given over to embassies. Turn left into De Vere Gardens where, towards the far end, two great writers lived opposite each other for a short period. Henry James (1843–1916) moved into No. 34 in March 1886 and Robert Browning (1812–1889) moved into No. 29 the following year. James loved his fourth-floor apartment, declaring, 'I shall enter it for life and I shall be as cossu [well-off] and bourgeois as my means will permit, & and have large fat sofas…everywhere.' He was also pleased to have Kensington Gardens up the road, referring to it as 'that paradise which is a wondrous thing to find in the heart of a great city'.

James already knew Browning and, as neighbours, their lives often overlapped. For example, in 1888 they shared a carriage to Kensal Green Cemetery to attend the burial of a mutual friend. During the long, slow ride, the 76-year-old Browning was 'infinitely talkative', James recalled. The American believed Browning to be 'the writer of our times of whom…the English tongue may be most proud.'

Turn right, left and right, which will take you through pretty (and very expensive) streets, to come out on St Albans Grove. Turn right into Kensington Court Place and cross to the left-hand pavement to get a better view of the red-brick mansion block opposite. In April 1957 T. S. Eliot (1888–1965) moved into No. 3 Kensington Court Gardens with his wife and former secretary from Faber, Valerie Fletcher. Like Henry James, Eliot liked to walk in Kensington Gardens: he particularly enjoyed watching children sailing their boats on the Round Pond. Although he was happy, his health began to deteriorate over the next few years. In December 1963 he was rushed from his home here to the Brompton Hospital, having collapsed in one of London's four-day 'smogs'. Although he initially seemed to recover and shouted 'Hurrah! Hurrah! Hurrah!' when he was carried over the threshold on his return home, he was on continuous oxygen and too weak to take solid foods. He relapsed into a coma at Christmas and regained consciousness only once to speak his wife's name; he died in the flat on 4 January 1965.

Turn left into the village-like Thackeray Street, named after the 19th-century novelist, whose house at No.16 Young Street is found by taking the next right. 'It has the air of a feudal castle', the author wrote after seeing the house for the first time. And indeed it still does, although it is dwarfed all around by new developments.

Look into the distance to the left of the house, and you will see a roof garden. This is Kensington Roof Gardens, which you find by retracing your steps, turning right into Kensington Square and right into Derry Street. The entrance is on the left. Sadly, the gardens are often closed for private functions, but they are well worth visiting. It was in the Spanish-themed gardens here that Thomas Eidson's acclaimed novel *St Agnes' Stand* was celebrated when it won WH Smith's £5,000 Thumping Good Read Award in 1995.

The Poet who didn't Like the Sound of Bells
Continue up Derry Street and cross busy Kensington High Street. Turn left and then immediately right into the easily missed Kensington Church Walk, a pretty walkway that winds through gardens and leads to St Mary Abbots Church, which boasts the highest spire in London. The poet and novelist G. K. Chesterton (1874–1936) was married here in 1901, and the poet Ezra Pound in 1914. Pound (1885–1972) had in fact already been living virtually in the shadow of the church's spire, at No. 10 Kensington Church Walk, which you find when it opens out into a courtyard on your left. He had rooms on the top floor of the last house on the right. He loved the place, apart from the noise of the church bells, which he campaigned against with typically eccentric zeal: '…the act of bell-ringing', he wrote, 'is symbolical of all proselytising religions. It implies the pointless interference with the quiet of other people.' Just before he married, he moved to a flat at 5 Holland Place Chambers, an inlet off Kensington Church Street found by turning right at the end of Kensington Church Walk and then left. It was here that Eliot first met Pound, on 22 September 1914. Eliot said his fellow American reminded him of Sinclair Lewis's Irving Babbitt, while Pound remarked of Eliot's own Americanness: '[He] has it perhaps worse than I have – poor devil.'

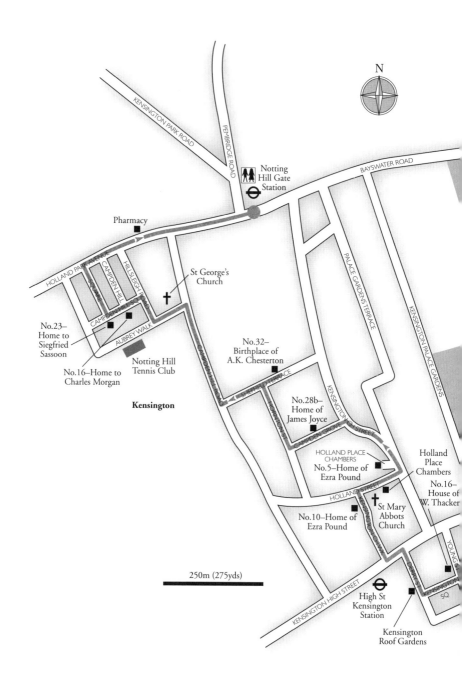

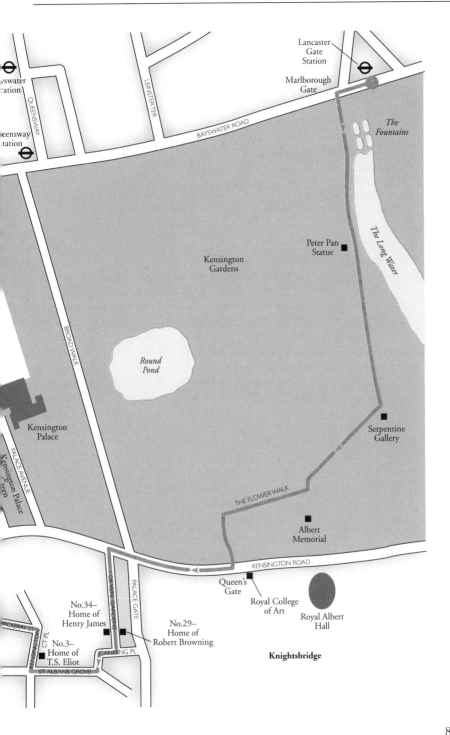

Follow Kensington Church Street up its slope until you turn left into Campden Grove, where you should take the right-hand pavement. In 1931 James Joyce (1882–1941) and family made what he called their 'fifth hegira', moving to England and settling in this quiet street at No. 28b, for what they thought would be an indefinite stay. He had come to England both to be near his ailing father and to marry Nora Barnacle, the tall brunette from Galway, whom he had met in Dublin in 1904. But theirs was a short stay. Kensington was too dull for Joyce, who complained that their street was full of mummies and should be renamed 'Campden Grave'.

Continue to the end and turn right into Hornton Street, which leads to Sheffield Terrace. A few yards along, on your right, is No. 32, where G. K. Chesterton was born on 29 May 1874, close to the 'great grey water-tower/That strikes the stars of Campden Hill'. The water tower featured in his novel *The Napoleon of Notting Hill* and stood next to St George's Church, which you pass shortly. The tower has now been demolished.

A Most Distinguished Square

Go back along Sheffield Terrace and turn right into Campden Hill Road. The hill rises up to St George's, which is found in Aubrey Walk, where you turn left. A little further along this road is Notting Hill Tennis Club, where publishers hold an annual tennis tournament. Lady Antonia Fraser occasionally plays at the club and was described by a member in *Publishing News* in 1998 as looking like a 'spinnaker in full sail' when on court. Lady Antonia and her husband, the playwright Harold Pinter, live close by in Campden Hill Square, one of London's most distinguished addresses. It is found by turning right into Hillsleigh Road and then first left.

The square has many blue plaques, although the first, which you find by walking along the top end of the square, is rather obscure – few people have heard of the English author Charles Morgan (1894–1958), who lived at No. 16. Further along, a plaque records that the poet and novelist Siegfried Sassoon (1886–1967) lived at No. 23 from 1925 to 1932, but there is nothing to indicate how involved J. M. Barrie was with this house from 1907 to 1918. He helped Sylvia Llewellyn Davies buy it, and when she died she left it to him and it continued to be home to her five boys, with Barrie trying to act as substitute mother and father.

Turn right and walk down the slope, leaving the square at the bottom and turning right onto busy Holland Park Avenue, home to crime novelist P. D. James. This soon rises into Notting Hill, passing on the left a white building squeezed between two blocks of flats. This is Pharmacy, a fashionable restaurant occupying a former chemist. Jay McInerney's novel *Model Behaviour* was launched here, but had he wished to find any of the 'Bolivian marching powder' that he wrote about in his acclaimed debut *Bright Lights, Big City* he would have had no luck – all the samples on the shelves are fakes. Now continue along to Notting Hill Station, where the walk ends.

Plate 17: St Paul's Cathedral where John Donne was Dean from 1621–1631. Scorch marks from the Great Fire of London in 1666 can be seen on his tomb (see page 72).

Plate 18: Bust of the diarist Samuel Pepys in Seething Lane Gardens (see page 77).

Plate 19: Ribbon adorns William Blake's tombstone in Bunhill Fields (see page 82).

Plate 20: *The statue of Peter Pan in Kensington Gardens was commissioned and paid for by J. M. Barrie himself. Children have worn smooth the tops of the animals (see page 83).*

Plate 21: Birthplace of Robert Graves at No.1 Lauriston Road, Wimbledon (see page 93).

Plate 22: No. 4 Whitehall Court, where George Bernard Shaw lived (see page 99).

Plate 23: Statue of Athena and frieze of the Elgin Marbles on the front of the Athenaeum in Waterloo Place. Dickens and Thackeray made up in this club after a quarrel (see page 98).

Plate 24: *Highgate's most distinguished address, No. 3 The Grove. Samuel Taylor Coleridge lived here from 1823 to 1834 and it was J. B. Priestly's home from 1933 to 1939 (see page 111).*

Plate 25: *Keats and Coleridge both used to walk on Hampstead Heath – while Wilkie Collins talked about its 'white winding paths' (see page 119).*

Putney to Wimbledon

Summary: This long walk takes you over the Thames and across Wimbledon Common, which has a real feeling of the countryside about it. You will be following in the footsteps of the poet Algernon Charles Swinburne and also see where one of England's most popular contemporary novelists sets his stories. If you feel like getting away from the traffic of central London, this walk is a good choice.

Start:	Putney Bridge Underground Station (District Line).
Finish:	Wimbledon Station (District Underground Line; overground trains to Waterloo Station).
Length:	9.5 kilometres (6 miles).
Time:	3–3.5 hours.
Refreshments:	There are plenty of pubs, cafés and restaurants in both Putney and Wimbledon Village, although those in the latter are more pleasant. The Wimbledon Windmill Café, approximately halfway, is an excellent place for a break.

Turn left on leaving the station and walk along Ranelagh Gardens. Bear left at the end, taking the short road leading to some flats. Turn the corner, walk through the foot tunnel, and take the steps up to Putney Bridge. With the river on your right, you now have a superb view of Putney Embankment on the far shore, where J. R. Ackerley (1896–1967), author of the classic memoir *My Father and Myself*, used to walk his beloved Alsatian, Queenie. She attained literary immortality in his novel *We Think the World of You* and the memoir *My Dog Tulip*.

The Poet who 'Cooed like a Dove'

Continue up Putney High Street. Cross to the left-hand side after Putney Station and continue over the lights to climb Putney Hill. A short way up on the left at No.11 is The Pines, the Victorian mansion in which the critic Theodore Watts-Dunton (1832–1914) provided refuge for the poet Algernon Charles Swinburne (1837–1909), who had become ill while living at the home of poet and painter Dante Gabriel Rosetti (1828–1882) in Chelsea. Swinburne's room was on the first floor. He lived a life of relative seclusion, save for his daily walk up to Wimbledon Common – a walk that you will now follow. The English writer and caricaturist Max Beerbohm (1872–1956) visited Watts-Dunton and Swinburne here, and recalled:

As soon as the mutton had been replaced by the apple-pie, Watts-Dunton leaned forward and 'Well, Algernon' he roared 'How was it on the Heath today?' Swinburne, who had merely inclined his ear to the question, now threw back his head, uttering a sound that was like the cooing of a dove and forthwith rapidly, ever so musically, he spoke to us of his walk... The wonders of this morning's wind and sun and clouds were expressed in a flow

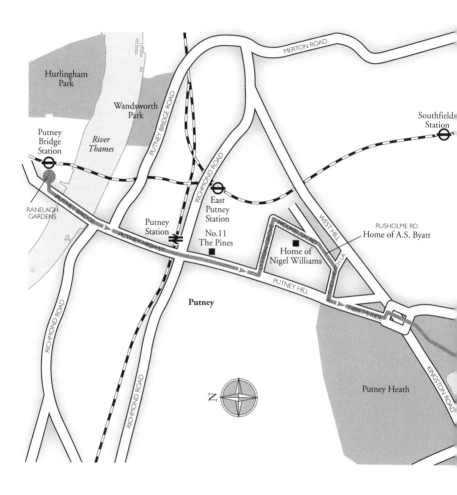

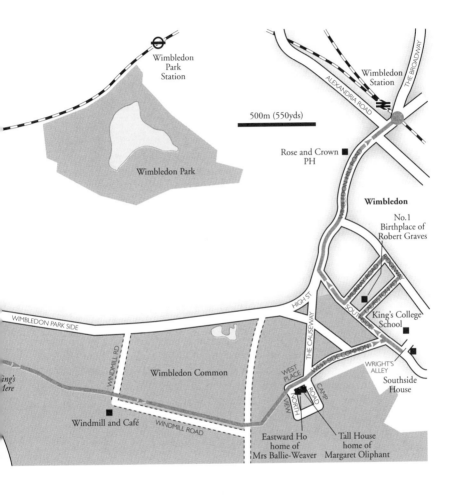

Wimbledon
Park
Station

Wimbledon
Station

THE BROADWAY

ALEXANDRIA ROAD

500m (550yds)

Rose and Crown ■
PH

Wimbledon

No.1
Birthplace of
Robert Graves

King's College
School ■

WIMBLEDON PARK SIDE

Wimbledon Park

Wimbledon Common

WINDMILL RD

WEST
PLACE

THE CAUSEWAY

HIGH ST

SOUTHSIDE

WEST SIDE COMMON

WRIGHT'S
ALLEY

Southside
House

ing's
lere

Windmill and Café ■

WINDMILL ROAD

NORTH
VIEW

CAMP
ROAD

Eastward Ho
home of
Mrs Ballie-Weaver

Tall House
home of
Margaret Oliphant

of words so right and sentences so perfectly balanced that they would have seemed pedantic had they not been clearly as spontaneous as the wordless notes of a bird song.

Head up the hill, turn left into Lytton Grove, and right into Holmbush Road. One of the large houses on the right is home to Nigel William, author of a successful trio of Wimbledon-based comic novels, *The Wimbledon Poisoner*, *They Came from SW19*, and *East of Wimbledon*.

The Booker Prize Winner on TV Sport

After a little green, turn right into Rusholme Road, home of A. S. Byatt, who won the Booker Prize in 1990 for *Possession*. She works in an attic room and relaxes by watching sport on cable television. She told *Publishing News* in 1998:

> *It's a kind of post-modernist cliché that sport is narrative… But as the TV gets worse, it's the only thing I watch – I feel it's the only tense narrative left. I'm keen on tennis, football, as long as it's top level, and athletics as long as it's a race and it's measurable.*

Turn right into Putney Heath Lane and then left onto the busy Tibbetts Ride. By the bus-stop take the quiet road to the left and just before it ends, opposite a block of flats called Sylvia Court, take the path into the trees. This eventually takes you under a busy road, where you turn left. Follow the path round and pass under the second bridge, ignoring the one on the left. You are now on Wimbledon Common.

The Common in Words and Duels

Carry on along a gravel path that enters the trees. Keep straight ahead. Wimbledon Common is protected by the Wimbledon and Putney Commons Act of 1871 and is looked after by a Board of Conservators so that it can be used 'for purposes of exercise and recreation,' and remain 'for ever open and uninclosed [*sic*] and unbuilt on.' You will quite likely see horses during your walk. The common is a special place that has its own mounted 'police' force, the Wimbledon Common Rangers. Thackeray (1811–1863) described this splendid piece of land – so close to London– as 'noble', and the air and green country 'delightfully fresh'. The poet and essayist Leigh Hunt (1784–1859) loved these 1,100 acres too, speaking of their 'Cloth of gold covering of furze'.

Presently you will come to the windmill, built in 1817 but disused since 1864. During the 19th century, the millers acted as policemen, watching for duels from the windmill's balcony. Several prime ministers are recorded as having fought here, including George Canning (1770–1827), who in 1798 was shot in the leg by another ex-minister, and William Pitt the Younger, who faced the local MP – neither was a seasoned marksmen and after two attempts and two misses, the duel was called off. Lord Baden-Powell (1857–1941) stayed in the mill house briefly and worked on *Scouting for Boys* – The buildings became a museum; there is also a very popular café here.

Continue along your original path, passing a horses' paddock behind the windmill. After 10–15 minutes you will come to a major junction, with a white cottage away to your right and wooden bollards across the bridle path to your left. Go straight over, and after approximately 70 metres (75 yards), take the path on the left, where there are two concrete posts in the ground. This takes you through a glade of young oak trees to the corner of North View and West Place, opposite two houses. The one on the left is Eastward Ho, its neighbour Westward Ho – their interesting blue-and-white murals show the sun rising and setting next to local churches. During the 1920s a Mrs Baillie-Weaver, a novelist (long forgotten now) who had connections with the Theosophical Society, lived at Eastward Ho. Local resident Constance Curry, remembers seeing a 'strange man…dark-skinned, dressed in white' walking along the middle of the road to visit Mrs Baillie-Weaver; and it was some time before Curry learned that this strange figure was the so-called 'New Messiah', the Indian mystic and philosopher, Jiddu Krishnamurti, who died in 1986 and whose teachings had wide appeal, from young hippies to old intellectuals such as Aldous Huxley. According to Curry, Krishnamurti was 'not at all friendly, least of all to the children who were gathered in small groups to see him go by', which rather takes the shine off his holiness.

Continue along West Place, with the common on the left, passing an attractive row of cottages. Cross Camp Road and pass into West Side Common. Continue to the end and then cross at the zebra opposite King's College School, which Robert Graves attended briefly. Turn right and almost immediately you come to Wright's Alley, next to which is Southside House, almost completely hidden by trees. Built at the end of the 17th century, this was once the home of the Swedish doctor Axel Munthe (1857–1949), who wrote the best-selling *The Story of San Michele*.

Robert Graves on Wimbledon
Retrace your steps along Southside and turn right into Lauriston Road. The poet and novelist Robert Graves (1895–1985) was born at No. 1. In *Goodbye to All That* he recalls 'being loyally held up at a window to watch a procession of decorated carriages and waggons for Queen Victoria's Diamond Jubilee in 1897.' He didn't much like Wimbledon, saying, 'I always considered [it] a wrong place: neither town nor country.'

Turn left into the Ridgeway and then left into Murray Road to rejoin Southside, where you turn right. Follow this road into Wimbledon Village where, appropriately, you come out opposite the Rose and Crown, final destination of Swinburne's walks up the hill from Putney. Graves remembers Swinburne in *Goodbye to All That*, too:

Nor had I any illusions about Algernon Charles Swinburne, who often used to stop my per-ambulator when he met it on Nurses' Walk, at the edge of Wimbledon Common, and pat me on the head and kiss me: he was an inveterate pram-stopper and patter and kisser. Nurses' Walk lay between 'The Pines'…and the Rose and Crown public house, where he went for his daily pint of beer; Watts-Dunton allowed him two pence and no more. I did not know that Swinburne was a poet, but I knew that he was a public menace.

The Rose and Crown dates from the early 17th century. Swinburne drank his beer in full view of passers-by until he fell foul of the paparazzi of the day – the newspaper artists who began to sketch him. He moved to a more obscure part of the pub, where a chair was eventually named after him.

Walk through the village, going straight over two roundabouts. Continue down Wimbledon Hill to the town centre and the station, where the walk ends.

Westminster and St James's

Summary: This walk passes the riverside home of millionaire novelist (and disgraced former London mayor hopeful) Jeffrey Archer, as well as the rather more modest attic in which T. E. Lawrence wrote *The Seven Pillars of Wisdom.* You will also pass the site of one of Oscar Wilde's favourite male brothels and a number of London's gentlemen's clubs, including the one in which Dickens and Thackeray famously 'made up' after a long-standing disagreement.

Start:	Pimlico Underground Station (Victoria Line).
Finish:	Embankment Underground Station (Northern and Bakerloo Lines).
Length:	5.6 kilometres (3½ miles).
Time:	2–2.5 hours.
Refreshments:	Many of the pubs and cafés on the first half of the walk are closed at weekends. The café/restaurant in St James's Park, on the second half of the walk, is a pleasant place to stop.

At Pimlico Station take the ramp exit and follow the signs for the Tate Gallery. At the traffic lights on Vauxhall Bridge Road you will see to your left the UK headquarters of Random House, one of the world's largest book publishing groups, whose authors include John Grisham, Robert Harris and Michael Crichton, as well as more literary names like A. S. Byatt, Roddy Doyle and Sebastian Faulks. The balconied room at the top belongs to the chief executive and is occasionally used for book launches. The e-mail gossip network went stratospheric here in March 1998, when staff learnt that the company had been bought by Bertelsmann, the giant German publishing and media group. The group is now often referred to as 'Random Haus'.

Cross at the lights and turn right. This is Bessborough Gardens, where Joseph Conrad (1857–1924) took rooms from 1889 to 1890. He had returned from two years at sea with the Merchant Navy and began his first novel *Almayer's Folly* here, before taking to the ocean again in May 1890, when he sailed for the Congo.

The Novelist with the Best View in London

At the junction with Millbank cross over, turn left and when you reach the Henry Moore sculpture 'Locking Piece', walk to the river wall. Now look for a black-and-white tower almost directly opposite. A dramatic two-storey penthouse with large panoramic windows and a 360-degree balcony sits on top of it. This is the £4m

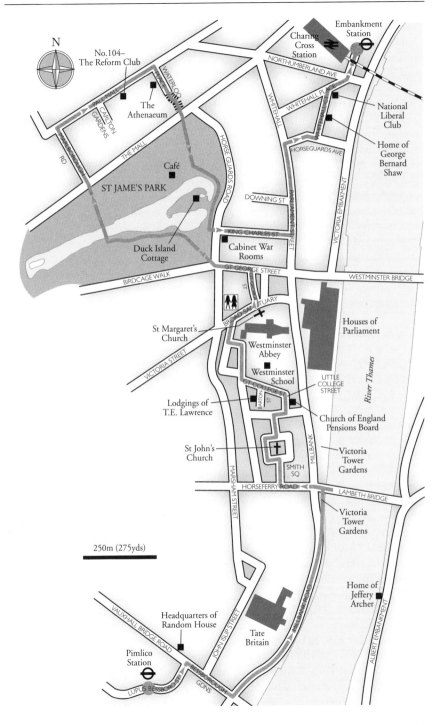

N

No.104–
The Reform Club

The
Athenaeum

PALL MALL

CARLTON
GARDENS

MARLBOROUGH
RD

WATERLOO
PLACE

THE MALL

Café

ST JAME'S PARK

HORSE GUARDS ROAD

Charing
Cross
Station

Embankment
Station

NORTHUMBERLAND AVE

WHITEHALL

WHITEHALL PLACE

WHITEHALL

HORSEGUARDS AVE

National
Liberal
Club

Home of
George
Bernard
Shaw

DOWNING ST

PARLIAMENT STREET

VICTORIA EMBANKMENT

KING CHARLES ST

Duck Island
Cottage

Cabinet War
Rooms

BIRDCAGE WALK

GT GEORGE STREET

WESTMINSTER BRIDGE

BROAD SANCTUARY

ST

St Margaret's
Church

Westminster
Abbey

Houses of
Parliament

VICTORIA STREET

Westminster
School

GT COLLEGE ST

BARTON ST

LITTLE
COLLEGE
STREET

River Thames

Lodgings of
T.E. Lawrence

Church of England
Pensions Board

St John's
Church

MILLBANK

SMITH
SQ

Victoria
Tower
Gardens

MARSHAM STREET

HORSEFERRY ROAD

LAMBETH BRIDGE

Victoria
Tower
Gardens

250m (275yds)

VAUXHALL BRIDGE ROAD

Headquarters of
Random House

JOHN ISLIP STREET

MILLBANK ROAD

Home of
Jeffery
Archer

ALBERT EMBANKMENT

Tate
Britain

Pimlico
Station

BESSBOROUGH GDNS

LUPUS ST

BESSBOROUGH ST

London home of millionaire novelist and former Conservative MP, Jeffrey Archer, who bought it in 1976. One of the previous owners was John Barry, composer of the James Bond theme. When Archer moved in he was apparently particularly taken with Barry's personalized telephone number – 0077.

The Wordsworths and Westminster Bridge

Keep to the Thames Path signs, ducking into Victoria Tower Gardens in front of Lambeth Bridge. Climb the steps and cross at the zebra. Take a few steps onto the bridge, which affords a good view of Westminster Bridge. It was while crossing this bridge 'in' the Dover coach at dawn on 31 July 1802 that William Wordworth (1770–1850) began one of the most quoted verses in poetry, which begins: 'Earth has not anything to show more fair…' The poem now greets visitors to the giant London Eye wheel, which can be seen in the distance. What is less well-known is Wordsworth's sister Dorothy's (1771–1855) account of the same view, recorded in her journal: 'We mounted the Dover coach at Charing Cross. It was a beautiful morning. The City, St Paul's, with the River and a multitude of little boats, made a most beautiful sight as we crossed Westminster Bridge.' Had they crossed it five years later they might have seen a fellow poet in the water. In 1807, Byron (1788–1824) swam from Lambeth to Blackfriars, watched by the poet and essayist Leigh Hunt (1784–1859).

Now walk directly away from the river, up Horseferry Road, turning right into Dean Bradley Street, which leads to St John's Smith Square. This former church is now used as a concert hall. Its unusual shape, with its four towers, did not appeal to Dickens (1812–1870) who, in *Our Mutual Friend*, called it 'a very hideous church, with four towers at the corners, generally resembling some petrified monster, frightful and gigantic, on its back with its legs in the air.'

Oscar Wilde and a Male Brothel

Continue around the square on the left-hand side, noting the elegant, listed 18th-century houses on the far side. Turn left into Lord North Street where, on the wall of No. 16, there is a rare echo of the Blitz. Painted on the bricks are the words, 'Public Shelters In Vaults Under Pavements In This Street.' Turn right and then first left into Little College Street. These streets are quiet and reserved now, but in the 19th century the slums here were so bad that the area was known as 'the Devil's Acre'. Oscar Wilde (1854–1900) frequented a male brothel at No. 13, run by the pimp Alfred Taylor, a former schoolboy at Marlborough whose father was a wealthy cocoa manufacturer. Today, the site of the brothel is occupied by the Church of England Pensions Board, which would no doubt have greatly amused Wilde.

How Chocolate Helped T. E. Lawrence

Turn left into Great College Street and then left again into Barton Street where, in the attic of No. 14, T. E. Lawrence (1888–1935) worked on *The Seven Pillars of Wisdom* in 1920. The rooms were provided by Herbert Baker, an architect friend, who had offices below. 'I work best utterly by myself,' Lawrence wrote, 'and speak to no one for days.' Already famous, he enjoyed the anonymity of the address. Baker gives this description of how his 'lodger' worked:

*He refused all service and comfort, food, fire or hot water; he ate and bathed when he hap-
pened to go out; he kept chocolate – it required no cleaning up, he said – for an emergency
when through absorption or forgetfulness he failed to do so. He worked time-less and sometimes around the sun...*

Poets' Corner

Return to Great College Street and continue to the end, where you turn right
through the gates into the quadrangle of Westminster School, one of the top schools
in the country, whose pupils have included Ben Jonson (1572?–1637), John Dryden
(1631–1700) and A. A. Milne (1882–1956). Keep to the right-hand pavement and
exit at the far corner. This brings you out at the entrance to Westminster Abbey. A
whole book could be written on the literary funerals that have taken place here.
Poets' Corner, roughly in the middle of the church, near to the St Faith Chapel, is
worth visiting. After Dickens's funeral in 1870 his grave in the abbey was left open
for two days. At the end of the first day, there were still one thousand people outside waiting to pay their respects. For two days the crowds of people passed by in
procession, many of them dropping flowers onto his coffin – 'among which', his son
Henry said, 'were afterwards found several small rough bouquets of flowers tied up
with pieces of rag.'

At the funeral of the Poet Laureate Lord Tennyson (1809–1892), the nave was
lined by men of the Balaclava Light Brigade. 'The Charge of the Light Brigade'
remains a title with which even those who say they know no poetry at all are familiar today. The congregation at the funeral included more or less every poet in the
country who had some sort of reputation. However, the long procession was swollen
by what the critic and essayist Edmund Gosse (1849–1928) called a stream of non-
entities, and even Henry James (1843–1916), recalling the day afterwards, wrote: '[It
was] a lovely day, the Abbey looked beautiful, everyone was there, but something –
I don't know what – of real impressiveness – was wanting.'

The Funeral of Ted Hughes

On Thursday, 13 May 1999 a memorial service for another Poet Laureate, Ted
Hughes, took place. Fellow poets and writers in the congregation included Seamus
Heaney, Simon Armitage, Wendy Cope, Andrew Motion (who was to succeed
Hughes as Laureate), Alan Sillitoe and Graham Swift. Heaney said, 'Ted was a great
man and a great poet through his wholeness, simplicity and unfaltering truth to his
whole sense of the world.' Surrounded by busts and memorials of poets and kings,
he added: 'In this abbey, it is impossible not to think of Ted Hughes as one of the
tapestry, who would have been as much at home with Caedmon, the first English
poet in his monastery, as he would have been with Wilfred Owen in the trenches.'
A recording of Hughes reading Shakespeare's *Cymberline* was played. This is the book
that Lord Tennyson had in his hand when he was buried.

A Pleasant Park

Turn right on leaving the abbey and enter the gardens, heading for the small white
church of St Margaret's, in which Samuel Pepys (1633–1703) and John Milton

(1608–1674) were both married. Cross at the traffic lights outside and head down Little George Street behind a statue of Abraham Lincoln. Turn left into Great George Street and cross Storey's Gate to enter St James's Park. It was Charles II who, in the second half of the 17th century, made this park a more formal affair and had a canal dug that would eventually be redeveloped by Nash in the 19th century to make the lake we see today. On 15 July 1666 Pepys wrote in his diary, 'lay down upon the grass by the canalle and slept awhile.'

A Literary Peep-hole

Continue through the park along the side of the lake, watching out for the famous pelicans that have been resident here since 1684, when the Russian ambassador presented them as a gift to Charles II. Cross the lake at the bridge, which affords a superb view of Buckingham Palace, and carry straight on to the gates. Cross the Mall into the unmarked Marlborough Road and, when it meets Pall Mall, turn right. After Carlton Gardens on your right you find No. 104, the Reform Club where Jules Verne's hero Phileas Fogg bet that he could travel round the world in 80 days. Founded in 1836, the Reform's members have included the writers William Thackeray (1811–1863), Henry James (1843–1916), Hillaire Belloc (1870–1953) and H. G. Wells (1866–1946). Anthony Trollope (1815–1882) mentions the club in his novel *Phineas Finn* and the room favoured by James had a hole bored in the door so that staff could check before knocking so as not to disturb him while he was writing. The club is often used for publishing parties today, among them the luncheon for the *Daily Mail*/John Llewellyn Rhys Prize. Virago also held a special reception for the American writer Maya Angelou. It was a joy to see this powerful lady recite her sensuous, rhythmic poetry in such formal surroundings.

The Athenaeum

Turn right into Waterloo Place and walk to the central pavement to get a better view of the Athenaeum, with its pillared entrance beneath its Elgin Marbles frieze. Founded in 1824 by John Wilson Croker (1780–1857), Secretary of the Admiralty and editor of Boswell's *Johnson*, the Athenaeum has a formidable reputation for 'intellectuality, gravity [and] deep respectability', according to Anthony Lejeune's *The Gentlemen's Clubs of London*. That may be so, but Rudyard Kipling (1865–1936) wasn't keen, describing it as 'like a cathedral between services'. W. B. Yeats (1865–1939) liked it though, confessing in a letter that he had always had 'a childish desire to walk up those steps & under that classical face – it seems to belong to folk lore like "London Bridge" & that is my subject.'

Among writers who spent time working in the club are the historian and essayist Lord Macaulay (1800–1869), Anthony Trollope and the poet Matthew Arnold (1822–1888). Charles Dickens was a member but was evidently not particularly clubbable. One member said: 'He seldom spoke to anyone unless previously addressed.' Another said: 'He used to eat his sandwich standing at the centre table, or striding about.'

Walk up to the doors of the Athenaeum and peer in. You should be able to see the staircase at the bottom of which occurred one of literature's great reconciliations. In 1863 the Scottish man of letters Sir Theodore Martin (1816–1909) was talking to Thackeray, when Dickens entered the club. Thackeray and Dickens had not spoken for years after a quarrel. Martin recalls: '[He passed us] without making any sign of recognition.' Then Thackeray broke away and reached Dickens as he began to climb the stairs. 'Dickens turned to him, and I saw Thackeray speak and presently hold out his hand to Dickens. They shook hands, a few words were exchanged, and immediately Thackeray returned to me saying, "I'm glad I have done this."' After Dickens died, his chair was brought from his home at Gad's Hill, near Rochester in Kent, and a member presented it to the club.

Continue down Waterloo Place, descend the steps and cross the Mall again to re-enter St James's Park to the right of the statues. Walk down to the café and then bear left round the side of the lake. The fairytale Duck Island Cottage was built in 1837 for a birdkeeper and is now the headquarters of the London Historic Parks and Gardens Trust. Cross opposite the Cabinet War Rooms and ascend the steps into King Charles Street, which comes out on Whitehall, where you turn left.

Whitehall's Writers and a Library That isn't All it Seems
Whitehall might seem a distinctly un-literary road given over to government ministries and their many civil servants, but it has a number of literary associations. T. E. Lawrence worked at the Colonial Office in 1921, and during the Second World War Iris Murdoch (1919–1999) worked at the Treasury, while John Betjeman (1906–1984) and Richard Hughes (1900–1984), author of *A High Wind in Jamaica*, were at the Admiralty. Ian Fleming, creator of James Bond, also did a spell at the Admiralty, and more recent 'literary' civil servants include John le Carré (Foreign Office) and P. D. James (Home Office).

Long before the prime ministers arrived, the 18th-century writers Horace Walpole (1884–1941) and Tobias Smollett (1721–1771) both lived in Downing Street, which you pass shortly on your left. Cross at the lights to enter Horseguards Avenue, on the right, and then turn left into Whitehall Court. The huge apartment block on your right, with the Parisian-style entrances, is where the playwright George Bernard Shaw (1856–1950) had his London pied-à-terre, No. 4, from 1928 to 1945. He had a corner flat with five rooms and a surrounding balcony overlooking the Embankment and the river. At the end of this street you come to No.1 Whitehall Place, home to the National Liberal Club. When the novelist Beryl Bainbridge won the 1999 £10,000 WH Smith Literary Award for *Master Georgie*, the awards lunch was held in the Gladstone Library on the first floor here. The 35,000 antique books are not as impressive as they seem, though – they are all wooden fakes, the real ones having been sold to Bristol University in 1977 to avert a financial crisis.

Continue to the end of Whitehall Place, where you will see a green taxi drivers' shelter opposite. Cross over and read the plaque on the door. Restoration of this shelter was supported by both Jeffrey Archer and the Seven Pillars of Wisdom Trust. As we have passed both Archer and T. E. Lawrence's homes, this seems an appropriate conclusion to the walk. Embankment Station now lies just the other side of the railway bridge, where the walk ends.

Richmond

Summary: Richmond is an up-market suburb lying to the south-west of the capital. Richmond Park, created in the 17th century, is London's largest park and, together with the river, has enclosed the town and prevented the sprawling development that has ruined so many other suburbs. The two literary figures most associated with Richmond are Virginia Woolf and T. S. Eliot – it was from a house here that Virginia Woolf and her husband Leonard published *The Waste Land*. The walk also takes in a pleasant corner of the park and offers a splendid – and unlikely – view of St Paul's.

Start and finish:	Richmond Station (Underground District Line; overground trains from Waterloo and Clapham Junction).
Length:	7.7 kilometres (4¾ miles).
Time:	3 hours.
Refreshments:	There are lots of pubs, cafés and restaurants in the town centre. The café at Pembroke Lodge in Richmond Park offers excellent views.

Turn right on leaving the station and cross the road to go down the tiny Sun Alley next to the Duke of York pub. At the bottom turn left into Parkshot to find the magistrates' court on your right, built on the site of the house in which Marian Evans first used the pseudonym George Eliot. Eliot (1819–1880) lived here with the writer and journalist Henry Lewes (1817–1878) from 1855 to 1859. The house was covered in ivy and had a long, narrow walled garden at the back. It was while living here that she started *Adam Bede*.

After crossing the railway, Parkshot becomes Little Green and you pass Richmond Theatre. This elegant theatre, which featured briefly in the 1995 film *Jack and Sarah*, starring Richard E. Grant, opened in 1899 with *As You Like It*. In the 1830s the orientalist and explorer Richard Burton (1821–1890), translator of *The Kama Sutra* and, most famously, *The Arabian Nights*, was a young boarder at Charles de la Fosse's school, now long gone, which stood on Little Green. He is buried in the cemetery of St Mary Magdalene in Mortlake, a mile or so away, in a tomb resembling an Arab tent.

A Literary Dog-walker

Keeping to the left-hand pavement, continue to Richmond Green, once a jousting ground and now the setting for gentle games of cricket on Saturday afternoons. In October 1914 Virginia Woolf (1882–1941) and her husband Leonard (1880–1969) rented rooms, while looking for more permanent accommodation, on the first floor of No. 17 The Green, which you find a short way along on the left. Today the rooms are above the Goods entrance to Boots the Chemists.

In the autumn of 1913 Virginia had attempted suicide and it had taken her most of the following 12 months to recover. Leonard felt she needed a break from the stresses of London and he thought that Richmond provided the ideal compromise, being not too far from the city but, importantly, a long way away from the tumult of the West End. People move here for the same reasons today, which is reflected in the house prices.

Virginia soon settled in. She would head off across the green to the river with her dog Grizzle, and in her letters began to refer to the Thames at Richmond as 'my river'. The household at No. 17 also provided entertainment. The Woolfs' landlady was a Belgian woman called Mrs le Grys, who was full of tales about previous lodgers. Lizzie the housemaid once nearly set the house on fire and Maud, her successor, claimed to be a colonel's daughter and sought to impress Virginia with genteel conversation and sophisticated views.

Continue past The Prince's Head pub into the pretty Paved Court, passing The Lion and Unicorn children's bookshop at the end. The Open Book, another bookshop, is opposite. The latter is worth a visit since it sells facsimiles of Virginia Woolf's Hogarth Press titles, some of which she printed herself in a house that you will pass shortly.

The Woolfs and the Hogarth Press

Turn left into King Street and when you reach the busy main road, go straight over and turn left into Red Lion Street, passing Waterstone's bookshop. Continue until the elegant, Georgian Hogarth House appears on your left, just beyond a zebra crossing. Built in the early 18th century, it was originally divided into two – Suffield House on the left and Hogarth House on the right. Virginia Woolf was very excited with their find, writing to a friend in February 1915: 'I do hope you'll come and see us often in our new house – Hogarth House – It's far the nicest house in England.' But just as the Woolfs were ready to move in, Virginia had another breakdown and was admitted to a nursing home. Leonard moved in to Hogarth House by himself on 25 March 1915, with Virginia following at the beginning of April under the care of four nurses. Her novel *The Voyage Out* had just been published but she was too ill to read the favourable reviews.

In March 1917 the Woolfs took delivery of a small, hand-operated printing press – an idea that they'd had some two years previously but abandoned when Virginia became ill. Though amateurs, they were both interested in the art of printing, and Leonard thought that the venture would provide therapeutic distraction for his wife. Virginia wrote to her sister, Vanessa Bell, describing the exciting arrival of the press. Upon unpacking it, she and Leonard discovered that it was broken in two. This did not appear to discourage her, though: she was confident that it could be put right, and in the meantime spent hours placing the various letters and fonts into their appropriate partitions.

The Woolfs' first publication was *Two Stories*, containing a short story each by Virginia and Leonard. Future Hogarth Press titles included a Mansfield short story and Virginia's own *Kew Gardens*, which was very successful. Facsimile copies of the latter, complete with 'decorations' by Vanessa Bell (1879–1961), may be found in The Open Book, which you passed earlier.

The Waste Land and 'That Strange Young Man'

The Hogarth Press's most famous publication is their edition of T. S. Eliot's *The Waste Land*, published in September 1923, complete with misprints, which were a result of Eliot's poor proofreading. Copies of this edition are extremely rare. Eliot (1888–1965) first visited the Woolfs at Hogarth House in November 1918. 'That strange young man', was Virginia's assessment. On 18 June 1922 he recited *The Waste Land* to them here and Virginia noted in her diary, 'He sang it & chanted it, rhymed it. It has great beauty & force…What connects it together, I'm not so sure.'

Retrace your steps along Paradise Road, turn left into Halford Road and right into The Vineyard. This brings you out on Richmond Hill, where you turn left. Opposite Richmond Hill Court, cross over to walk along the Terrace, from which Virginia Woolf watched the peace celebrations and fireworks in 1919. 'Rising over the Thames, among trees, these rockets were beautiful', she wrote in her diary.

The panorama at the top of Richmond Hill, with views over what the Scottish poet James Thomson (1700–48) called 'The matchless Vale of Thames', is splendid.

The enormous Star and Garter Home for disabled soldiers stands on the site of the Star and Garter Inn where, in 1850, Tennyson and Thackeray were Dickens's guests to celebrate the publication of *David Copperfield*. Dickens (1812–1870) also liked to host dinners here on his wedding anniversary.

From Philosophy to Children's Books

Enter Richmond Park, London's largest open space, and turn right. Follow the tree-lined path and pass through the gate into Pembroke Lodge Gardens. After the covered laburnum walk, take the left-hand path up the slope to King Henry's Mound, from which Henry VIII allegedly saw the smoke signal that told him that Anne Boleyn had been beheaded. Turn round and look through the hole in the hedge behind you. There, 16 kilometres (about 10 miles) away, cleverly framed by the trees, is the dome of St Paul's Cathedral.

Come down from the mound and continue along the path to Pembroke Lodge, where tea on the terrace with its view over the river is a must. Named the Molecatcher's Cottage in the 18th century – after the humble occupation of its resident – it had successive owners until, in 1847, Queen Victoria presented it to her Prime Minister, Lord John Russell. It stayed in the Russell family for many years and it was here that the philosopher Bertrand Russell (1872–1970) spent his childhood. Later, in writing his autobiography, he recalled the hours he spent in the garden here, the intimacy with which he knew each part of it, and the delight that he took in each season's plant and bird life.

Before you head out of the park, it is worth noting two more of Richmond Park's connections to the world of books. Colin Dann's popular *Animals of Farthing Wood* stories, published in 1979, are loosely set here and, by complete contrast, it was here that in November 1917 trials were carried out on H. G. Wells's 'aerial rope-way'. This was the writer's ingenious invention for moving supplies and wounded men, which he developed after being shocked by the deaths of soldiers carrying rations and ammunition up to the front line in the Third Battle of Ypres. Unfortunately, the generals rejected it. 'The tin hats did not like it', Wells remarked.

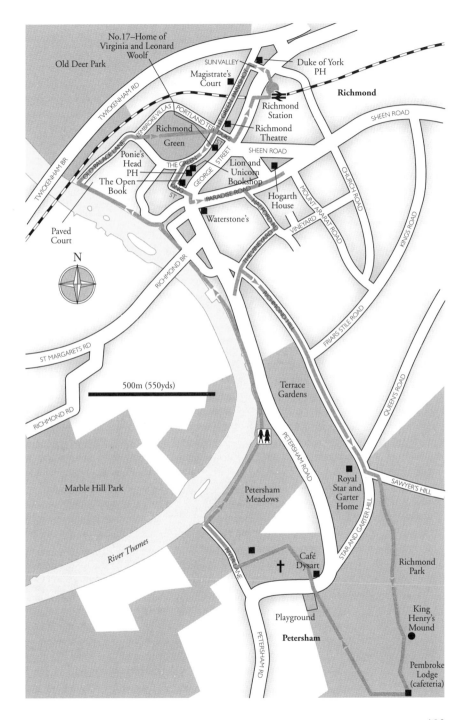

Dickens Takes a Swim

Take the steps down from the terrace and follow the path to the left to a gate. On the other side take the path in front of you and turn right when it meets the main path. Follow this past a playground to come out opposite the Café Dysart, established in 1787, and probably where Dickens stayed whilst on holiday in 1836. Cross the busy Petersham Road and take the narrow path in front of you to begin a surprisingly rural route to the river. Turn right after the churchyard and follow the road round to the left. Pass along the alley on the left and turn right at River Lane, passing the house called Petersham Lodge. This leads down to the river, where you turn right to follow the tow-path back into Richmond. Petersham Farm is on your right. It is surreal – pleasantly so – to see cows grazing so near to London. Dickens stayed in a cottage on Petersham Road in 1839 and often swam along this stretch of the river to Richmond Bridge, which now comes into view. Built between 1774 and 1777, this is the oldest bridge on the Thames.

Keep to the river for some distance, until you reach the White Swan pub sign before the railway bridge. Turn right here, into Old Palace Lane, passing some pretty cottages before rejoining Richmond Green. Take the path diagonally across the green and turn right into Duke Street, where the Woolfs had to engage the services of The Prompt Press when the Hogarth Press machinery broke down. At the traffic lights turn left and follow the road until you come to Richmond Station, where the walk ends.

Islington

Summary: This longish walk takes you through one of London's most fashionable districts. You will see where the Artful Dodger gave Oliver Twist his first lessons in pick-pocketing, and pass the former homes of George Orwell and Evelyn Waugh. You will also see the house in which Salman Rushdie was living when the Ayatollah Khomeini issued his *fatwa*, and walk along one of the capital's least-known waterways.

Start:	Farringdon Underground Station (Bakerloo, Circle and Hammersmith Lines).
Finish:	Highbury and Islington Underground Station (Victoria Line).
Length:	6.6 kilometres (4 miles).
Time:	2–2.5 hours.
Refreshments:	There are numerous bars, cafés and restaurants in Islington. The Marquess Tavern along New River Walk is very pleasantly located.

Turn left on leaving Farringdon Station and left into Turnmill Street. Cross busy Clerkenwell Road and then turn right into Clerkenwell Green, where the Artful Dodger instructed Oliver in the art of picking pockets in *Oliver Twist*. The narrow court from which the boys emerged onto the green is generally assumed to be Pear Street Court, found by turning left into Clerkenwell Close. Pear Street Court is on your left, surrounded by late Victorian Peabody Estate buildings. It brings you out, appropriately enough, opposite the Betsey Trotwood pub, which takes its name from David Copperfield's aunt.

Turn right into Farringdon Road, passing the offices of the *Guardian*, then right into Bowling Green Lane. The atmosphere becomes Dickensian again here, especially in Corporation Row, when you pass an old London Board School with one of its entrances marked 'Special Girls'. Continue into Skinner Street and turn left at the lights into St John Street to begin the rise to Islington. When you cross Rosebery Avenue look to your left to see Sadler's Wells theatre. This famous place of entertainment was named after Thomas Sadler (1888–1957) who, influenced by the success of Tunbridge Wells, founded a health spa and music house here in the 17th century. It is one of London's oldest theatres, having been in existence since 1683.

Wordsworth (1770–1850) was among the theatre's famous visitors, and wrote in his autobiographical poem 'The Prelude' of the many acts he saw here. Dickens (1812–1870) also has many associations with the theatre. The ending of *Oliver Twist* was performed here with – in true pantomime style – a woman playing Oliver, much to Dickens's displeasure. As a boy, Dickens saw the clown Joe Grimaldi perform here, and in 1837 he was offered a partly written biography of Grimaldi to complete. George Cruikshank (1792–1878), who lived close by, provided the illustrations.

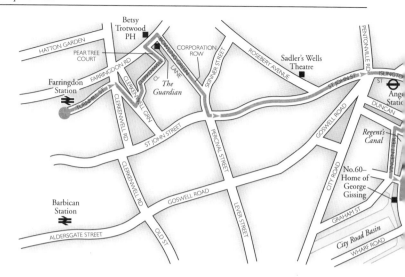

Cross over to begin the walk up into Islington proper. The domed building ahead used to be the Angel Inn, a popular stopping place during the 17th and 18th centuries for travellers arriving in London late in the day. Rather than risk being attacked by highwaymen, who lay in wait along the road to the City, they would stay the night at the inn. Dickens mentions the Angel in *Oliver Twist*, and it is alleged that Tom Paine wrote *The Rights of Man* while staying there.

Grisly Death near a Pretty Canal

Pass Angel Station on Islington High Street and turn right into Duncan Street. Cross Duncan Terrace, home to the novelist and Dickens biographer Peter Ackroyd, and at the second road take the descending steps on the right, hidden in the trees. These lead down to the Regent's Canal, where you'll probably see some attractive houseboats. Ascend the steps at the end, go left over the bridge and left again into Noel Road. A short way up on your right, marked by a plaque, is No. 25, where the playwright Joe Orton (1933–1967), who wrote *Entertaining Mr Sloane, Loot* and *What the Butler Saw*, lived with his lover Kenneth Halliwell from 1959 to 1967. Today, the pair are chiefly remembered for stealing and defacing 83 books from local libraries, and the grisly manner of their death. In the early hours of 9 August 1967 Halliwell battered Orton to death with a hammer and then killed himself by taking a drug overdose.

Retrace your steps and cross to the other half of Noel Road to find No. 60, where George Gissing (1857–1903) lived. His novel *The Nether World*, published in 1889, is regarded as one of the most graphic accounts of Victorian poverty ever written. Return to the crossroads and turn right into Danbury Street.

Salman Rushdie's House

At the end of Danbury Street turn left into St Peter's Street where, a few yards up on your right and marked by a rowan tree, is No. 41. This four-storey, mid-Victorian house, with its cast iron boot scrapers, iron railings and bank of ivy facing the base-

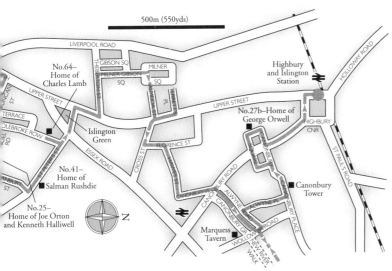

ment windows, is possibly one of the most famous literary houses in the country. Yet you won't find it mentioned in any guidebooks, nor is it on any tourist itinerary. It was while living in this house that the writer Salman Rushdie was forced into hiding after Ayatollah Khomeini of Iran proclaimed his *fatwa* on the author of *The Satanic Verses*. 'I would like to inform all the intrepid Muslims in the world,' read the *fatwa*, 'that the author of the book entitled *The Satanic Verses*, which has been compiled, printed and published in opposition to Islam, the Prophet and the Koran, as well as those publishers who were aware of its contents, have been sentenced to death.'

So began an extremely troubled time that is not, at the time of writing, completely over. Bookshops have been fire-bombed and the staff of Rushdie's publisher, Penguin, have received death threats, some written in blood. For a long time there was a police officer permanently stationed outside Penguin's offices. Rushdie's house is still a literary one. It was later sold to Robert McCrum, sometime novelist and former Faber editor, and at the time of writing Literary Editor of the *Observer*.

Continue up St Peter's Street and turn left into Colebroke Row where, a short way down on the right, hidden by a sycamore and bushes, is No. 64, Colebroke Cottage, where the essayist Charles Lamb (1775–1834) lived from 1823 to 1827. A visitor described it as a 'white house, with 6 good rooms, the New River (rather elderly by this time) runs (if a moderate walking pace can be so termed) close to the foot of the house; and behind is a spacious garden, with vines (I assure you), pears, strawberries…' The New River, which you will pass later, is covered over now, but wasn't when another of the Lambs' friends, the myopic George Dyer, paid them a visit. After an enjoyable evening – perhaps too enjoyable – he left the house and plunged straight into the water.

Anyone for a 'Literary Swim'?

Return to St Peter's Street, where you turn left. Cross Essex Road to Islington Green, passing Waterstone's bookshop, and then turn right into Upper Street.

Islington Green was originally the 'waste' of Canonbury Manor, a grand house long since demolished. The children's illustrator Kate Greenaway (1846–1901) used to live above a shop on Upper Street just north of here.

Turn left into Theberton Street and then right into Gibson Square, one of Islington's many smart squares. Penelope Lively, who won the Booker Prize in 1987 with *Moon Tiger*, lives here, and at the time Stephen Fry's first novel, *The Liar*, was published, he had a house here too, on the right-hand side, along which you are walking. Continue into Milner Square and take the alley-way on your right, into Almeida Street. Rejoin Upper Street and turn left to find the tiny Terrett's Place, which dates back to the 18th century. The odd, narrow house at the end, No. 3, with the worn step and seat-like entrance, is generally identified with the house of Tom and Ruth Pinch in *Martin Chuzzlewit* – 'a singular, old-fashioned house, up a blind street.' Indeed, it used to have a plaque identifying it as such, but it has vanished.

Return to Upper Street, turn right, and cross over into Cross Street. Turn left into Florence Street, noting a wonderful 19th-century wall advertisement for a veterinary practice, and follow it around into Hawes Street. Follow this until you come to a children's playground. Take the path in front of you, turn left, and walk through the playground, coming out on Canonbury Road. Cross straight over into Canonbury Grove, where a gate takes you to the New River Walk, one of London's best-kept secrets.

This delightful walk follows part of the course of the river cut in the 17th century to bring fresh water 61 kilometres (about 38 miles) from Hertfordshire into London. Note the curious watchman's hut, used by the 'linesman' to prevent people from fishing and bathing when this was still drinking water. Keep to the path, ignoring the first exit, and enjoy the quiet, the ducks, the weeping willows and the back views of some of London's most expensive houses, the gardens of which run down to the water's edge. Coleridge (1772–1834) and Lamb swam in the New River, but you may wish to forgo joining the ducks.

George Orwell and Gentleman's Relish

Leave the walk by the Marquess Tavern, cross the bridge and turn left into Alwyne Road, then right into Alwyne Place. Turn left at the top, where you will see Canonbury Tower, which dates from 1562 and was home for a time to Sir Walter Raleigh. Pass the tower and continue into Canonbury Square where, in the left-hand corner, two wildly contrasting writers lived during the first half of the 20th century. In 1945 George Orwell (1903–1950) moved into the top-floor flat of No. 27b with his wife Eileen and their baby son Richard. Eileen, who was ill, died on the operating table at the end of March and soon afterwards Orwell employed a live-in housekeeper, Susan Watson, to help look after his son. Susan has left fascinating glimpses of life at 27b: Orwell was fond of Gentleman's Relish on toast or kippers, washed down by incredibly strong tea, for high tea. He would then go back to work, often writing until the early hours. Michael Shelden records in his authorized biography that Susan became so accustomed to sleeping at night with the sound of the typewriter in the background that she would wake when it stopped. Undaunted by the fact that T. S. Eliot, no less, had just rejected *Animal Farm*, Orwell did a little work on *Nineteen Eighty-Four* here, eventually finishing it at the cottage he owned on the island of Jura.

Evelyn Waugh the Decorator

A writer of a very different kind had lived in the same street 20 years earlier. In 1928 the newly married Evelyn Waugh (1903–1966) and Evelyn Gardner ('He-Evelyn' and 'She-Evelyn', as they dubbed themselves) moved into the first floor of No. 17a. They bought cheap furniture in the junk shops of Upper Street and Essex Road and the writer enjoyed repairing and decorating his finds. He pasted magazine covers on to an old black chest and brightened up a coal scuttle with used postage stamps bought at a local stationer. The writer Sir Harold Acton (1904–1994) called one day to 'find him squatted on the floor, deeply preoccupied, surrounded by confetti-like pools of these bright little stamps which he would stick in elaborate patterns on an ugly coal-scuttle, his hair all tousled and his fingers dabbled in glue…' The flat had the air, he continued, 'of a sparkling nursery'.

Continue round this half of the square and then turn right on Canonbury Road, which rises up to cross the lights. Now continue down the slope to Highbury Corner and find Highbury Station at the far left-hand corner, where the walk ends.

Highgate

Summary: Much of Highgate used to belong to the Bishop of London and this elegant hilltop village takes its name from the gate that led to the Bishop's park. Today, like Barnes in south-west London, it exists in a kind of splendid isolation, squeezed between Hampstead Heath on the one side and Archway Road on the other. Strict planning laws help maintain the character of the village which, despite the traffic, remains genteel. This walk passes the houses of Samuel Taylor Coleridge and A. E. Housman, and the graves of George Eliot and Karl Marx. You will also see where T. S. Eliot briefly taught the young John Betjeman.

Start:	Highgate Underground Station (Northern Line).
Finish:	Archway Underground Station (Northern Line).
Length:	5.6 kilometres (3½ miles).
Time:	3–3.5 hours.
Refreshments:	Highgate has plenty of cafés, bars and restaurants. Lauderdale House in Waterlow Park has a café, although the fare is perhaps rather more meagre today than it would have been when Pepys dined there in 1666.

Take the Archway Road exit from Highgate Station. Turn left and walk down to the lights, where you turn right into Jacksons Lane. Bear to the left into Southwood Lane and breathe a sigh of relief as the road levels out. Turn right into Castle Yard, with its pretty row of artisans' cottages, then left into North Road, continuing until you reach the Red Lion and Sun pub. Cross at the lights to find No. 17, Byron Cottage, almost directly opposite, the left-hand house in an elegant Georgian terrace set back from the road behind a little grove of trees.

A. E. Housman, the Bashful Lodger

Despite its name, the house seems to have no associations with Lord Byron. Rather, as a plaque notes, this three-storey building with the slightly crooked roof was the home of the poet and scholar A. E. Housman (1859–1936) from 1886 to 1905. He wrote *A Shropshire Lad* here while employed as a Professor of Latin at London University. His landlady was a Mrs Hunter and he was the sole lodger. The best rooms, on the ground floor, were used by Mrs Hunter. Housman had rooms on the floor above, where the bathroom and toilet were also situated. As his sister Clemence observed, this arrangement suited the shy poet: 'He was exceedingly bashful about being seen *déshabillé.*' When Mrs Hunter moved to Pinner, Housman moved too. She is reported to have said that though sorry to lose him, she hoped that by living in a college he 'would be taken out of himself, shaken up, and made to chatter like the rest of the world...'

Continue to the roundabout, with Highgate School to your left. Literary pupils here include the poets Gerald Manley Hopkins (1844–1889) and John Betjeman (1906–1984). The latter was taught, for three terms in 1916, by T. S. Eliot (1888–1965), 'The American master, Mr Eliot/That dear good man, with Prufrock in his head/And Sweeney waiting to be agonized.' The young Betjeman was well known at school for reciting his own verses in the playground and some of his fellow pupils persuaded him to present a manuscript entitled *The Best Poems of Betjeman* to Eliot. Years later Eliot kindly reminded Betjeman of the incident.

Although their work was markedly different, Betjeman always defended Eliot, who was sometimes attacked for being too serious or obscure. He certainly felt that, when it came to religion, they shared common ground. '[Eliot's] soul journey', Betjeman wrote in 1948, using a very Betjeman-esque rail analogy, 'travels in the same carriage as mine, the dear old rumbling Church of England...'

Coleridge and his Opium Addiction
Turn right into Hampstead Lane, then left into The Grove, Highgate's most distinguished address. Walk along the right-hand, gravelled pavement, until you reach No. 3, home of the poet, critic and 'philosopher of Romanticism' Samuel Taylor Coleridge (1772–1834), who lodged here with Dr James Gillman and his family from 1823 until his death in 1834.

The arrangement was an unusual one. It had begun in 1816, in another house, which you will pass shortly. Gillman had agreed to take Coleridge in as a 'patient/lodger', in an attempt to cure him of his opium addiction. The poet warned the doctor that it would be difficult for both of them, admitting that he would have to be 'watched carefully'. His cravings would drive him to 'Evasion and the cunning of a specific madness.' For the first week 'I must not be permitted to leave your House, unless I should walk out with you...both the Servant and the young Man must receive absolute commands from you on no account to fetch anything for me.' The following years were to show how Coleridge continued to crave – and obtain – opium.

Coleridge's Highgate
Coleridge had a large attic bedroom, to which was added an extension looking westwards over Hampstead Heath. Decorated with pictures of Coleridge's family and friends, the room had a long wall of bookshelves and numerous pot plants on the table at which he worked, including a myrtle, which he described in a poem as the symbol of love lost and found.

Coleridge *is* Highgate – every inch of this pretty village is suffused with the great man. Indeed, such is the interest in the poet that in 1999, the librarian at the Highgate Literary and Scientific Institution admitted that she could simply not get enough copies of *Coleridge: Darker Reflections*, the second volume of Richard Holmes's masterly biography and the one that deals with the Highgate years.

Literary Visitors
During his time in the village Coleridge received an array of distinguished visitors. Thomas Carlyle, Dante Gabriel Rosetti, John Stuart Mill, James Fenimore Cooper,

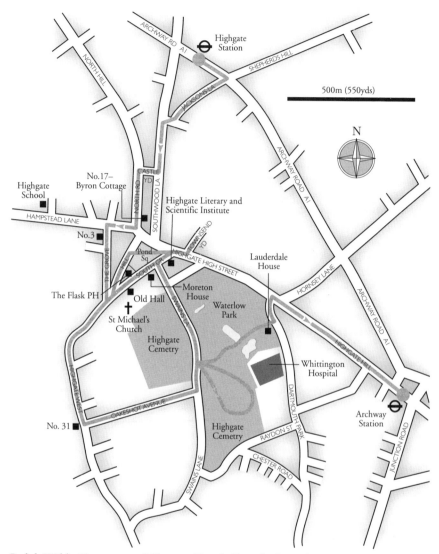

Ralph Waldo Emerson and Thomas Hood all made the trek up the hill to hear the brilliant conversation of the 'white-haired, shuffling sage' (Holmes's phrase). John Keats (1795–1821) never saw him at The Grove, but bumped into him on Hampstead Heath on 11 April 1819 (see pages 119–20).

No. 3 The Grove is one of the few houses in London to bear two plaques. The writer J. B. Priestly (1894–1984) lived in the same house from 1933–1939, having bought it on the proceeds from his best-selling novel *The Good Companions*, published in 1931. He loved the house, describing it as one 'of the loveliest things you ever saw. I sit in Coleridge's old room typing this letter; I see nothing from my window but Kenwood and the slope of the Heath, and our own flower beds below, or our neighbour, Gladys Cooper, still beautiful, eating breakfast outside in pyjamas.'

Continue along The Grove and then turn sharp left back on yourself, with the Flask pub on your right. Follow this short road, with the reservoir on your left, then turn right into Pond Square. Coleridge was a well-known and popular figure in the village and it is easy to imagine him descending the narrow steps and alley-ways here, followed by the gaggles of small boys who found the old gentleman eccentric and appealing.

Exit at the far corner, passing the phone boxes, and come out on to Highgate High Street, where you turn right. A short way down on the left is Townsend Yard. The building on its left-hand corner is now Litchfields estate agents, but in Coleridge's day it was occupied by the chemists T. H. Dunn. Unknown to Dr Gillman, it was from here that Coleridge managed to secure a private supply of opium, receiving it by a discreet side door, which is perhaps the low one that can be seen today. A young assistant felt sympathy for him and became something of a friend, seeking the poet out on his afternoons off when, 'whether reading or making notes' Coleridge would break off to talk to him.

Return to Pond Square and turn left into South Grove. The white-fronted Highgate Literary and Scientific Institute, founded in 1839, 'to excite and cultivate an intelligent interest in the objects of literature and science', contains an extensive Betjeman archive as well as a small but well-stocked library. It has hosted lectures for over 100 years. In 1899 Mary Kingsley (1862–1900), author of *Travels in West Africa*, gave a talk on her adventures and in 1998 the future Poet Laureate, Andrew Motion, another Highgate resident, spoke about his biography of Keats.

Almost immediately you reach Moreton House, on the left, where Coleridge first began living with Dr Gillman and his family in April 1816, before the move to The Grove. A little further along is the Old Hall, former home of the novelist Rumer Godden (1907–1998). Next door is St Michael's Church, where Coleridge is buried. His memorial stone lies in the central aisle; photocopied brass-rubbings of the stone may be purchased. There is also a memorial tablet from the Gillmans on the north wall of the nave, which reads: 'this truly great and good man…the gentlest and kindest teacher; the most engaging home companion.' Richard Holmes brought a group of London booksellers here on his own Coleridge walk in 1998, before *Darker Reflections* was published. He remarked on how fitting it was that he could see the spire of the church from the windows of his flat down the hill.

Betjeman's Highgate

Retrace your steps from the church and turn left into Highgate West Hill to find No. 31, the childhood home of John Betjeman, of which he wrote: 'At that hill's foot did London then begin,/With yellow horse-drawn trams clopping past the planes…' From here the young Betjeman would walk to school up in the village, feeling 'very sorry for horse chestnuts if they were left on the road' because he believed that 'inanimate objects could feel and think.'

Almost directly opposite is Oakeshott Road, which leads through Holly Lodge Estate. Continue until you reach Swain's Lane, where you turn left to find the twin entrances to Highgate Cemetery. Founded in 1839 and 1854 respectively, the Western and Eastern Cemeteries are both impressive. Around 166,800 people are buried here in 51,800 graves. The Western Cemetery is probably the more famous. The extraordinary Gothic architecture of some of its tombs led Betjeman to describe it as a 'Victorian Valhalla'. Literary graves here include those of Margaret Radclyffe Hall (1886–1943), author of *The Well of Loneliness*; the poet Christina Rosetti (1830–1894); Stella Gibbons (1902–1989), author of *Cold Comfort Farm*; and Frederick Warne, Beatrix Potter's publisher. But to visit it you have to join an organised tour.

Our route goes through the Eastern Cemetery. Follow the main path and look out for an open-book tombstone on the right, just after the first junction. This is the grave of William Foyle (1885–1963), founder of the famous Charing Cross Road bookshop (see page 47). At the next junction take the left-hand, gravelled path. Cross two junctions to find the famous, sphinx-like tomb of Karl Marx (1818–1883). Retrace your steps and turn right at the first junction. A short way up on the right, with an obelisk pointing at the sky, is the tomb of Mary Ann Evans, better known as George Eliot (1819–1880). Retrace your steps, turn right on to the main path, and follow it to the exit.

Where Pepys heard too much Scottish Music

Turn right and then immediately right again into Waterlow Park. Go left at the first junction, ignoring the path immediately to your left, then turn right, heading for the bridge between the ponds. Take the middle path to the left and turn left in front of the flower beds. Ignoring the steps, take the entrance to the right, which leads up to the 17th-century Lauderdale House, where Pepys (1633–1703) dined with Lord Lauderdale in July 1666 and heard perhaps rather more Scottish tunes 'upon the viallin' than he cared for. The poet Andrew Marvell (1621–1678) lived in a house very close by, hence the quote from his poem 'The Garden' on the sundial.

Leave the gardens of Lauderdale House and turn right. Follow this path round to leave Waterlow Park, then turn left. A few yards up there is a curious plaque on the wall, dating from 1898, which informs pedestrians that 'Four feet below this spot is the stone step formerly the entrance to the cottage in which lived Andrew Marvell…'

To complete the walk, descend Highgate Hill, which offers views right across London to the Millennium Dome in Greenwich. Continue down to Archway Station, where the walk ends.

Hampstead (1) North

Summary: Hampstead, perched on a hilltop some 120 metres (400 feet) above London in a very pleasant setting, has long attracted both the wealthy and the artistic, and is perhaps London's most literary neighbourhood. Here there are probably more 'plaqued' houses commemorating distinguished people than in any other quarter of the capital, and practically every bench one passes on the famous Hampstead Heath seems to be dedicated to a writer or philosopher. This walk takes in the homes of writers D. H. Lawrence, Katherine Mansfield and H. G. Wells, and follows in the footsteps of the poets Keats and Coleridge out on to the Heath.

Start and finish:	Hampstead Underground Station (Northern Line).
Length:	7 kilometres (4⅓ miles).
Time:	3.5 hours.
Refreshments:	Jack Straw's Castle and The Spaniards are two pubs with numerous literary associations, although today neither has a particularly literary atmosphere. Keats used to lodge next door to the Wells Tavern. There are many cafés and restaurants in Hampstead village.

On leaving Hampstead Station, cross straight over into Heath Street, almost immediately passing the Pullman Everyman Cinema, formerly the Everyman Theatre, where Noel Coward's play *The Vortex* opened in 1924. Turn right into Church Row, with its elegant line of Georgian townhouses standing to attention on the left. Lord Alfred Douglas, or 'Boysie' (1870–1945), as Oscar Wilde called him, lived at No. 26, the third house along, in 1913–1914. Douglas's father, the 8th Marquis of Queensberry, had some years earlier objected to Wilde's relationship with his son, provoking the legal action that saw Wilde's downfall and imprisonment in Reading Gaol. While in prison, Wilde (1854–1900) wrote *De Profundis*, a long and bitter letter to Boysie.

H.G. Wells and his Long-suffering Wife
Towards the end of Church Row, No. 17, also on the left, was the home of H. G. Wells (1866–1946) from 1909 to 1912. D. H. Lawrence (1885–1930) once came to dinner here and complained all evening because he'd had to borrow a dinner jacket. Wells had insisted on the correct attire. The author of such early science fiction classics as *The Time Machine* and *The War of the Worlds* lived a curious life in Hampstead. He was having an affair with Amber Reeves, an enlightened 'new' woman, the daughter of Fabian parents who were advocates of social change and sexual liberation. Wells's wife Jane knew of her existence and even knew that the pair had rented a house in Le Touquet on the Normandy coast, the better to continue their affair. But when Amber became pregnant, Wells lost interest in her. Jane Wells

still stuck by her husband, as she would do throughout his numerous subsequent affairs, until her death in 1927.

Pass into the attractive lane by the side of the Parish Church of St John-at-Hampstead, where the poet Gerard Manley Hopkins (1844–1889), who grew up locally and whose father was churchwarden, used to worship. The elegant interior of the church includes a memorial to Keats (1795–1821) erected in 1894 by American admirers. The landscape painter John Constable (1776–1837) is buried in the graveyard. Turn right into Frognal Gardens, where the children's writer and illustrator Kate Greenaway (1846–1901) lived, and then right again into Frognal itself. Note the extremely pretty Bay Tree Cottage opposite, which itself looks as though it is from a children's book.

Robert Louis Stevenson

After a short distance, take the passage on the right, up Mount Vernon. The house immediately on the right was the home of E. V. 'Evoe' Knox, editor of *Punch* from 1932 to 1949. The solid, squat, brick house at No. 7, on the corner of Holly Walk and Mount Vernon, is Abernethy House, where the writer Robert Louis Stevenson (1850–1894), having been advised to come south for the sake of his health, lodged briefly with his friend Sir Sidney Colvin (1845–1927), Slade Professor of Fine Art at Cambridge. Although Colvin was not homosexual, his appreciation of Stevenson was intensely physical: 'The most robust of ordinary men', he wrote, 'seemed to turn dim and null in the presence of the vitality that glowed in the steadfast, penetrating fire of the lean man's eyes, the rich, compelling charm of his smile, the lissom swiftness of his movements and lively expressiveness of his gestures, above all in the irresistible sympathetic play and abundance.'

Continue up Mount Vernon, passing No. 3, where the English poet Coventry Patmore (1823–1896) lived. At the top, follow Mount Vernon round to the left on a high walkway, which offers delightful views, through the trees, over Holly Hill. Follow the walkway down to a small green. Opposite you, on Windmill Hill beneath a horse chestnut tree, is the gateway to Bolton House. A plaque, which is impossible to read, indicates that this is the former home of the poet and dramatist Joanna Baille (1762–1851). Practically unknown today, she was described by Wordsworth – a visitor, along with Keats – as 'the ablest authoress of the day.'

A Donation to the English Language

Turn right into Hampstead Grove, passing Fenton House before you come to No. 28 on the right, once home to the *Punch* illustrator and novelist George du Maurier (1834–1896). Du Maurier shares with Joseph Heller and J. M. Barrie the rare distinction of having given the English language a word or phrase. His 1894 novel *Trilby* told the story of a young singer who comes under the mesmeric influence of another musician, Svengali. Dictionaries now define 'Svengali' as 'somebody who controls and manipulates somebody else, usually for evil purposes'.

Turn immediately left into Admiral's Walk, at the bottom of which you will find Grove Lodge, where the novelist and playwright John Galsworthy (1867–1933) lived from 1918 until his death. This 17th-century house, in which John Constable also

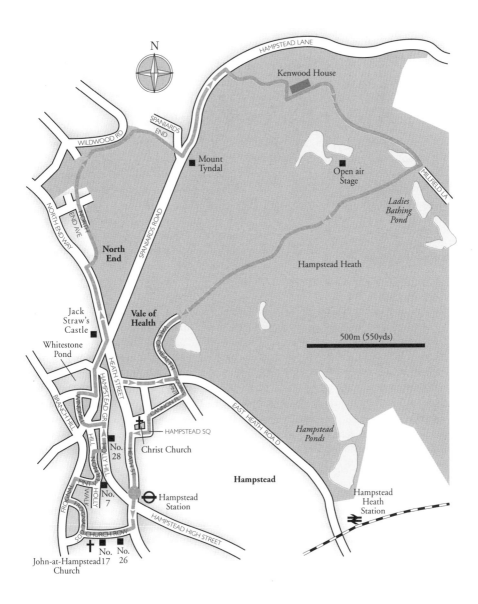

N

HAMPSTEAD LANE

Kenwood House

WILDWOOD RD

SPANIARDS END

Mount
Tyndal

Open air
Stage

MILLFIELD LA

*Ladies
Bathing
Pond*

NORTH END WAY

NORTH END AVE

SPANIARDS ROAD

North
End

Hampstead Heath

Jack
Straw's
Castle

Vale of
Health

VALE OF HEALTH

500m (550yds)

Whitestone
Pond

HEATH STREET

HAMPSTEAD GR

EAST HEATH ROAD

BRANCH HILL

WINDMILL HILL

CANNON PL

HAMPSTEAD SQ

*Hampstead
Ponds*

HOLLY HILL

No.
28

HOLLY HILL

HEATH ST

Christ Church

FROGNAL

MNT VERN

FROGNAL

HOLLY WALK

No.
7

Hampstead
Station

Hampstead

Hampstead
Heath
Station

CHURCH ROW

HAMPSTEAD HIGH STREET

John-at-Hampstead
Church

No.
17

No.
26

117

lived for a period, is deceptively small, an effect that is emphasised by the extraordinary, enormous clapboard 'Admiral's House' next door (which appears as Admiral
Boon's House, Cherry Tree Lane, in P. L. Travers's *Mary Poppins*). The ground floor of
Grove Lodge included a dining-room, study and drawing-room, all overlooking the
garden. The drawing-room was extended to include a bay, in which Galsworthy's
wife would play the piano – something that apparently helped the writer when
working on a particularly 'knotty passage'. He would call out to her to 'play something' to make the words come. Galsworthy wrote the last five volumes of *The Forsyte
Saga* here. When he was too ill to travel to Stockholm to receive the Nobel Prize for
Literature in 1932, the medal and illuminated scroll were brought to Grove Lodge.

Continue past Galsworthy's house, then turn right at the tiny island, into Lower
Terrace. Cross straight over, walk along the side of Fountain House, beneath a weeping willow, and continue up Windmill Hill, noting the white, architect-designed
home on your left – such expensive, new buildings, sandwiched between those of old
Hampstead, are a typical sight in this exclusive London suburb. Soon you reach
Judges Walk, with the Heath beyond. Turn right and then left on to Lower Terrace,
keeping to the left, which brings you out by Whitestone Pond. Carry straight on to
the far side of the pond. Continue, bearing to the left, until you reach busy North
End Way, where you turn left. The large, handsome, Georgian house beyond the war
memorial is Heath House, once the home of Sir Samuel Hoare, a 19th-century
Quaker banker. He was a generous host to many poets and his frequent guests included George Crabbe (1754–1832), William Cowper (1731–1800) and William
Wordsworth (1770–1850).

Jack Straw's Castle, on your left, is a famous old coaching inn named after one of
the leaders of the Peasants' Revolt. Wilkie Collins, William Thackeray and Charles
Dickens all patronized it. Continue along North End Way and when the road bends
to the left at a traffic island, cross over and take the path on to the Heath. Take the
right fork, keep to the main track, and ignore all turns. This takes you through the
trees to North End Avenue. Follow it down and go straight over into North End.
The path becomes a gravel track leading past Wildwood Terrace, an elegant row of
tall houses on the left. No. 2 was the home of Sir Nikolaus Pevsner (1902–1983),
author of Penguin's famous *The Buildings of England* series, who lived here from 1936
until his death.

Is this London or is it the Country?

This is an extraordinary part of London: in the capital, yet also in what amounts to
a country lane. Follow the track round to find a house with dark weather-boarding,
almost the last house on the left. This, together with its neighbour, used to form
Wyldes Farm, a 17th-century farmhouse that belonged for a time to the artist John
Linnell (1792–1882). Although there have been alterations over the years, parts of the
original farmhouse still exist. William Blake (1757–1827) visited Linnell here, but
would later complain that Hampstead's fresh air 'always laid me up the day after.' In
1832 Charles Dickens stayed here after the death of his sister-in-law, Mary Hogarth.

Follow the track along and to the left to Wildwood Road, where you turn right.
Just before Spaniards Rise, as the road bends to the left, take the path into the Heath

and climb up past houses with conservatories giving dramatic views over the tree-tops. Turn left at the top into Spaniards Way, passing the Mount Tyndal development. The Spaniards pub dates back to the 16th century and, with the toll house opposite (in which the highwayman Dick Turpin stabled his horse Black Bess), forms one of the best known chicanes in London. Shelley (1792–1822), Keats and Byron (1788–1824) all patronized the pub, while Dickens has Mrs Bardell and her friends plot the downfall of Mr Pickwick here.

From Julia Roberts to Dr Johnson

Drop down along Hampstead Lane and enter the grounds of Kenwood House on your right. Take the left-hand drive to the house. Built in the 17th century and owned by the descendants of Lord Mansfield until 1922, it has a tenuous literary connection through the film *Notting Hill*, starring Hugh Grant and Julia Roberts. The scene filmed here shows Roberts's character acting in the film of a Henry James short story. Grant walks on to the set and is instructed to 'drink tea' by Roberts.

Take the right-hand path at the front of the house. Dr Johnson's summer-house, which originally stood in the garden of his friend Mrs Thrale in Streatham, used to overlook the lawn on the right. Sadly, it was burned down by vandals in 1993. Duck through the Ivy Walk and turn left, walking past the front of the house, noting the glorious views over the magnificent landscaped gardens. At the far end there is a café, a good place to pause before you head out on to the Heath in the footsteps of Keats and Dickens.

A Famous Meeting on the Heath

Continue along the gravel path and when you reach the concert stage, go left through a gate, and then right. This becomes Millfield Lane – although it is still really a path – and presently there are views across to St Michael's in Highgate, one of the most distinctive spires in north London. Samuel Taylor Coleridge (1772–1834) is buried in St Michael's (see page 113), and it was on this lane that he had a famous meeting with John Keats. At the time, Coleridge was in conversation with a companion, J. H. Green, who had taught Keats at Guy's Hospital. Coleridge later recounted:

A loose, slack, not well-dressed youth met Mr Green and myself in a lane near Highgate. Green knew him and spoke. It was Keats. He was introduced to me and staid [sic] a minute or so. After he had left us a little way, he came back and said: 'Let me carry away the memory, Coleridge, of having pressed your hand!' – 'There is death in that hand', I said to Green when Keats was gone; yet this was, I believe, before the consumption showed itself distinctly.

It is fascinating to read Keats's account of the meeting. He wrote to his brother George:

In the lane that winds behind the side of Lord Mansfield's Park [what is now Kenwood] I met Mr Green our Demonstrator at Guy's in conversation with Coleridge... I walked with him at his alderman-after-dinner pace for near two miles I suppose. In these two miles he approached a thousand things...Nightingales, Poetry...Different genera and species of Dreams...the difference explained between Will and Volition...Monsters...the Kraken...

It is also interesting to note that both writers, living on opposite sides of the Heath, were listening to the nightingales that year. They got on Coleridge's nerves somewhat – the Heath was 'incessant with song', he complained – but Keats sat in his Hampstead garden and wrote 'Ode to a Nightingale', one of the most famous poems in the English language.

Literary Walkers

After a large, partly hidden pond, turn right and climb the slope. Eventually the path enters the trees, and Canary Wharf can be glimpsed in the distance. Hampstead Heath's literary associations are numerous: in *The Woman in White* Wilkie Collins talks about the 'white winding paths across the lonely heath'; Dickens was well-known for setting a fearsome pace on his walks. He once asked his future biographer, John Forster (1812–1876): 'You don't feel disposed, do you, to muffle yourself up and start off with me for a good brisk walk over Hampstead Heath? I know of a good house where we can have a red-hot chop for dinner and a glass of wine.' The 'good house' was Jack Straw's Castle, which you passed some time ago. The son of the painter Samuel Palmer recalls that after William Blake's winter visits to the Linnells at Wyldes Farm, Blake (1757–1827) was 'wrapped up in a shawl by Mrs Linnell and sent on his homeward way, with the servant, lantern in hand, lighting him across the Heath.' On the night of 8 September 1915 D. H. Lawrence (1885–1930) and his wife Frieda watched the first major Zeppelin raid on London from the Heath. 'Guns boomed and searchlights raked the sky, and a fire burned far off in the City', he recalled. He used the incident in his novel *Kangaroo*.

D. H. Lawrence, Keats and the Vale of Health

Presently you come to a fairly large, open junction containing a little green and two benches. To your right is a path through a gate. Take the second path to its left (as you look at it), passing a large, gnarled oak. Carry straight on, eventually passing an open area to your right, where a television tower protrudes from the trees. A switchback follows before the land opens out on either side of the path. A church spire appears above the trees on your left. Continue along the top path and then take the left-hand path, down through the trees. Continue, passing a car park-cum-fairground, then turn right, passing an ugly block of flats (Spencer House). The little network of streets and passageways you are now entering is called the Vale of Health and is one of the most literary areas in all Hampstead.

Continue up the street to find Byron Villas at the top on the left, where D. H. Lawrence and his wife Frieda lodged on the ground floor of No. 1 in 1915. They had plans to form a community of like-minded people, among them the writers Katherine Mansfield (1888–1923) and John Middleton Murry (1889–1957), who both lived locally and would join them for picnics on the Heath. At the time, Lawrence was also trying to set up a new critical magazine called *Signature* with Middleton Murry. Numerous other writers visited the Lawrences here, among them

E. M. Forster, Aldous Huxley, Bertrand Russell, W. B. Yeats and Ezra Pound. But according to Frieda, her husband was not happy: 'He didn't like the Vale of Health, and he didn't like the little flat and he didn't like me or anybody else.' After six months they left Byron Villas for Cornwall, but Lawrence's short story 'The Last Laugh' has a Hampstead setting.

Turn right at the top of the Vale of Health and note the first white wooden door on your left. Look at it carefully. It should say 'Woodbine Cottage', this being the tiny former home of Compton Mackenzie (1883–1972), author of *Whisky Galore*. Follow the road up and round. The large house facing the Heath at the end, behind the brick wall, is Vale Lodge, home of the poet and essayist Leigh Hunt (1784–1859). When Hunt lived here it became one of the most literary houses in London. Keats and Shelley visited often. Keats wrote much of the poem 'Sleep and Poetry' on a sofa Hunt let him use when he stayed overnight 'in a parlour no bigger than an old mansion's closet'. The house was chaotic. Manuscripts were strewn about and Hunt's children darted from room to room. He called it his 'philosophy of cheer'. In complete contrast, the English writer turned Hollywood scriptwriter Edgar Wallace would live in the same house many years later.

Follow the road round and take the passageway to the left, which comes out on an attractive little island. The house behind you, No. 3 Villas on the Heath, is where the Indian poet and philosopher Rabindranath Tagore (1861–1941) stayed in 1916. Tagore received the Nobel Prize for Literature in 1913, the first Asian to do so, and was also knighted in 1915 – an honour he resigned in 1919 in protest against British policy in the Punjab. Keep going, and after the houses cross over and take the path on to the Heath to visit the pond on which Shelley floated paper boats with Hunt's 11-year-old son Thornton.

Katherine Mansfield and 'The Elephant'

Return to the road and turn left. Shortly you meet East Heath Road where, slightly to the left, Katherine Mansfield moved with her new husband John Middleton Murry in 1918. Like Robert Louis Stevenson, she had come to Hampstead for her health, in the hope that the clean air would cure her tuberculosis. But she was ambivalent about the house, often referring to it as 'The Elephant', probably because of its size and its grey bricks. On other occasions, as Claire Tomalin observes in her biography of the writer, she thought it 'the charming house it actually appears today, elegant, tall and airy, with pretty windows under lintels shaped like eyebrows...' Mansfield herself wrote in her *Journal* (1927), in an entry headed 'October, Hampstead: Geraniums': 'I went to London and married an Englishman, and we lived in a tall grave house with red geraniums and white daisies in the garden at the back.'

Cross over into Squires Mount, passing the former home of the actor/manager Sir Gerald du Maurier, and turn right into Cannon Place. Continue into Hampstead Square, bearing left past Christ Church into Elm Row, where D. H. Lawrence stayed in one of the townhouses on the right in 1923. Turn left into Heath Street, which drops down to the traffic lights, where you turn left. Continue to Hampstead Station, where the walk ends.

Hampstead (2) South

Summary: The second Hampstead walk visits the home of its most famous literary resident, John Keats. You will also climb John Betjeman's beloved Parliament Hill, before passing buildings associated with writers as diverse as George Orwell, Lytton Strachey and Alex Garland. The walk then drops down to Belsize Park, the equally up-market suburb that nestles on Hampstead's shoulder.

Start:	Hampstead Underground Station (Northern Line).
Finish:	Belsize Park Underground Station (Northern Line).
Length:	6 kilometres (3¾ miles).
Time:	2.5 hours.
Refreshments:	Establishments with literary connections include the Flask pub, the forerunner of which is mentioned in Samuel Richardson's *Clarissa*. John Keats once lived next door to the Wells Tavern, then called The Green Man. The South End area has plenty of cafés and an attractive, continental atmosphere.

Turn left out of the station and then left into Flask Walk, a narrow paved alley-way of secondhand bookshops and small boutiques, which takes its name from the spa that grew up in the early 18th century around the spring that rises on the Heath. Hampstead Spa became a fashionable resort with a coffee house and wells of spa water, hence Well Walk, which you enter shortly. But the spa's proximity to London meant that too many 'common' people visited and eventually it declined. Perhaps this is why The Lower Flask Tavern, now simply called The Flask, which you pass shortly, is described by Samuel Richardson (1689–1761) in his novel *Clarissa* as 'a place where second-rate persons are to be found occasionally in a swinish condition.'

Kipling and Burgh House
Follow Flask Walk round to the right, passing charming cottages and secret gardens behind ancient brick walls. At the junction with Willow Road, Burgh House appears on your left, behind enormous London plane trees. Built in 1703, this splendid Queen Anne building was the home from 1934 to 1937 of Captain George Bambridge and his wife Elsie, daughter of Rudyard Kipling (1865–1936). The writer visited the house often and Elsie recalled, 'the delightful old house and garden which we rented in Hampstead was a source of happiness to my father to the end of his life.' In fact, Kipling's last trip before his death in 1936 was a visit to Burgh House to see his daughter and son-in-law. Today, the house, which has a café in the basement, is home to a local history museum and arts centre and is also used for exhibitions and concerts.

In 1918 the birth-control pioneer Marie Stopes (1880–1958) lived directly opposite Burgh House, at No. 13 Well Walk. That was the year in which her controversial book *Married Love* was published, heralding a greater openness about sexual matters. Continue along Well Walk and, just before Christchurch Hill, find No. 27, the large white house on the right, home to the writer J. B. Priestly (1894–1984) from 1929 to 1931. It was here that he wrote the last chapters of *The Good Companions*, in 'a little empty room near the roof' during the great cold spell of 1929. He wrote of the experience: 'Day after day the temperature sank, the streets became like glass, pipes were bursting on every side…but all this was nothing more to me than a vague fantastic dream. I would return to my typewriter after dinner and go on until the small and dreadfully freezing hours…Out it came like a flood and down it went.' He didn't much like the house, though, describing it as 'one of the tallest and ugliest houses in London.' However, his novel met with success and on the proceeds he was able to buy Samuel Taylor Coleridge's old house in The Grove, Highgate.

John Keats in Well Walk

Cross Christchurch Hill and continue along Well Walk. In April 1817 John Keats (1795–1821) and his brothers George and Tom, fed up with the dampness in their Cheapside rooms, took lodgings in the house of Mr Bentley, the postman, on the first floor of No.1 Well Walk (since demolished), next door to the Wells Tavern, which was then known as The Green Man. John Keats's room overlooked an avenue of lime trees leading on to the Heath, '…where sweet air stirs/Blue hare-bells lightly, and where prickly furze/Binds lavish gold.' Although he had obtained a licence from the Society of Apothecaries, he did not want to become a doctor or continue training to be a surgeon. He wanted to devote his life to poetry. Part of the reason for his move to Hampstead was the fact that it was the home of the critic Leigh Hunt (1784–1859), whom he had often visited and where he had met many other writers, among them his fellow poet Percy Bysshe Shelley (1792–1822). But Keats used some of his medical skills to nurse his 19-year-old brother Tom, who died of consumption, 'quietly and without pain', at Well Walk on 1 December 1818.

Keats's Bench

If the proximity of fellow writers and the Heath was an inspiration, the proximity of Bentley's young family was sometimes a hindrance. 'Bentley's children are making a horrid row', Keats wrote once; on another occasion he complained about the cramped conditions and having to 'breathe worsted stockings'. But Well Walk was then a country lane and soothing nature was all around, and there was a seat with a view towards the Heath that for years was known as Keats's Bench. Today you'll find two benches at the end of the road. Sadly, they are often covered with graffiti. Before you reach them, however, note No. 13 on your left, an elegant, gabled house that rises high above the road. Its plaque commemorates the Socialist leader Henry Hyndman (1842–1921), but the house was also home to John Masefield (1878–1967), a contemporary of Kipling's who, like Kipling, was a writer who had made many journeys by sea, having served his apprenticeship at sea but been driven

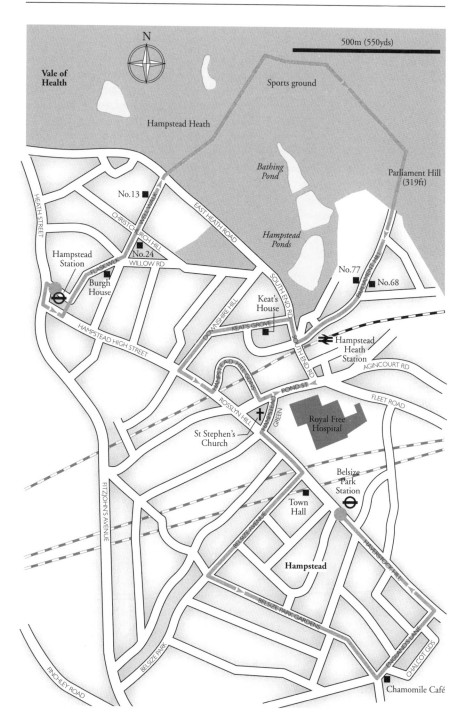

N

500m (550yds)

**Vale of
Health**

Sports ground

Hampstead Heath

*Bathing
Pond*

Parliament Hill
(319ft)

No.13

HEATH STREET

CHRISTCHURCH HILL

EAST HEATH ROAD

*Hampstead
Ponds*

Hampstead
Station

No.24

WILLOW RD

FLASK WALK

No.77

No.68

PARLIAMENT HILL

Burgh
House

Keat's
House

SOUTH END RD

DOWNSHIRE HILL

KEAT'S GROVE

HAMPSTEAD HIGH STREET

Hampstead
Heath
Station

SOUTH END RD

AGINCOURT RD

HAMPSTEAD HILL GDNS

HAMPSTEAD GREEN

POND ST

ROSSLYN HILL

FLEET ROAD

St Stephen's
Church

Royal Free
Hospital

Belsize
Park
Station

FITZJOHN'S AVENUE

Town
Hall

BELSIZE AVENUE

HAVERSTOCK HILL

Hampstead

BELSIZE PARK GARDENS

ENGLAND'S LANE

CHALCOT GDS

BELSIZE PARK

FINCHLEY ROAD

Chamomile Café

ashore by ill health. The author of one of the best-known lines in English poetry – 'I must go down to the seas again…' – Masefield lived here from 1914 to 1916.

Out on to the Heath

At the end of Well Walk cross straight over onto the Heath. Descend into an avenue of trees and follow this path until you come to a playing field on your right. The pavilion in the corner appears in *Smiley's People* by John le Carré, another local writer. Continue up the avenue and take the path to the right behind the pavilion. Keep to the path between the trees and, after you descend, take the tarmac path straight ahead. Soon the land opens out to your left, when you should take the path up the slope. This brings you out on the top of Parliament Hill, so called, as one legend has it, because Guy Fawkes and his conspirators planned to watch the Houses of Parliament burning from here. London is spread out before you, while Highgate is over to your left and behind you. It is easy to spot the very narrow spire of St Michael's, Highgate, where Coleridge is buried (see page 113).

Orwell the Nature-lover

Retrace your steps and take the path off to the left, down the grassy bank, to the street called Parliament Hill. In 1935 George Orwell (1903–1950) was living at No. 77, the last house on the right. His second novel, *A Clergyman's Daughter*, had just been published and he was working in a secondhand bookshop down the road. A friend had found him the flat, thinking that being close to the Heath would benefit his troublesome lungs. Hampstead's history is peppered with people coming to its heights for similar reasons: Samuel Johnson (1649–1703) brought his wife Tetty here in 1746 to lift her spirits, and Katherine Mansfield (1888–1923) moved to the village in 1918, in the hope that it would cure her tuberculosis (see page 121).

Orwell enjoyed walking on the heath with Kay Welton, a bookish friend whom he had met through the shop. She discovered that he knew much about the trees and plants and that he was 'passionately fond' of birds. She was amused that he was also fond of cats and could 'never square the fact that cats killed birds'.

The alcoholic writer Malcolm Lowry (1909–1957), author of *Under the Volcano*, was a frequent visitor to No. 68, almost directly opposite Orwell's house, during the autumn of 1932. The house, nicknamed 'Bourgeois Towers', was the home of the Australian poet Anna Wickham (1889–1947) and her three sons, one of whom, James, was a Cambridge friend of Lowry's. James was alarmed to discover Lowry living in squalor in Bloomsbury and brought him to stay here. Opposite, at No. 67, was where Harold Brighouse (1882–1958), author of *Hobson's Choice*, lived until his death.

Keats House

Continue to the bottom of the road and turn right into South End Road, passing a pleasant, village-like row of shops and cafés. Turn left into Keat's Grove to find one of London's best-kept literary sites, Keats House, halfway up on the left. A little archway leads to a pretty garden, which is often pervaded by a strong smell of lavender – a smell that would have appealed to the poet, who famously sat in a kind of swoon beneath a plum tree here one May morning in 1819 and wrote his legendary 'Ode to a Nightingale'. Over the years a succession of plum trees has been planted in approximately the same spot, and a plaque relates the story of the poem's creation. Keats House was built in 1815 as a pair of houses for Keats's friends Charles Wentworth Dilke (hence its proper name, Wentworth Place) and Charles Armitage Brown. One half of Wentworth Place was rented for a time to a family called Brawne. While living in nearby Well Walk, Keats met Mrs Brawne's 18-year-old daughter, Fanny, at Wentworth Place, and fell in love with her. After the Brawnes took lodgings a few minutes away, and following the death of his brother Tom in 1818, Keats moved in to Wentworth Place himself. The Brawnes returned to the neighbouring house the following year, so that in 1819 Keats and Fanny were living next door to each other. Keats wrote many of his most famous poems here, including 'Ode on a Grecian Urn'.

In the silence of the rooms today – particularly in Keats's study – and in the poignant displays, including the engagement ring Keats gave to Fanny, it is possible to reach back across the years and feel the poet's breath. The house is a literary pilgrimage point, receiving some 22,000 visitors a year. Thomas Hardy (1840–1928) was moved to write a poem after his visit in July 1920, and in Vita Sackville-West's novel *All Passion Spent* a character describes the house as, 'that little white box of strain and tragedy marooned among the dark green laurels.' The Poet Laureate Andrew Motion spent six months working on his biography of Keats here.

Upstairs is the bedroom in which the poet, having caught a chill on a walking tour, coughed a drop of blood on to his sheet. 'I know the colour of that blood', the poet told Charles Brown. 'It is arterial blood – I cannot be deceived in that colour – that drop of blood is my death-warrant – I must die.' Keats and Fanny never married. He left Hampstead in September 1820 and died in Rome, aged 25, on 23 February 1821.

There are other, more recent, literary associations with Keats Grove. The playwright Alan Ayckbourn lived almost opposite Keats House for a time, and the literary agent David Higham, founder of the eponymous award for fiction, lived at No. 12. Continue to the end of the road, turn left into Downshire Hill, with its impressive cream villas, left into Rosslyn Hill, and then left again into Hampstead Hill Gardens. The Studio House at No.1, entered via a gate in the wall on the left, was the home of the critic William Empson (1906–1984), author of *Seven Types of Ambiguity*. The novelist and arts broadcaster Melvyn Bragg also lives in this street.

Orwell the Bookseller

Turn left into Pond Street and follow it down to South End Green. At the very bottom of Pond Street, just before it meets South End Road, look at the wall on your left. There is an unusual, rather macabre memorial, which looks like a miniature death-mask. It commemorates George Orwell's spell working in Booklovers' Corner in 1934–5. The shop occupied the corner plot (currently a pizza outlet) and Orwell lived in a flat above the shop. It was while living here that he wrote *Keep the Aspidistra Flying*, which features a similar secondhand bookshop. Although being faced by thousands of books every day was 'boring and even slightly sickening', Orwell did find great pleasure in going through back-numbers of the *Girl's Own*

Paper, chuckling at the absurdities of its letters page. He was particularly amused over the recurring question as to whether it was 'ladylike' for women to ride tricycles.

Retrace your steps up Pond Street and, after the Royal Free Hospital, take the unmarked passageway to the left in front of St Stephen's Church. This brings you out on Rosslyn Hill/Haverstock Hill, where you turn left. The newly renovated Hampstead Town Hall soon appears on your right, a fine example of Victorian civic pride if ever there was one. It was here that the biographer Lytton Strachey (1880–1932), author of *Eminent Victorians*, was brought in 1917 to face questioning about his stance as a conscientious objector. Asked how he would react if he saw a German soldier attempting to molest his sister, he replied that he would attempt to interpose his body between them.

Turn right into Belsize Avenue, walking alongside the Town Hall, then turn left into Belsize Park Gardens, where Strachey's family lived, first at No. 6, on the left, and then at No. 67. Once known as 'Cut-Throat Alley' because of the murders committed here, this road has long been respectable. Strachey actually found it too respectable and claimed that it made him depressed.

A Favourite Author of the Backpack Generation

At the end of the road, turn left into England's Lane, which has an attractive, village-like atmosphere. The young writer Alex Garland, author of *The Beach* and *The Tesseract*, lived here in 1998, in a flat above the shops on the left-hand side of the road, opposite the laundry. At the time, *The Beach* was being filmed in Thailand, and Garland was writing his more difficult second novel, *The Tesseract*. The Chamomile Café at No. 45 was one of his favourite haunts. A shy man who does not like publicity, Garland told *NorthWest* magazine: 'For eight years my whole life revolved around getting money together from crap jobs to go travelling. And almost invariably I'd go to the Philippines. It's very different from anywhere else in South East Asia because of the Hispanic influence. It's very, very beautiful and also very edgy. At the age of 18 that mixture of beauty and edginess was extremely seductive.'

Continue to the end of England's Lane and turn left to climb Haverstock Hill to Belsize Park Station, where the walk ends.

Southwark

Summary: Despite developments along the river bank and the splendid Globe Theatre, most of Southwark is still distinctly off the tourist route. Yet this quarter of London is steeped in literary history because of its many associations with Charles Dickens, who lodged here as a child. This walk passes the location of the workhouse in *Oliver Twist*, the church in which Little Dorrit is christened and married, and takes in the museum that has an exhibit that inspired the crime writer Minette Walters. It also covers some pleasant stretches of the river.

Start:	Blackfriars Underground Station (District and Circle Lines).
Finish:	Monument Underground Station (District and Circle Lines).
Length:	5 kilometres (3 miles).
Time:	2.5–3 hours.
Refreshments:	There are lots of places to stop at the beginning and the end, but not many in between. The Globe has a café, and The George, London's only remaining galleried inn, is an absolute must.

Take the Blackfriars Bridge exit from Blackfriars Station and cross the bridge. In 1824 the 12-year-old Charles Dickens (1812–1870) used the earlier Blackfriars Bridge when he walked home from his miserable days at Warren's Blacking Factory off the Strand. Take the steps down to the river and turn right. Pass under the railway bridge and duck in around the Founders Arms pub. The apartments here are built on Falcon Point, named after the Falcon, a 17th-century inn. This part of the riverside is called Bankside and it was from an inn here that Samuel Pepys (1633–1703) watched the Great Fire of London in September 1666: '[We] stayed until it was dark almost and saw the fire grow; and as it grow darker, appeared more and more, and in Corners and upon steeples and between churches and houses, as far as we could see up the hill of the City, in a most horrid malicious bloody flame...'

Continue past the monolith of the new £134m Tate Modern gallery, with its Millennium Bridge that crosses the river towards St Paul's, and immediately afterwards find a pretty row of Georgian cottages. A plaque on the tall house next to Cardinal Cap Alley claims that Sir Christopher Wren lived here. This is fanciful nonsense that dates back to the time the house belonged to Malcolm Munthe, son of Axel Munthe, Swedish author of *The Story of San Michele*.

Shakespeare's Globe

In Elizabethan times Bankside was a cross between the Soho and West End of today. Because it lay outside the jurisdiction of the City authorities, activities looked down

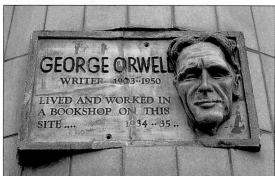

Plate 26: *Keats's House, Hampstead. He wrote* Ode to a Nightingale *in the garden (see page 125).*

Plate 27: *Macabre memorial to George Orwell in Pond Street, Hampstead (see page 126).*

Plate 28: *The George in Southwark, built in 1677, appears in Dickens's* Little Dorrit *(see page 133).*

Plate 29: *The reconstruction of Shakespeare's Globe Theatre opened in 1996 thanks to the vision and persistence of American actor and director Sam Wanamaker (see page 128).*

Plate 30: *The stage ceiling of the Globe includes a divinely-lit cloud (top right) which conceals a trap-door to lower a god or goddess over the stage (see page 128).*

Plate 31: *The Trafalgar Tavern in Greenwich where Dickens was fêted on his return from America in 1842 (see page 139).*

Plate 32: Ye Olde Cheshire Cheese in Wine Office Court off Fleet Street is a tourist trap but splendidly atmospheric. Dickens, Thackeray and Mark Twain were among its customers (see page 147).

Plate 33: Dr Samuel Johnson's House at 17 Gough Square, off Fleet Street, where he lived from 1748 to 1759 (see page 147).

Plate 34: Hangman's gibbet outside The Prospect of Whitby pub where Dickens and Pepys used to drink (see page 152).

upon elsewhere went on here. There were numerous brothels, a bear-baiting ring and four theatres – including the legendary Globe, which stood on a site not far from the splendid replica in front of you, which opened in 1996. The first Globe burned down in 1613, when a canon fired during a performance of *Henry VIII* set fire to the thatched roof. No one was injured, although one man had to have his breeches doused with 'pottle ale'. To find the entrance to Shakespeare's 'wooden O', as the original Globe was dubbed, turn right into New Globe Walk.

Return to the river and turn right and then right again into the tiny, cobbled Bear Gardens. After some new buildings this widens to give a flavour of the area's trading past. Note the hoists on the warehouse on the right. You will see these throughout the walk. The Globe Education Centre on the left is built on the site of Davies Amphitheatre, one of Bankside's last bear-baiting rings, which was visited by the diarists Samuel Pepys and John Evelyn (1620–1706). Ben Jonson's play *Bartholomew Fair* was first performed near here.

Where Dickens Lodged

Turn right, then left into Emerson Street, then right onto Sumner Street briefly and then left into Great Guildford Street. Carry straight on over Southwark Street and under the railway bridge. This is quiet, non-tourist London. Cross Union Street and pass David Copperfield Street on your right just before the end. The buildings here have a distinctly Dickensian feel. Indeed, Southwark is riddled with Dickens references, commemorating both the writer's short stay here and characters from *David Copperfield*, *Little Dorrit* and *The Pickwick Papers*, parts of which are set in the area.

Turn right into Southwark Bridge Road and cross at the zebra by Sawyer Street, going straight over into Lant Street. St Michael's Church on the left and the blocks of cheap council flats have a flavour of the author too, since in 1824 the 12-year-old Dickens lodged in a back attic (now demolished) in this street. You soon come to Charles Dickens School, built after his death and named in his honour. Earlier in 1824 John Dickens, Charles's father, had been arrested for debt and placed in the New Marshalsea Debtors' Prison, one of a number of grim prisons that existed in Borough, as this area was, and still is, known. It was a traumatic period for the young Charles and the impressions it made – the stories of his father's fellow inmates, the atmosphere of the surrounding streets – were to recur time and time again in his writing. And he would use his landlord and landlady as the models for the Garland family in *The Old Curiosity Shop*. He would remember in later years that, 'my old way home by the Borough made me cry, after my eldest child could speak.' Lant Street was one of many locations visited by Peter Ackroyd during the writing of his masterly *Dickens*, and the biographer cried 'on this same spot'.

Other prisons close by included the King's Bench, in which Daniel Defoe (1660?–1731) was locked for a week for writing subversive pamphlets, and the Horsemonger Gaol, in which Leigh Hunt (1784–1859) was imprisoned between 1813 and 1815 for calling the Prince Regent 'a fat Adonis of fifty'. Today there is a Leigh Hunt Street commemorating the English poet and essayist's brief, uncomfortable sojourn in Borough.

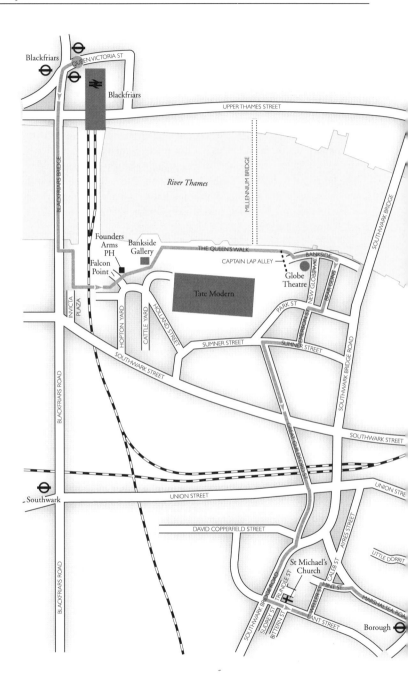

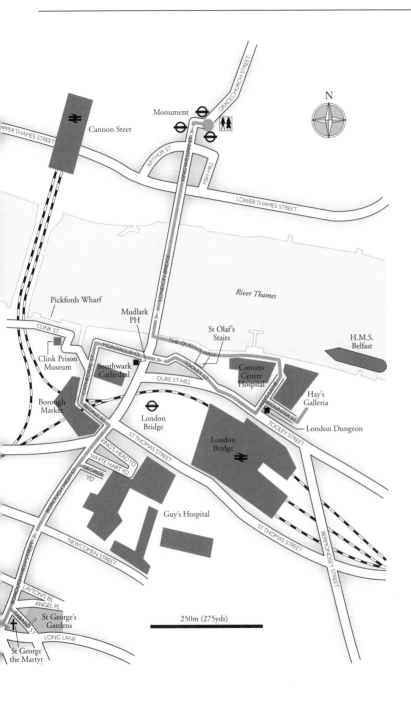

N

Monument

Cannon Steet

UPPER THAMES STREET

GRACECHURCH STREET

ARTHUR ST

KING WILLIAM ST

FISH HILL

LOWER THAMES STREET

River Thames

LONDON BRIDGE

Pickfords Wharf

Mudlark PH

St Olaf's Stairs

H.M.S. Belfast

CLINK ST

MONTAGUE CL

THE QUEEN'S WALK

Clink Prison Museum

Southwark Cathedral

TOOLEY ST

Cottons Centre Hospital

Hay's Galleria

CATHEDRAL ST

DUKE ST HILL

HAY'S LANE

COUNTER ST

Borough Market

BEDALE ST

London Bridge

London Dungeon

TOOLEY STREET

KING'S HEAD YD

ST THOMAS STREET

London Bridge

BOROUGH HIGH ST

WHITE HART YD

GEORGE YD

Guy's Hospital

ST THOMAS STREET

BERMONDSEY STREET

NEWCOMEN STREET

250m (275yds)

LAYTON'S BS

ANGEL PL

TABARD ST

St George's Gardens

LONG LANE

St George the Martyr

Little Dorrit's Church

Turn left into Weller Street – named after Sam Weller from *The Pickwick Papers* – and then right into Mint Street, believed to be the location of St George's workhouse, which formed the basis of the workhouse descriptions in *Oliver Twist*. The poet W. H. Davies (1871–1940) stayed in a lodging house here called Farm House (since demolished). In a poem called 'An Old House in London' he writes about Southwark's 'Three hundred children [who] show/Rags and white faces at thy door/For charity…' Born in Wales in 1871, Davies emigrated to the States when he was 22 and lived partly as a tramp and partly as a casual workman, until the loss of a leg while 'jumping' a train caused him to return to England. Here he began to write and lived the life of a tramp and pedlar in order to raise sufficient money to have his poems printed by a jobbing printer. George Bernard Shaw (1856–1950) helped him find a proper publisher and Davies went on to achieve considerable success with his *Autobiography of a Super-tramp*, published in 1908.

Mint Street soon meets Marshalsea Road, where you turn right. The church ahead of you on the other side of the busy junction is St George the Martyr, built in 1736 and known as 'Little Dorrit's church' because of its associations with the novel. It is here that Little Dorrit is christened and later marries Arthur Clennam. But it is another scene from the book that is commemorated by one of the church's windows. At one time Little Dorrit lived in the Marshalsea Debtors' Prison with her father. Returning late one night, she is locked out and has to sleep in the vestry, using one of the old registers as a pillow. Today, her kneeling figure can be seen in the bottom of the east window behind the altar.

Dickens's Prison

On leaving the church, turn right into Tabard Street, named after the long-gone Tabard Inn on Borough High Street, from which Chaucer's 29 pilgrims set out on the journey to Canterbury – the journey that gave rise to *The Canterbury Tales*. Go left, through the railings, into a small garden that is the former burial ground of the church. The brick wall on the far side is all that remains of the Marshalsea Debtors' Prison. To stand here and scroll back the years is a moving experience. In *Little Dorrit* Dickens writes of, 'the games of the prison children as they whooped and ran, and played at hide-and-seek, and made the bars of the inner gateway "Home".' In *David Copperfield*, Mr Micawber remembers, 'the shadow of that ironwork on the summit of the brick structure…reflected on the gravel of the Parade, I have seen my children thread the mazes of the intricate pattern, avoiding the dark marks.'

Retrace your steps back to Borough High Street and turn right. You can walk up Angel Place, immediately on your right, to get an impression of the size of the Marshalsea's wall. The main entrance to the prison and the turnkey's lodge was at the end of this narrow court. Continuing down the High Street, note Little Dorrit Court on the other side and the rather Chaucerian-sounding Newcomen Street. Borough High Street was once the only route south from the City and was lined with coaching inns, each one serving different destinations on the south coast. At No. 103 a plaque marks the site of the old Queen's Head Inn, which was owned by members of the Harvard family. John Harvard, born in Southwark in 1607, emigrated to North America in 1637, where he died the following year. In his will he left 'one half of his estate towards the erecting of a college, and all his library'. Thus Harvard University was born.

The Stuff of Ghost Stories
A few yards on and you come to George Inn Yard, home to The George, London's only remaining galleried inn. The building dates from 1677, but John Stow mentions an earlier George in his *Survey of London* of 1598. It is worth exploring at your leisure. You can walk along the first floor gallery, but try to ignore the dreadful view of the surrounding modern developments.

Dickens captured the atmosphere of Southwark's inns perfectly in *The Pickwick Papers*: 'In the Borough, especially, there still remains some half-dozen old inns which have preserved their external features unchanged, and which have escaped alike the rage for public improvement and the encroachment of private speculation. Great, rambling, queer old places they are, with galleries and passages and stairways, wide enough and antiquated enough to furnish material for a hundred ghost stories.' It is in The George that Edward 'Tip' Dorrit composes a begging letter to Arthur Clenman.

The Dickens associations continue next door. The White Hart once stood in White Hart Yard, where Sam Weller meets Mr Pickwick: 'Number twenty-two wants his boots', Weller is told. To which he famously replies: 'Ask number twenty-two, whether he'll have 'em now, or wait till he gets 'em...'

Cross at the lights and turn left into Bedale Street, then left into Borough Market. Said to be the oldest fruit and vegetable market in London, it has retained its original steel-and-glass structure, dating from 1851, as well as numerous splendid original signs. Its magnificent setting beneath the railway arches that carry trains into London Bridge Station is truly Victorian and gives a perfect idea of what the original Covent Garden market would have been like.

The 'Scold's Bridle'
Continue to Southwark Cathedral, parts of which date from 1520. Walk down the far aisle first, where there are memorials to John Bunyan (1628–1688) and John Gower (1330?–1408), the poet and friend of Chaucer. Pass the Harvard Chapel, restored with donations from the Friends of Harvard University., and continue round to the Shakespeare Memorial, erected in 1911. Note the statue's worn knee, hand and arm, reminiscent of the worn rabbit's ears on the statue of Peter Pan in Hyde Park. You can see the Globe Theatre in the panorama of Southwark behind the statue while, above, various characters from Shakespeare's plays are depicted in the windows. Next to the Shakespeare memorial is a memorial to the actor and director Sam Wanamaker (1919–1993), 'whose vision rebuilt Shakespeare's Globe Theatre.'

Leave the cathedral and grounds and turn right, then slightly left, walking towards the ship in the distance. This is the *Kathleen and May*, one of London's last surviving three-masted trading schooners. It is worth popping down to the river here to enjoy the views – or you can follow the signs along Pickfords Wharf to the Clink Prison Museum, site of the Clink Prison mentioned by Dickens in *Barnaby Rudge*. Although touristy, the museum and its setting capture the dark and barbaric side of 19th-century Southwark. Among grim displays is a 'scold's bridle', an iron gag, sometimes spiked, once used to silence women who were deemed too talkative. One of Minette Walters's popular crime novels takes its title from this cruel device.

Keats and the 'Turnings and Windings'
Retrace your steps back to the cathedral, turn left, walk past the modern Minerva House and keep to the cobbled road that takes you past the Mudlark Pub and under London Bridge. Continue along Tooley Street, which eventually brings you out by the London Dungeon. Before turning left into Hay's Lane, look at the dark tunnel opposite – all that remains of the old Dean Street, where John Keats (1795–1821) lodged while a medical student at nearby Guy's Hospital. It was to these cramped lodgings that he returned at 6am one October morning in 1816, composing as he walked what would become one of his most anthologised verses, 'On First Looking Into Chapman's Homer'. He had been visiting his friend Charles Cowden Clarke in Clerkenwell and had been shown a translation of Homer by George Chapman. He was tired when he left, but as soon as he had made his way through the 'turnings and windings' of Borough, he was able to sit down and write the famous sonnet, which begins with the line: 'Much have I travelled in the realms of gold.' He found a messenger to deliver the sonnet to Clerkenwell by 10am that very morning. Clarke read it with an admiration that would remain undiminished for the rest of his life.

The Rush Hour Immortalized
Turn left into Hay's Lane, right into Counter Street and left into Hay's Galleria – a bustling development of shops and restaurants and a good example of the development that has taken place at a furious rate since the demise of London's docks and wharves. The Riverside Bookshop on the right is a well-stocked independent bookshop. At the end there are good views of HMS *Belfast* and London Bridge. Look too at the pink, 'modern Gothic' building with the two pointed towers on the opposite bank. This is the London Underwriting Centre. Find the circular window in the tower on the right. It was in this room on 11 August 1999 that Little, Brown launched *The Business* by Iain Banks, the acclaimed Scottish author who alternates between writing conventional novels and science fiction, the latter as Iain M. Banks.

Now head left along the river, soon taking the pink granite steps up to London Bridge, where you turn right. In *Oliver Twist*, the fateful meeting between Nancy and Rose Maylie and Mr Brownlow takes place on the steps of London Bridge, 'on the same side...as St Saviour's Church.' 'St Saviour's' was the name of Southwark Cathedral until 1905.

Continue over London Bridge and imagine the scene on cold winter's mornings before the Clean Air Act was passed. All across this wide pavement the suited and hatted commuters would swarm, heading north from London Bridge Station, a scene captured in *The Waste Land* by T. S. Eliot, who briefly worked in the City himself (see page 76). Continue into King William Street and up to Monument Station, where the walk ends.

Blackheath to Greenwich

Summary: Blackheath and Greenwich, lying to the south-east of London's centre, offer welcome relief from the traffic and density of the West End. This walk explores their surprising connections with the authors of *The Scarlet Letter* and *Moby Dick*, as well as their numerous associations with Dickens.

Start: Blackheath Station (overground trains from London Bridge, Charing Cross and Canon Street).

Finish: Greenwich Station (overground trains to London Bridge, Docklands Light Railway to Canary Wharf and Bank).

Length: 5.5 kilometres (3⅖ miles).

Time: 2.5–3 hours.

Refreshments: The Royal Observatory in Greenwich Park has a café. The Trafalgar Tavern on the river has Dickens associations.

Cross the road outside Blackheath Station and turn right. Climb the hill, keeping to the left, then turn left into Blackheath Park. After the church, turn left into tree-lined Pond Road. On the right, obscured by tall trees, is No. 4, the squat, double-fronted villa in which the American writer Nathaniel Hawthorne (1804–1864) lived in 1856, six years after his most famous book, *The Scarlet Letter*, was published. With its clean lines and classical pillars, the house would not look out of place in Boston – that most English of American cities – which is perhaps why Hawthorne chose it. Hawthorne had worked in the custom-house in Boston in 1839, before being appointed US consul in Liverpool in 1853 by President Franklin Pierce, an old schoolfriend. He wrote a series of articles about his time in England for *Atlantic Monthly*, which were collected as *Our Old Home* in 1863. Although there are far more houses here today, much of what he says about Blackheath remains true:

> *The scene is semi-rural. Ornamental trees overshadow the sidewalks, and grassy margins border the wheel-tracks. The houses, to be sure, have certain points of difference from those of an American design, through seldom of individual taste; and, as far as possible, they stand aloof from the street, and separated each from its neighbour by hedge or fence, in accordance with the careful exclusiveness of the English character, which impels the occupant, moreover, to cover the front of his dwelling with as much concealment of shrubbery as his limits will allow. Through the interstices, you catch glimpses of well-kept lawns, generally ornamented with flowers, and with what the English call rockwork, being heaps of ivy-grown stones and fossils, designed for romantic effect in a small way.*

At the end of Pond Road, you can see the winking tower of Canary Wharf in the distance. Turn right, pass Cator Manor, and find the splendid Paragon, arguably London's finest Georgian terrace. These elegant houses were built at the end of the

135

18th century by John Cator, a businessman who ran a timber business on the site of what is now the new Tate Modern gallery at Bankside. He was greatly admired by Samuel Johnson (1649–1703), although the latter's friend Mrs Thrale declared Cator's voice 'so loud and his manners so rough that disgust gets the better of curiosity.'

The Dangerous Heath and Charles Dickens

Cross directly over to the Heath, take the path behind the pond, and continue right across the Heath. The famous spire of All Saint's Church appears on your left, almost as striking, in its 19th-century way, as Canary Wharf. Once the haunt of highwaymen, for years the Heath had a reputation as dark as the soil from which it takes its name. Samuel Pepys (1633–1703), on his way to see his fellow diarist John Evelyn (1620–1706), passed a gibbet from which a bloated body was swaying ('a filthy sight

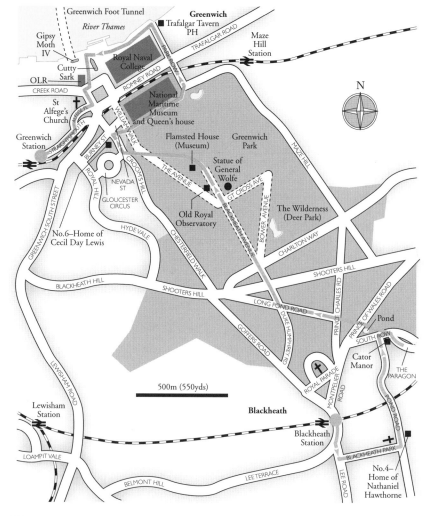

it was to see how the flesh is shrunk from his bones'). It was not until residential development began in the 18th century that this open expanse was considered safe. There has been ordinary activity on the Heath, too. Considered a fine place for an assembly, it was here that Henry V was welcomed after the battle of Agincourt in 1415. The space has also been used for agricultural fairs and military reviews.

Blackheath has various associations with Dickens (1812–1870). The writer's parents lived here for a while, and Salem House, 'a square brick building with wings, of a bare and unfinished appearance', where David Copperfield receives his first formal education, was situated 'down by Blackheath'. During his lonely trek to Dover to find his aunt, the young Copperfield spends a night under a haystack close by. *A Tale of Two Cities* begins with the Dover mail coach lumbering up Shooters Hill (whose name hints at the area's dangerous past) 'on a Friday night late in November 1775.'

The Millennium Dome

Continue into Long Pond Road. When it bends to the left, take the cycle path to the gates ahead of you, which lead into Greenwich Park, laid out in 1433 by Henry VI. Greenwich takes its name either from the Anglo-Saxon for 'green village', or from a Scandinavian name given by the Danes, meaning 'green reach'. Follow the avenue of horse chestnuts until you come to the statue of General Wolfe, who lived in Greenwich from 1752 to 1757. In front of you, away to your right, you can see the controversial £780m Millennium Dome. The structure is enormous – big enough to contain the Eiffel Tower (also controversial in its day) laid on its side, or 18,000 double-decker buses. Each of its 'spikes' is 100 metres (328 feet) long.

Daniel Defoe and the Seamen's Hospital

The white house directly in front of you, with its pillared walkway, is the Queen's House, designed by Inigo Jones (1573–1652) and completed in 1637 for Henrietta Maria, mother of Charles I. In order that she would have a clear view of the river, the former Seamen's Hospital beyond was divided in two, and its twin towers can still be clearly seen. The hospital, completed in the early years of the 18th century, was designed by Sir Christopher Wren (1632–1723) and built of bricks provided by none other than Daniel Defoe (1660?–1731), part owner of a brick factory at Tilbury. The diarist John Evelyn became the hospital's treasurer at the age of 75, and it was largely through his persistence that the money for its completion was found. The buildings are now occupied by the Royal Naval College and the new University of Greenwich.

Samuel Johnson liked to walk along the river here, and mentions it in his poem 'Irene in Greenwich Park': 'On Thames' bank in silent thought we stood/Where Greenwich smiles upon the silver flood.' Although he undoubtedly found the surroundings pretty, they couldn't compare with his beloved central London, as recorded by Boswell (1740–1795), his biographer:

We walked in the evening to Greenwich Park. He [Johnson] asked me, I suppose by way of trying my disposition: 'Is not this very fine?' Having no exquisite relish of the beauties of nature and being more concerned with 'the busy hum of men', I answered: 'Yes, sir; but not equal to Fleet Street.' Johnson replied 'You are right, sir.'

The complex of buildings to your left make up the Old Royal Observatory, erected for the first Astronomer Royal John Flamsteed, appointed in 1675. He wrote that 'some wood, iron and lead from a gatehouse demolished in the Tower' were used in their construction. Of particular interest is the Octagon Room, which has a 'time ball' on its roof that has been dropped daily at 1pm since 1833 to enable sailors on ships on the Thames to set their clocks by it. The prime meridian (0° longitude) that divides the earth's eastern and western hemispheres passes through the main building. In 1884 Greenwich Mean Time became the basis of time measurement for most of the world.

In literary terms the word 'longitude' means only one thing – Dava Sobel's extraordinary best seller of 1995, *Longitude*, which tells the story of John Harrison, the Yorkshire clockmaker who developed the marine chronometer and solved the centuries-old problem of how to accurately measure longitude at sea. The book has sold over two million copies, and formed the basis for a successful two-part television film.

In Joseph Conrad's 1907 novel *The Secret Agent*, in which an anarchist plans to blow up the Royal Observatory, but the bomb explodes in the hands of his simpleton brother-in-law, Conrad (1857–1924) comments, 'the whole civilised world has heard of Greenwich…the very boot-blacks in the basement of Charing Cross Station know something of it.'

Greenwich Fair

Leave the statue of General Wolfe and the observatory and take the path to the left, passing the Octagon House. Follow this diagonal down to the road. Cross to the part of the park in which the Greenwich Fairs of the 19th century took place, famously described by Dickens as, 'a periodical breaking out…a sort of spring rash; a three days fever which cools the blood for six months afterwards, and at the expiration of which London is restored to its old habits of plodding industry.' He wrote of, 'the screams of women, the shouts of boys, the clanging of gongs, the firing of pistols, the ringing of bells, the bellowings of speaking trumpets, the squeaking of penny dittoes, the noise of a dozen bands, with three drums in each, all playing different tunes at the same time, the hallooing of showmen, and an occasional roar from the wild beast shows.'

Hawthorne and the 'Common People of England'

One of the most popular pastimes of the period was for young couples to climb the hill to the Royal Observatory, where the young men would pull the women down again as quickly as possible, 'greatly to the derangement of their mobs and bonnet-cap', Dickens observed. In *David Copperfield,* a servant to Dora and David 'a young person of genteel appearance…went to Greenwich Fair in Dora's bonnet.' The novelist William Thackeray mentioned the fair in his *Sketches and Travels in London*, and Nathaniel Hawthorne witnessed the last one in 1857. Recalling the throng of Londoners, the American wrote: 'It taught me to understand why Shakespeare, in speaking of a crowd, so often alludes to its attribute of evil odor. The common people of England, I am afraid, have no daily familiarity with even so necessary a thing as a washbowl, not to mention a bathing-tub.'

Leave the park through the gates opposite Gloucester Crescent and turn right into Croom's Hill, which has some of London's best-preserved housing dating from the 17th, 18th and 19th centuries. Sadly, the house Pepys visited here and found 'very pretty' has gone, but at the bottom there is an elegant Georgian terrace on the left, where the Poet Laureate Cecil Day Lewis (1904–1972) lived at No. 6 from 1954 to 1972. The plaque omits to mention Lewis's pseudonym, Nicholas Blake, under which he wrote some 20 sophisticated detective novels.

Dickens and the 'Whitebait Suppers'

Turn right into Nevada Street, and at the end re-enter the park through the entrance on the right. Turn left and pass the National Maritime Museum. Note the splendid views up the hill to the statue of Wolfe. On the other side of the park, before the pond, turn left into Park Row. Follow this to the river, passing the Royal Naval College on your left. Soon the Trafalgar Tavern appears ahead, with Canary Wharf looming behind it – a classic 'old against new' view of London. The Trafalgar was famous for its 'whitebait suppers' in the 19th century, and they became a great tradition of the capital. The meals were popular with writers too, with the exception of Thackeray, who described them as a 'hotchpotch of all sorts of fishes'. Dickens was fêted at The Trafalgar after his return from America in 1842. 'There is no next morning hangover like that which follows a Greenwich dinner.' he wrote. In *Our Mutual Friend*, Bella persuades her Pa to take her out for dinner. 'The little expedition down the river was delightful, and the little room overlooking the river into which they were shown for dinner was delightful…' The Trafalgar is still delightful today, and the window seats of its dining-room afford a splendid view of both the river and the Millennium Dome.

Poetic Ships

Outside the Trafalgar, turn left and follow the river front until you come to Greenwich pier and the towering masts of the *Cutty Sark*. Built in 1869, this majestic vessel is the last of the great tea clippers whose world Eric Newby captured so evocatively in *The Last Grain Race* and in photographs in *Learning the Ropes*. The ship takes its curious name from Robert Burns's poem 'Tam O'Shanter', in which Tam is pursued by witches as he rides drunkenly home. The fastest witch is young and beautiful and wears only a short linen shift or 'cutty sark'. She just manages to grasp the tail of Tam's horse and they gallop to safety. Thus began a tradition whereby sailors make a grey mare's tail from an old end of rope and place it in the hand of the ship's figurehead. You can easily see the one at the front of the *Cutty Sark*.

Just beyond the dome (another one!) that marks the Greenwich Foot Tunnel, lies *Gipsy Moth IV*, in which Sir Francis Chichester (1901–1972) made a successful solo circumnavigation of the world in 1966–7. In July 1967 the Queen knighted him at the waterside here, using the same sword with which her ancestor Elizabeth I had knighted Sir Francis Drake.

Turn inland and head for St Alfege's church tower in the distance. This is often called Greenwich Church. In *Our Mutual Friend* Bella and John Rokesmith are married here: 'the church porch, having swallowed up Bella Wilfer for ever and ever, had it not in its power to relinquish that young woman, but slid into the happy sunlight, Mrs John Rokesmith instead.' Continue past the church and follow the main road up to Greenwich Station, where the walk ends.

Clapham Junction
to Wandsworth Village

Victorian London, passes a grim prison with literary associations, and finishes in a village suburb that was once, surprisingly, home to Thomas Hardy. You will also see roads associated with Paul Theroux and the best-selling novelist Douglas Kennedy.

Start:	Clapham Junction Station (overground trains from Victoria and Waterloo).
Finish:	Wandsworth Common Station (overground trains to Victoria).
Length:	4.5 kilometres (2¾ miles).
Time:	2 hours.
Refreshments:	There are plenty of pubs and some particularly attractive cafés and restaurants in Wandsworth Village.

Clapham Junction might seem the least literary location in London, but it does have one very important association with the world of letters. Everyone knows that Oscar Wilde (1854–1900) was imprisoned in Reading Prison. Rather fewer know how he got there. On 21 November 1895, handcuffed and in prison uniform, and accompanied by prison officers, he was brought from Wandsworth Prison to Clapham Junction. His train would have left from the far side of the station, where platforms five and six are today. It was a rainy afternoon and he had to wait on the platform for the Reading train from 2 to 2.30pm. A crowd gathered, first laughing and then jeering at the prisoner. One man recognized Wilde and spat at him. 'It was the single most humiliating experience of Wilde's prison life', Richard Ellmann observes in his classic biography. Wilde himself wrote in *De Profundis*: 'For a year after that was done to me I wept every day at the same hour and for the same space of time.'

Turn right at the bottom of the platform stairs and right again on leaving the station to walk up St John's Hill, passing The Grand music venue. This was opened as The Grand Theatre in 1900 by the music-hall singer, dancer and world clog-dancing champion (*sic*) Dan Leno, who was immortalized in Peter Ackroyd's novel *Dan Leno and the Limehouse Golem*. Just beyond the church, cross over and turn left into Spencer Road and then turn first right into Elsynge Road. These roads are full of attractive, expensive Victorian villas. It is a 'specimen' area, so called because builders and architects were invited to submit designs – hence the varied nature of the housing. In the 1980s novelist and travel writer Paul Theroux lived at No. 35, a solid, detached, four-storey house on the left. He describes these south London double-parked streets perfectly in his novel *The Family Arsenal*.

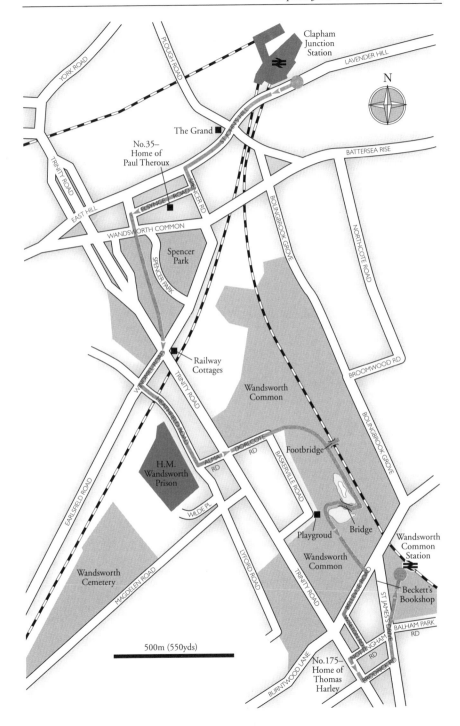

Clapham Junction Station

LAVENDER HILL

N

PLOUGH ROAD

YORK ROAD

TRINITY ROAD

The Grand ■

No.35–
Home of
Paul Theroux

ST JOHN'S HILL

BATTERSEA RISE

EAST HILL

ELSYNGE ROAD

SPENCER RD

WANDSWORTH COMMON

Spencer
Park

BOLINGBROOK GROVE

NORTHCOTE ROAD

SPENCER PARK

WINDMILL ROAD

TRINITY ROAD

HEATHFIELD ROAD

■— Railway
Cottages

Wandsworth
Common

BROOMWOOD RD

BOLINGBROOK GROVE

EARLSFIELD ROAD

ALMA RD

DORLCOTE
RD

BASKERVILLE ROAD

Footbridge

H.M.
Wandsworth
Prison

WILDE PL

Playgroud

Bridge

Wandsworth
Common
Station

Wandsworth
Cemetery

MAGDELEN ROAD

LYFORD ROAD

Wandsworth
Common

TRINITY ROAD

NOTTINGHAM RD

ST JAMES'S DRIVE

BELLEVUE ROAD

Beckett's
Bookshop

BALHAM PARK
RD

500m (550yds)

BURNTWOOD LANE

BROOMWOOD RD

No.175–
Home of
Thomas
Harley

141

Turn left at the end, cross at the zebra and take the tree-lined path across Wandsworth Common. Continue to the lights, where you turn right into Windmill Road, with the common on your right. At the lights turn left into Heathfield Road and go past a little gate leading to some fascinating, sunken railway cottages. After the railway bridge cross to the left-hand pavement to fully appreciate the grim edifice of Wandsworth Prison that now appears.

Oscar Wilde and Wandsworth Prison

Another fact not widely known about Oscar Wilde is that he spent a miserable four-and-a-half months in Wandsworth Prison before his transfer to Reading. After the failure of his libel action against the Marquess of Queensberry, Wilde began something of a tour of the penal system. He was taken first to Newgate Prison, then to Holloway and then to Pentonville, where he was admitted on 9 June 1895. Weak from lack of sleep and diarrhoea, he was then transferred to Wandsworth on 4 July 1895. By a strange irony he had visited this prison in happier circumstances 12 years previously, when he was earning money lecturing. On 24 September 1883 he had spoken here without notes and wearing a waistcoat with a salmon-coloured silk handkerchief. On his transfer in 1895 he wore drab prison clothing and when his own clothes were sent on, one of his waistcoats was missing. He was furious and threw a tantrum until it was found. He then apologised to his warder, saying, 'Pray pardon my ebullition of feeling.'

HMP Wandsworth is a classic Victorian prison that seems little changed since it opened in 1851. The outer walls are new, but the darker inner ones are the originals. It is a forbidding structure, built on the familiar Victorian penal design of wings radiating from a raised, central tower. Ignore the cars and replace the sound of Gatwick-bound electric trains with the chuff and whistle of steam engines, and you are back at the end of the 19th century, when Wilde arrived at the prison.

The regime was rigorous. Prisoners spent the day in almost total solitary confinement, working, eating and sleeping alone in their cells. Despite the arrival from Pentonville of some books from Wilde's personal library on 17 August – including works by St Augustine, Pascal and Cardinal – Wilde was visibly suffering the effects of his incarceration. A visitor on 26 August observed that his hands were disfigured and his nails broken and bleeding, his hair was unkempt and he had a small straggly beard. His face had grown appallingly thin.

Wilde's Degeneration

By the following month, Wilde's condition had deteriorated further. His abject despair was graphically described by the prison chaplain, W. D. Morrison, quoted in Ellmann's biography:

When he first came down here from Pentonville he was in an excited flurried condition, and seemed as if he wished to face his punishment without flinching. But all this has passed away. As soon as the excitement aroused by the trial subsided and he had to encounter the daily routine of prison life his fortitude began to give way and rapidly collapsed altogether. He is now quite crushed and broken… I need hardly tell you that he is a man of decidedly morbid disposition… In fact some of our most experienced officers openly say that they don't think he will be able to go through the two years…

Never one to keep silent, Wilde would talk to the other inmates, contrary to the prison regulations. His prison 'work' – picking oakum – was poor and he described many of the warders as brutes. Weak from dysentery and hunger, he was nonetheless forced to attend chapel, where he collapsed and injured his ear on one occasion. He was admitted to the infirmary, where he stayed for two months. His wife's brother Lily visited him there on 22 October and wrote: 'He is hungry but cannot eat the food and at present is only allowed a little beef tea. Mentally he is very unhappy… He is very altered in every way.' Eventually Wilde was transferred to Reading, where he remained until 18 May 1897.

A little beyond the prison is Wilde Place, which commemorates the few months the writer spent here, but you turn left into Alma Terrace, a pretty row of gentrified cottages. Continue to the end and cross over into Dorlcote Road. Take the path to the left at the end of the road onto Wandsworth Common, and at the junction choose the middle path. At the footbridge take the right-hand path, which follows the railway line. Much of the common was lost to the railway or to property developers before it fell under the protection of an Act of Parliament in 1871. However, like all London's green open spaces, it is still pleasant and helps to make Wandsworth an attractive, if expensive, place to live.

After the first pond, take the right-hand path over the little bridge. Opposite the children's playground, go left, taking an unofficial path round the pond. On the other side of the pond, take a similar unofficial path to the right, towards an avenue of trees. Continue straight over (don't take the left-hand path) until you come to the parade of shops that marks Wandsworth Village. You emerge opposite Beckett's Bookshop, opened in the 1980s and particularly cosy in the winter, with its flickering fireplace. Visitors include local novelists Elizabeth Buchan, Graham Swift and Douglas Kennedy, best-selling author of *The Big Picture*. Kennedy in fact lives just behind the shop and likes to visit every week. Louis de Bernières, author of the extraordinarily successful *Captain Corelli's Mandolin*, also lives nearby.

Thomas Hardy: The Tooting Years
After visiting the shop, turn left and left again into Wiseton Road. This is a typical Wandsworth Village road, full of pretty houses that have been endlessly refurbished and tinkered with by architects. Turn right at the end of Wiseton Road and then left at the top of Nottingham Road to reach one of London's most surprising blue-plaques – at No. 172 Trinity Road, on the corner of Brodrick Road. The discovery that Thomas Hardy (1840–1928) lived in Wandsworth for a spell is a shock; it's like being told that some quintessentially urban author like Will Self lives in Sherborne. Actually, Hardy called Wandsworth, Upper Tooting. Still, it is hard to think of a location less like Hardy's Dorset than this busy road with the buses to Tooting and Clapham rattling past every few minutes.

The writer took a three-year lease on The Larches, at No. 1 Arundel Terrace (the latter sign is still there) on Trinity Road, partly on the urging of his wife Emma, who thought that the air from the River Stour, which they overlooked in their house in north Dorset, was bad for her husband. How strange to think that the air in Wandsworth could once have been deemed better than that of north Dorset! They moved in on 1 March 1878. Hardy wrote to Kegan Paul that, 'for such utter rustics as ourselves Tooting seemed town enough to begin with.' Hardy was already a successful author – *Far from the Madding Crowd* had been published in 1874 – and Emma felt that a location nearer to London was better suited to his status. Hardy, too, felt that more work might come his way by being closer to publishers, editors and agents.

But their stay in Wandsworth was not a happy one: Hardy suffered a severe internal haemorrhage in 1880 and was bedridden for several weeks. He seems to have felt some unease at being so close to London, famously describing the city as a 'monster whose body had four million heads and eight million eyes.' It was during this time that *The Return of the Native* was published, and Hardy met writers like Matthew Arnold and Tennyson at the house of publisher Alexander Macmillan on the edge of Tooting Common, but none of this was enough. With some relief he and Emma moved to back to Dorset in June 1881.

Walk down Brodrick Road, turn left into St James's Drive, and pause at the top of Balham Park Road on your right. Douglas Kennedy was living in this road in 1999, almost certainly having bought his house outright, thanks to the movie deals on *The Big Picture*, *Dead Heart* and *The Job*. At the postbox, take the diagonal path across the common to Wandsworth Common Station, where the walk ends.

Holborn to Chancery Lane

Summary: This walk through the London of Dickens and Johnson visits two unmarked buildings in which the former gave readings or worked, and which provided locations for many scenes in his novels. This is also legal London, and the walk through its squares, courts and alleys will take you from noise to quiet and back again within yards.

Start: Holborn Underground Station (Central and Piccadilly Lines).

Finish: Chancery Lane Underground Station (Central Line).

Length: 1.8 kilometres (1 mile).

Time: 2 hours.

Refreshments: There are lots of pubs and cafés en route. Ye Olde Cheshire Cheese is the nearest one can get to stepping back 200 years, and although it is very much on the tourist itinerary, it is still worth a visit.

Turn left out of the station's main exit onto Holborn, and immediately left into Gate Street. At the end of this passage you will see the curiously named Little Turnstile on your left, which marks the days when cattle grazed on Lincoln's Inn Fields and revolving stiles were set up at each corner to prevent them from straying onto the highway. In *Bleak House* Mr Snagsby tells his apprentices of a time when 'a brook "as clear as crystal" once ran down the middle of Holborn, leading slap way into meadows.'

Where Dickens Made his Audience Cry

Turn right into Lincoln's Inn Fields and notice how the roar of Holborn fades away. This faintly Bostonian square, with its villas set back from the road, was completed towards the end of the 17th century. Keep to the right-hand pavement to find No. 57–58, with its pillared entrance and cobbled yard. No. 58 was the home of Dickens's good friend, adviser and eventual biographer, John Forster (1812–1876). It was also the inspiration for Mr Tulkinghorn's house in *Bleak House*. 'The crow flies straight across Chancery Lane and Lincoln's Inn Garden, into Lincoln's Inn Fields', wrote Dickens in that novel, continuing, 'Here, in a large house, formerly a house of state, lives Mr Tulkinghorn. It is let off in sets of chambers now, and in these shrunken fragments of its greatness lawyers lie like maggots in nuts.'

Here, at 6.30pm on 2 December 1844, a group of Forster's friends gathered to hear Dickens (1812–1870) read his new Christmas story 'The Chimes'. The early hour was chosen because the story would take more than three hours to read. The audience included the essayist Thomas Carlyle and Douglas Jerrold, one of the early contributors to *Punch*. 'There was not a dry eye in the house', said one listener.

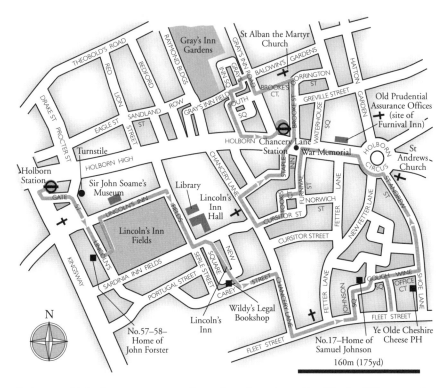

'I do not think there was ever such a triumphant hour for Charles.' The area also features in *David Copperfield*, where we are told that Aunt Betsey Trotwood stays 'at a kind of private hotel in Lincoln's Inn Fields.'

Enter the gardens opposite and turn left. Leave the gardens at the next gate, cross over and turn right, along Lincoln's Inn Fields. Halfway along on the left is Sir John Soane's Museum, which occupies the former home of one of England's greatest architects, who died in 1837. The best reason for visiting the museum is to get a feel for the late 18th and early 19th century, whose writers feature so much in this walk. According to an Act of Parliament of 1833, the house has been left 'as nearly as possible in the state in which he [Soane] shall leave it.' Among the exhibits are a Shakespeare recess, off the stairs, as well as Hogarth's famous *A Rake's Progress*.

On leaving the museum turn left, continue along the top of the square and turn right. The first building on your left is the Library of Lincoln's Inn, founded in 1497 and containing the oldest collection of books in London. The next building, parallel to the road, is Lincoln's Inn Hall, in which the Chancery court case of Jarndyce v. Jarndyce 'drones on' in *Bleak House*. Enter Lincoln's Inn proper at the gates on your left (it is closed to the public at weekends, in which case you should carry straight on and turn left after Wildy's legal booksellers, into Carey Street, to rejoin the route).

Lincoln's Inn is one of the four Inns of Court. Some of the buildings in this square date back to the 15th century and now house the chambers of various barristers and lawyers, whose names can be seen on wooden boards in the doorways. A number of writers have studied at the Inn, among them Wilkie Collins (1824–1889), Thomas Hughes (1822–1896), author of *Tom Brown's Schooldays*, and H. Rider Haggard (1856–1925). The poet John Donne (1572–1630) inaugurated Lincoln Inn Chapel. Head for the far left-hand corner, away down to your right, and leave the square through the archway by Wildy's legal booksellers.

Johnson's 'Counting House'

Turn left into Carey Street and at the end turn right into Chancery Lane. At the bottom turn left into Fleet Street and, after crossing Fetter Lane, look for the pavement sign to Dr Johnson's House. This is soon reached at Johnson's Court on your left. The 19th-century *Monthly Magazine* had its offices here. In October 1833 Dickens submitted some of his first fictional sketches to the magazine, posting them 'with fear and trembling into a dark letter-box, in a dark office, up a dark court in Fleet Street.' He met with success, and when he saw his work in the magazine he walked to Westminster Hall and 'turned into it for half an hour because my eyes were so dimmed with joy and pride that they could not bear the street, and were not fit to be seen there.'

Follow the court up and round to find Gough Square. Of the 17 London addresses listed for Samuel Johnson by Boswell, his biographer (1740–1795), it is only this five-storey house at No. 17 Gough Square that survives. Johnson (1649–1703) would have been impressed by this walk: 'If you wish to have a just notion of the magnitude of this great city,' he wrote, 'you must not be satisfied with seeing its great streets and squares but must survey the innumerable little lanes and courts.' Notice how clean these windings are, and then imagine the stink that must have pervaded the air in the 18th century, before London had a proper drainage system.

Johnson lived at Gough Square from 1748 to 1759, and it was here, in the top-floor garret, that six copyists stood and transcribed the entries for his famous *A Dictionary of the English Language* – the first ever comprehensive English dictionary – which was published in 1755. It became the basis for all subsequent English dictionaries. Boswell described the scene in the garret as being 'like a counting house'. The dictionary is remembered for its touches of Johsonsian wit, most famously in its definition of a lexicographer: 'A writer of dictionaries; a harmless drudge…'

A Literary Tavern

Leave Gough Square through the archway opposite No. 17 (not the one to the left), and at the canon in Gunpowder Square turn right into Wine Office Court to find Ye Olde Cheshire Cheese at the bottom. It is not certain that Johnson frequented this ancient pub – Boswell doesn't mention it – but it is widely assumed that he did, and highly likely. After all, it wasn't far for him to take his considerable bulk. The Cheshire Cheese certainly loses no sleep over claiming Johnson as its own, and has a 'Johnson's Restaurant' and one of his chairs by the fireplace. It is touristy, but don't be too cynical: this splendidly dark, oak-beamed hostelry is rich in atmosphere, being absolutely redolent of the London chophouses of the late 18th and 19th centuries. Dickens, Carlyle, Tennyson, Thackeray, Wilkie Collins, Mark Twain, Conan Doyle, Beerbohm and G. K. Chesterton are among its distinguished literary rollcall. In *A Tale of Two Cities*, Sydney Carton leads Charles Darnay down Ludgate Hill to Fleet Street and then up a covered way into a tavern, where they enjoy a 'good plain dinner and good wine'. The model for Dickens's tavern is widely believed to be Ye Olde Cheshire Cheese and Dickens himself allegedly chose to sit at the table to the right of the fireplace in the ground-floor room opposite the bar.

Retrace your steps to the canon, turn right, walking between dull modern buildings, then turn left into Shoe Lane. Continue past the zebra crossing and soon the white tower of St Andrew's Church will appear on your right. Charles and Mary Lamb were groomsman and bridesmaid at the wedding of the essayist William Hazlitt (1778–1830) here in 1808. Charles (1775–1834) later wrote that he was nearly 'turned out several times during the ceremony. Anything awful makes me laugh.' At the major junction take the second turning to the left, into High Holborn, heading for the large red brick building. This is the former offices of the Prudential Assurance Company and is built on the site of Furnival's Inn (demolished 1897), where Dickens was living when he wrote *The Pickwick Papers*, published in 1836. In *Martin Chuzzlewit* John Westlock has chambers in Furnival's Inn, 'a shady, quiet place, echoing the footsteps of the stragglers who have business there; and rather monotonous and gloomy on summer evenings.'

Turn left into Furnival Street and right into Took's Court, which is easily missed. This is the 'Cook's Court, Curistor Street' where 'Mr Snagsby, Law-stationer, pursues his lawful calling' in *Bleak House*. 'In the shade of Cook's Court, at most times a shady place, Mr Snagsby has dealt in all sorts of blank forms of legal process...' Dickens was both fascinated and appalled by the law. In honour of the area's connection with the great writer, No. 15 is called Dickens House. The 'Door Tennants' sign next door has a distinctly Dickensian ring.

A 'Nook...out of the Clashing Street'

Turn right into Cursitor Street and right into Chancery Lane. In November 1828 the young Dickens entered the employment of Charles Molloy, Solicitor, in now-vanished premises off Chancery Lane. Dickens was a fashionable young man by this time, often wearing a military-style cap at a jaunty angle. It seems that someone thought he was perhaps too pleased with himself because, while he was crossing Chancery Lane one morning, 'a big blackguard fellow knocked my cap off... He said "Halloa, sojer," which I could not stand, so I struck him and he hit me in the eye.'

Turn right into Southampton Buildings and continue through the brick archway at the end to find Staple Inn, one of London's little secrets. This small garden features twice in Dickens. In *Bleak House*, the law stationer Snagsby enjoys walking 'in Staple Inn in the summertime and to observe how countrified the sparrows and the leaves are.' In *The Mystery of Edwin Drood* it is described as, 'one of those nooks, the turning into which out of the clashing street, imparts to the relieved pedestrian the sensation of having put cotton in his ears, and velvet soles on his boots.'

The Tragic Story of Thomas Chatterton, 'Boy Poet'
Follow the passageway out to High Holborn again. Turn right, cross at the lights and opposite the war memorial turn left into Brooke Street. It was in lodgings here, on the night of 24 August 1770, that the 17-year-old poet Thomas Chatterton poisoned himself with arsenic. Chatterton's story is a curious one. The son of Bristol teachers, he was born in 1752 after his father had died and was brought up in poverty by his mother. As a child he was fascinated by antiques and claimed to have discovered some poems by a 15th-century priest called Thomas Rowley. In fact, he had written the poems himself. He sent them to Horace Walpole, who was initially deceived, and made his way to London to seek his fortune by the pen. But he met with little success in the capital, although he did sell an operetta. He was to last only four months in the city. His sad end was described by his biographer, John Davis: 'Pressed hard by indigence and its companions, gloom and despondency, the mind of Chatterton became disordered, and…he swallowed a large dose of poison, which caused his death…'

But his 'Rowley' poems, although forgeries, did have merit, and many of the Romantic poets posthumously adopted him as a kind of hero. 'The marvellous boy [who] perished in his pride', wrote Wordsworth. Henry Wallis's famous painting, 'The Death of Chatterton', in the Tate Gallery, depicting the boy poet on his deathbed, the light from the attic window caressing his face, is one of literature's most enduring images. Picador used it on the cover of *Brief Lives*, its anthology of short biographies of writers and artists whose lives ended prematurely.

Dickens, the Office Mimic
Sadly, Brooke Street is now a rather boring street, but it becomes more attractive at the far end. Here, take the passageway to the left, along the church wall of St Alban the Martyr, which the poet Gerald Manley Hopkins (1844–1889) occasionally attended before he became a Roman Catholic. Turn right onto Gray's Inn Road, cross at the zebra and pass straight through the archway into Gray's Inn Square. This has been a legal centre since the 14th century, and Dickens was once employed as a clerk here. The building in which he worked, although not marked, still exists, and it is odd to stand in front of it. Odd because, if you take away the cars, not much has changed. To find what were the offices of Ellis and Blackmore, where Dickens worked, walk past Gray's Inn Chapel and turn left into South Square. Look for the exit straight ahead of you and No. 1 South Square is just to the left. Note the date above the door: 1759. It was through this entrance that the 15-year-old Charles Dickens walked one May morning in 1827. He was taken on as a clerk/messenger and found the work dull in the extreme. However, according to a fellow clerk, George Lear, he was apparently a 'universal favourite' among the staff. He was a brilliant mimic and could, Lear said, 'imitate, in a manner that I have never heard equalled, the low population of the streets of London in all their varieties, where mere loafers or sellers of fruit, vegetables or anything else.' It was, of course, a skill that would serve him well when he later came to recreate these people on the page.

Leave South Square through the archway next to 'Dickens' chambers', rejoin High Holborn, and turn left to find Chancery Lane Station, where the walk ends.

Wapping to Westferry

Summary: No part of London has changed more in the last 15 years than Docklands. Effectively, a whole new city has been created since the decline of the docks. So this walk – with two notable exceptions – is very much a walk of the imagination. This former 'low-life' area inspired writers as diverse as Oscar Wilde and Celine, and there are also numerous Dickens locations, including a pub he frequented. There is also a 'literary' Tube station.

Start:	Wapping Station (East London Line).
Finish:	Westferry (Docklands Light Railway).
Length:	2.3 kilometres (1½ miles).
Time:	1.5 hours.
Refreshments:	There are surprisingly few cafés, considering how residential the area now is, but a number of good pubs. Both The Prospect of Whitby and The Grapes are essential stops, although the latter is not open at lunch-time at the weekend.

Wapping Station may seem a strange place to start a literary walk, but it isn't if you have former Poet Laureate Sir John Betjeman as your guide. Betjeman (1906–1984) described this vaulted brick station as 'the most interesting and most historic on the whole London Transport system', and he is right. The East London Underground line uses the Thames Tunnel, the world's first underwater tunnel, completed in 1843 by Marc Brunel (1769–1849), father of Isambard Kingdom Brunel (1806–1859). You can see the original splendid arches of Brunel's Thames Tunnel, looking like giant horseshoe magnets, at the river end of the platform. Visiting in 1957, Betjeman noted that if you stand at this end of the platform and look carefully, 'you can see the light from Rotherhithe shining on the rails at the other end as the tunnel dips down under the bed of the river.' This remains true today.

Spicy Smells

Another London enthusiast who liked this station was the writer and artist Geoffrey Fletcher, author of the minor classic *The London Nobody Knows*. He quite rightly extolled people never to use the lift at Wapping, 'for by so doing you lose the opportunity of seeing Brunel's work from the inside.' He wrote in *London's River*, published in 1966: 'Look up the shaft from a point about three-quarters of the way down, admire the great stone cornice and the sweep of the giant cylinder above you, and inhale the spicy smells drifting in from the warehouses, mingling with the damp, mouldy tang of the tunnel.'

This 'giant cylinder' was the access point for the tunnel. There are only 84 steps, so it's worth the effort. Incidentally, the surviving staircases, descending from lower lobby level, have Grade II listed status, as do Brunel's tunnel arches. But don't expect spicy smells. Some of the warehouses are still there – as you will discover – but they are now apartments.

Conrad and Celine's Docklands

Gone are the days when seemingly all the world's produce was stored along the river. Joseph Conrad (1857–1924) described the trading vessels that crowded the river moorings below London Bridge as forming 'one solid mass like an island covered with a forest of gaunt, leafless trees.' Docklands can seem a rather lifeless, sanitised place now, full of estate agents, 'show apartments' and 'sales offices'. Following the river has become difficult: there may be lots of helpful 'Thames Path' signs, but access to the river bank is often blocked by an apartment block or faulty 'buzzer' gate.

What changes the early 20th-century writers who wrote about this area would notice now. In his novel *Guignol's Band*, the French doctor and writer Louis-Ferdinand Celine (1894–1961) leaves Wapping Station and describes the warehouses he sees:

> *Treasure cliffs!...monster ships...phantasmagoric storehouses, citadels of merchandise, mountains of tanned goatskins enough to stink all the way to Kamchatka! Forest of mahogany in thousands of piles, tied up like asparagus, in pyramids, miles of materials!...rugs enough to cover the Moon, the whole world...all the floors in the Universe!... Enough sponges to dry up the Thames! What quantities!... Enough wool to smother Europe beneath heaps of cuddly warmth... Herrings to fill the seas!... Himalayas of powdered sugar... Matches to fry the poles!... Enormous avalanches of pepper, enough to make the Seven floods sneeze!...*

A Bedroom that 'Hung over the Thames'

How quiet and empty, almost anaemic, the streets seem today. Turn right on leaving the station and after a few yards follow the Thames Path sign to the river, passing through the first of many disconcerting access gates. Pause at the river wall. Opposite is Rotherhithe, which here presents a similar sanitised and scrubbed vista of apartment blocks and converted warehouses – very different from the view Betjeman would have seen from his tumbledown river-front house (demolished in the Sixties), with its bedroom that 'hung over the Thames'. He recalled his time here as 'the most restful few months' he ever spent in London. 'I put my bed on the river side of the room and it was delicious to go to sleep to the solacing sounds of water.'

The winking tower of Canary Wharf dominates the skyline, with the protruding yellow spikes of the Millennium Dome to the right. Further to the left is the square spire of Hawksmoor's St Anne's, Limehouse, which has the highest church clock in London and was for years an important landmark for sailors on the river. You can walk along some 50 metres or so – noticing the small white front of The Mayflower pub across the water, outside which *The Mayflower* was moored before setting sail for America – but your way may well be blocked by a gate that refuses to open. Retrace your steps and take the next Thames Path sign down New Crane Stairs. If the tide is out, this will give you access to the foreshore.

151

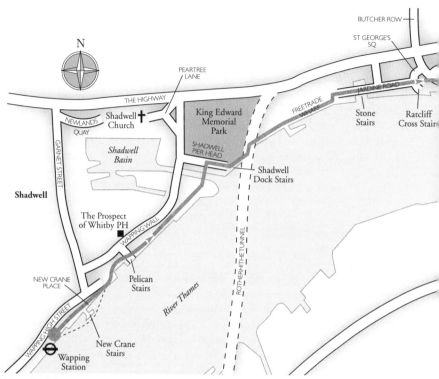

The Devil's Tavern

Return to New Crane Place and follow it round the corner into the cobbled Wapping Wall. This has refurbished warehouse after refurbished warehouse, their winching arms all pointing upwards, mirroring the rising prices of the apartments. At the end of the road you reach The Prospect of Whitby, one of London's oldest and most famous riverside pubs. It doesn't look much from the outside, but it is splendid within. Built in 1520, it was originally known as the Devil's Tavern, after its clientele of smugglers and criminals. It changed its name after *The Prospect*, a collier ship from Whitby, was moored outside. The tavern's seedy reputation appealed to Dickens, who was a customer, as were the artists Whistler (1834–1903) and Turner (1775–1851) and the diarist Samuel Pepys (1633–1703). Inside, it could still almost be a pirates' den – there is lots of dark wood, lovely open fires, old photos of the river, and an ancient foghorn on a shelf. Execution Dock was close by, described by the chronicler John Stow thus: 'The usual place for the hanging of pirates and sea-rovers, at the low-water mark, and there to remain until three tides had overflown them.' The gibbet on the foreshore that is visible through the windows (accessible via Pelican Stairs next to the pub if the tide is out) may not be original, but the newspaper reports framed near the door are. These reveal that in January 1953 a gang led by Robert 'Scarface' Sanders appeared out of the 'swirling riverside fog' and raided the party being hosted by Captain John Cunningham, a Mayfair oysterman, in the Pepys Room upstairs. Sanders was later given a life sentence for shooting a policeman.

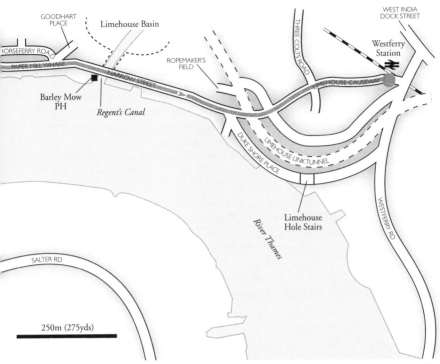

Turn right on leaving the pub and follow the sign to the river again. Walk past more new apartments before cutting in to cross the bridge at Shadwell Basin. Cross over and walk right into the basin, until Shadwell Church appears on your right. It was in this quiet stretch of water that Dickens boarded the Mormon emigrant ship, the *Amazon*, bound for the Great Salt Lake. He found, to his surprise, everything in order for the long voyage.

Literary Shadwell

It takes a real effort to imagine what these dockland streets must have been like in the days before the Second World War. The pubs would be packed with sailors from around the world, the air would be rich with the smell of the river – then much dirtier – and drunken fights would break out between prostitutes. The Ratcliffe Highway, where Dickens visited the sailors' dancing and drinking dens, wasn't far from here. He wrote:

> *Down by the Docks they 'board seamen' at the eating-houses, the public-houses, the slop-shops, the coffee shops, the tally shops…board them, as it were, in the piratical sense, making them bleed terribly and giving no quarter… You may hear the Incomparable Joe Jackson sing the 'Standard of England', with a horn pipe, any night, or any day may see at the wax-work, for a penny and no waiting, him as killed the policeman at Acton and suffered for it.*

Something of the dark, dangerous, foggy atmosphere of the area was captured by the war poet Wilfred Owen (1893–1918) in his poem 'Shadwell Stair': 'I am the ghost of Shadwell Stair./Along the wharves by the water-house,/And through the dripping slaughter-house,/I am the shadow that walks there.'

For the American writer Nathaniel Hawthorne (1804–1864), who visited this part of the river in the 1850s, the shore here was distinctly unappealing: '[It] is lined with the shabbiest, blackest and ugliest buildings that can be imagined, decayed warehouses with blind windows, and wharves that look ruinous...and the muddy tide of the Thames, reflecting nothing and holding a million of unclean secrets within its breast...is just the dismal stream to glide by such a city.'

Cross the bridge and follow the Thames Path sign again along the side of King Edward Memorial Park. Keep going for some way, until another apartment block (inevitably) blocks the path. Duck around it and keep to the riverside road, passing Dutch-looking warehouse conversions. Continue along Narrow Street and after Sun Wharf, turn right for the river again. Walk along until you find the Barley Mow pub, a 1905 conversion that occupies the former Dockmaster's House at Limehouse Marina.

The Lure of Opium

Limehouse has a number of literary associations, many of them thanks to the influx of Chinese sailors who brought with them a reputation for gambling and opium-smoking that attracted a certain kind of writer. The hero of Oscar Wilde's *The Picture of Dorian Gray* comes to Limehouse to smoke opium, and Dickens's last novel, *The Mystery of Edwin Drood*, opens in a dishevelled opium den just off the Ratcliffe Highway. Conan Doyle sent Sherlock Holmes to this part of London, too, and the Birmingham-born novelist Arthur Sarsfield Ward, better known as Sax Rohmer, uses the area as a backdrop for the activities of his sinister, sardonic, criminal genius villain, Fu Manchu, the 'devil doctor'. Fu Manchu's Limehouse den was 'a place of perfumed, slumberous darkness', surrounded by the 'smoke-laden vapours of the Lower Thames'.

The little-known English writer Thomas Burke (1886–1945) left this description of a dockside opium den:

> *Low couches lay around the wall and strange men decorated them: Chinese, Japs, Malays, Lascars, with one or two white girls; and sleek, noiseless attendants swam from couch to couch... On one of the lounges a scorbutic nigger sat with a Jewess from Shadwell. The atmosphere churned. The dirt of years, tobacco of many growings, opium, betel net, and moist flesh allied themselves in one grand assault on the nostrils.*

'A Tavern of Dropsical Appearance'

Cross the giant swing bridge over Limehouse Basin, which connects the Thames to Regent's Canal and the country's inland waterway system. Continue along Narrow Street until you come to a pretty 18th-century terrace, which is home to The Grapes, a pub immortalized by Dickens in *Our Mutual Friend* as The Six Jolly Fellowship Porters: '[It was] a tavern of dropsical appearance...long settled down into a state of hale infirmity. In its whole constitution it had not a straight floor, and hardly a straight line; but it has outlasted, and clearly would outlast, many a better-trimmed building, many a sprucer public-house.' Inside, 'the available space was not much larger than a Hackney-coach; but no one could have wished the bar bigger.' Seen from the river, it was, 'a narrow lopsided wooden jumble of corpulent windows…with a crazy wooden verandah impended over the water.'

Its verandah does still 'impend' over the water and inside it is still charmingly 'dropsical' in appearance. The long, dark, wooden downstairs bar has fascinating old photographs and drawings of the pub and of the river, as well as prints of numerous Dickens characters. In Dickens's day it had red curtains, which he said matched the customers' noses. From the wooden balcony the view is much changed from his day, consisting almost entirely of new apartment blocks. But the wooden jetty posts in front of you could be the originals, and it is lovely to hear the water lapping beneath your feet.

Dickens Sings for his Supper

Dickens knew the area well. His godfather, Christopher Huffam, a sail-maker and ship's chandler, lived close by and Dickens's father, John, would often take his son to visit him. The young boy would sometimes be sat on the table and prevailed upon to sing one of the popular ditties of the day. In *Our Mutual Friend* the Hexam family live in Limehouse Hole in a 'low building [that] had a look of once having been a mill. There was a rotten wart of wood upon its forehead that seemed to indicate where the sails had been, but the whole was very indistinctly seen in the obscurity of the night.'

Opposite the pub is Ropemaker's Fields, a park created by the London Docklands Development Corporation. In *Our Mutual Friend*, Dickens describes how Roger Riderhood 'dwelt deep and dark in Limehouse Hole, among the riggers, and the mast, oar and block makers, and the boatbuilders, and the sail-lofts.'

Duke Shore Wharf lies opposite the park. Pepys visited a porcelain factory here in 1660. The area's limekilns were originally used to provide quicklime for making building mortar, and later to make pottery. Keep to this road, passing pretty Dunbar Wharf and the curiously named Three Colt Street, until you reach Limehouse Causeway. Follow this to Westferry Station (with its platform views of the Millennium Dome), where the walk ends.

Further Information

Opening Times

SOHO

House of St Barnabas-in-Soho 1 Greek Street W1. Tel: 020 7437 1894. *Open* for short guided tours 14.30–16.15 Wed, 11.00–12.30 Thur. For parties for 10 or more, write for an appointment to the Guide, c/o the Warden's Office. Admission free, but donations are appreciated.
Underground: Tottenham Court Road (Central and Northern Lines).

COVENT GARDEN

Rules Restaurant 35 Maiden Lane WC2. Tel: 020 7836 5314. *Open* for lunch and dinner daily.
Underground: Covent Garden (Piccadilly Line).

AROUND THE STRAND AND FLEET STREET

Savoy Chapel Strand Steps Strand WC2. Tel: 020 7836 7221. *Open* 11.30–15.30 Tues–Fri. *Closed* Aug–Sept.
Underground: Charing Cross (Bakerloo, Northern and Jubilee Lines); Embankment (Bakerloo and Northern Lines).
Roman Bath 5 Strand Lane WC2. Tel: 020 7798 2063. *Open* only by prior request.
Underground: Temple (District and Circle Lines).
Prince Henry's Room 17 Fleet Street EC4. Tel: 020 7936 2710. *Open* 11.00–14.00 Mon–Sat. *Closed* public holidays.

Underground: Temple (District and Circle Lines); Chancery Lane (Central Line).
St Bride's Fleet Street EC4. Tel: 020 7353 1301. *Open* 8.00–17.00 Mon–Fri (last admission 16.45); 09.00–16.30 Sat; 9.30–12.30pm, 17.30–19.30 Sun. *Closed* public holidays.

PICCADILLY, MAYFAIR AND ST JAMES'S

St James's Church 197 Piccadilly W1 Tel: 020 7734 4511 *Open* 08.00–19.00 daily. *Underground*: Piccadilly (Bakerloo and Piccadilly Lines).

CHELSEA

Chelsea Old Church Cheyne Walk SW3. Tel: 020 77352 7978. *Open* 10.00–13.00, 14.00–17.00 Mon–Sat; 13.30–18.00 Sun.
Underground: Sloane Square (District and Circle Lines); South Kensington (District, Circle and Piccadilly Lines).
Carlyle's House 24 Cheyne Row SW3. Tel: 020 7352 7087. *Open* Apr–Oct, 11.00–17.00 Wed–Sun, public holidays (last admission: 16.30). *Closed* Good Friday. Admission charge.
Underground: Sloane Square (District and Circle Lines); South Kensington (District, Circle and Piccadilly Lines).
Royal Hospital Royal Hospital Road SW3. Tel: 020 7730 0161. *Open* 08.30–12.30, 14.30–16.30 Mon–Sat; 14.00–16.00 Sun. *Closed* public holidays.
Underground: Sloane Square (District and Circle Lines).

CHARING CROSS ROAD AND FITZROVIA

The Ivy 1 West Street WC2 Tel: 020 7836 4751. *Open* Lunch and Dinner daily. *Underground*: Leicester Square (Northern and Piccadilly Lines).

Fitzroy Tavern 16 Charlotte Street W1 Tel: 020 7580 3714. *Open* 11.00–23.00 Mon–Sat; Midday–22.30 Sun. *Underground*: Goode Street (Northern Line).

MARYLEBONE

St Marylebone Parish Church Marylebone Road NW1. Tel: 020 7935 7315. *Open* 12.30–13.30, Mon–Fri, Sun mornings.
Underground: Regent's Park (Bakerloo Line).

Sherlock Holmes Museum 221b Baker Street NW1. Tel: 020 7935 8866. *Open* 09.30–18.00 daily. *Closed* Christmas Day. Admission charge.
Underground: Baker Street (Bakerloo, Hammersmith & City, Circle and Metropolitan Lines).

BLOOMSBURY (1): TOTTENHAM COURT ROAD TO HOLBORN

Dickens House Museum 48 Doughty Street WC1. Tel: 020 7405 2127. *Open* 10.00–17.00 Mon–Sat (last admission 16.30). *Closed* some public holidays. Admission charge.
Underground: Baker Street (Bakerloo, Hammersmith & City, Circle and Metropolitan Lines).

BLOOMSBURY (2): RUSSELL SQUARE TO WARREN STREET

British Museum Great Russell Street WC1. Tel 020 7636 1555. *Open* 10.00–17.00 Mon–Sat; 12.00–18.00 Sun (last admission 15 mins before closing). *Closed* 24–26 Dec, 1 Jan, Good Friday, 8 May.

Underground: Tottenham Court Road (Central and Northern Lines).

THE CITY (1): ST PAUL'S TO THE TOWER

St Paul's Cathedral Ludgate Hill EC4. Tel: 020 7236 4128. *Open* 09.30–15.45 Mon–Sat; galleries 09.30–16.15; crypt and ambulatory 08.45–16.15. *Closed* for sightseeing on Sun. Admission charge.
Underground: St Paul's (Central Line); Mansion House (District and Circle Lines).

Guildhall Gresham Street EC2. Tel: 020 77606 3030. *Open* 10.00–17.00 Mon–Sun, May–Sept; 10.00–17.00 Mon–Sat. *Closed* 25–26 Dec, 1 Jan. The Great Hall and crypt are working buildings so may occasionally be closed to the public (call the keeper's office on the above number, ext 1460, to check). Conducted tours may also be arranged on this number.
Underground: St Paul's (Central Line).

St Magnus the Martyr Lower Thames Street EC3. Tel: 020 7626 4481. *Open* 10.00–16.00 Tues–Fri; 10.15–14.00 Sun.
Underground: Monument (DLR, District and Circle, Northern and Central Lines).

THE CITY (2): MANSION HOUSE TO OLD STREET

St Botolph, Aldersgate Aldersgate Street EC1. Tel: 020 7606 0684. *Open* 11.00–15.00 Wed–Fri.
Underground: St Paul's (Central Line).

St Bartholomew-the-Great West Smithfield Street. Tel: 020 7606 5171. *Open* 08.30–17.00 (16.00 in winter) Mon–Fri; 10.30–13.30 Sat; 14.00–18.00 Sun.
Underground: Barbican (Circle, Hammersmith & City and Metropolitan Lines).

St Giles without Cripplegate Fore Street EC2. Tel: 020 7606 3630. *Open*

09.15–17.15 Mon–Fri; 9.00–13.00 Sat. *Underground*: Barbican (Circle, Hammersmith & City and Metropolitan Lines); Moorgate (Northern, Metropolitan, Circle, Hammersmith & City Lines).
Bunhill Fields City Road EC1. Tel: 0207 8472 3584. *Open* Oct–Mar 07.30–16.00 Mon–Fri, Sat–Sun and Bank Holidays 09.30–16.00; April–Sept, Mon–Fri 07.30–19.00, Sat, Sun and Bank Holidays 09.30–16.00).

KENSINGTON
Kensington Roof Gardens 99 Kensington High Street (entrance in Derry Street). Tel: 020 7937 7997. *Open* daily 09.00–17.00 (unless booked for a function – always telephone).
Underground: Kensington High Street (District and Circle Lines).

PUTNEY TO WIMBLEDON
Wimbledon Windmill Museum Windmill Road SW19. Tel: 020 8947 2825. *Open* 14.00–17.00 Sat–Sun and Bank Holidays. April–October.
Underground and British Rail: Wimbledon (District Line).
Southside House Southside SW19. Tel: 020 8946 7643. *Open* Tues, Thurs, Sat 14.00, 15.00, 16.00, and 17.00, 1 Dec–Midsummer's Day. Admission charge.
Underground and British Rail: Wimbledon (District Line).

WESTMINSTER TO ST JAMES'S
Westminster Abbey Broad Sanctuary SW1. Tel: 020 7222 5152. Cloisters open 08.00–18.00 daily. Royal Chapels, Poet's Corner, Choir, Statemen's Aisle, Nave open 09.00–15.45 Mon–Fri, 09.00–13.45 Sat. Chapter House, Pyx Chamber and Museum open 10.30–16.00 daily. Admission charge.
Underground: Westminster (District, Circle and Jubilee Lines).
St Margaret's Church Parliament Square SW1. Tel: 020 7222 5152. *Open* 09.30–15.45 Mon–Fri; 09.30–13.45 Sat; 14.00–17.00 Sun.
Underground: Westminster (District, Circle and Jubilee Lines).

RICHMOND
Pembroke Lodge Cafeteria Richmond Park. *Open* April–Oct: Mon–Fri 10.00–17.30; Sat–Sun 10.00–19.00.
Underground and British Rail: Richmond (District Line).

ISLINGTON
New River Walk Entrance on Alwyne Road N1. *Open* daily during daylight hours.
Underground: Highbury & Islington (Victoria Line).

HIGHGATE
St Michael's Church South Grove N6. Tel: 020 8340 7279. *Open* Sat 10.00–12.00.
Underground: Highgate (Northern Line), Archway (Northern Line).
Highgate Cemetery Swains Lane N6. Tel: 020 8340 1834. *Open*: Eastern Cemetery: Apr–Oct: Mon–Fri 10.00–17.00, Sat and Sun 11.00–17.00; Nov–Mar: Mon–Fri 10.00–16.00, Sat and Sun 11.00–16.00. Western Cemetery: guided tours only, Apr–Oct: Mon–Fri: 12.00,

14.00 and 16.00. Sat and Sun on the hour every hour 11.00–16.00; Nov–Mar: same as for Apr–Oct except last tour is at 15.00; Dec–Feb: Sat and Sun on the hour every hour 11.00–15.00. Both cemeteries closed during funerals. Admission charge.
Underground: Archway (Northern Line).

HAMPSTEAD (1): NORTH

Wells Tavern 30 Well Walk NW3 1BX. Tel: 020 7794 2806 11.00–23.00 Mon–Sat, Midday–22.30 Sun.
Underground: Hampstead (Northern Line)
The Spaniard's Inn Spaniard's Road NW3. Tel: 020 8731 6571 11.00–23.00 Mon–Sat Midday–22.30 Sun.
Underground: Hampstead (Northern Line).
Jack Straw's Castle North End Way NW3. Tel: 020 7435 8885 11.00–23.00 Mon–Sat, Midday–22.30 Sun.
Underground: Hampstead (Northern Line).

HAMPSTEAD (2): SOUTH

Burgh House and Hampstead Museum New End Square NW3. Tel: 020 7431 2516. *Open* Wed–Sun 11.00–17.30. *Closed* Good Friday and Easter Monday and for two weeks at Christmas.
Keats House Keats Grove NW3. Tel: 020 7435 2062. *Open* Mon–Fri 14.00–18.00 (13.00–17.00 Nov–Mar), Sat: 10.00–13.00 and 14.00–17.00. Sun 14.00–17.00. NB. Under renovation at time of going to press so ring to check times.
Underground: Hampstead or Belsize Park (both Northern Line)

SOUTHWARK

Globe Theatre New Globe Walk SE1. Tel: 020 7902 1500. *Open*: mid–May–Sept 09.15–12.15; Oct–mid–May 10.00–17.00 daily. Performances: mid–May to Sept. Guided tours. Admission charge.
Underground: London Bridge (Northern and Jubilee Lines); Mansion House (District and Circle Lines); Southwark (Jubilee Line).
Southwark Cathedral Montague Close SE1. Tel: 020 7407 2939. *Open* 09.00–18.00 daily.
Underground: London Bridge (Jubilee and Northern Lines).
Clink Prison Museum 1 Clink Street SE1. Tel: 020 7378 1558. *Open* 10.00–18.00 daily. *Closed* 25 Dec. Admission charge.
Underground: London Bridge (Northern Line); Southwark (Jubilee Line).
Church of St George the Martyr There are services at 10.30 and midday on Sundays and on Wednesdays at 12.45 and Fridays at 21.00.

BLACKHEATH TO GREENWICH?

Trafalgar Tavern Park Row SE10. Tel: 020 8858 2437. *Open* 11.00–23.00 Mon–Sat. Midday–22.30 Sun.
Greenwich Station (overground trains from Charing Cross and London Bridge).

CLAPHAM JUNCTION TO WANDSWORTH VILLAGE

Beckett's Bookshop 6 Bellevue Road Wandsworth Common SW17 7EG. Tel: 020 86872 4413. *Open* 9.30–17.30 Mon–Sat.
Wandsworth Station (overground trains from Victoria).

HOBORN TO CHANCERY LANE
Sir John Soane's Museum 13 Lincoln's Inn Fields WC2. Tel: 020 7430 0175. *Open* 10.00–17.00 Tues–Sat. *Closed* Sunday and Monday, 24–6 Dec, 1 Jan, Easter and public holidays.
Underground: Holborn (Central and Piccadilly Lines).
Johnson's House 17 Gough Square EC4. Tel: 020 7353 3745. *Open* Apr–Sep: 11.00–17.30 Mon–Sat; Oct–Mar: 11.00–17.00 Mon–Sat. *Closed* 24–26 Dec, 1 Jan, Good Friday, public holidays. Admission charge.
Underground: Blackfriars (District and Circle Lines), Chancery Lane (Central Line), Temple (District and Circle Lines).

WAPPING TO WESTFERRY
Prospect of Whitby 57 Wapping Wall E1. Tel: 020 7481 1095. *Open* 11.30–15.00 and 17.30–23.00 Mon–Fri; 11.30–23.00 Sat; Midday–22.30 Sun.
Underground: Wapping (East London Line).
The Grapes 56 Narrow Street E14. Tel: 020 7987 4396 Midday–15.00 and 17.30–23.00 Mon–Fri, 19.00–23.00 Sat, Midday–15.00 and 19.00–22.30 Sun.
Westferry Station (DLR)

Authors and their Works

The following is not a comprehensive list of each author's works; only the titles mentioned in this book are listed here.

Ackerley, J. R. *My Dog Tulip, We Think the World of You, My Father and Myself*

Ackroyd, Peter *Dan Leno and the Limehouse Golem*

Amis, Kingsley *The Old Devils*

Baden-Powell, Lord Robert *Scouting for Boys*

Bainbridge, Beryl *Master Georgie*

Banks, Iain *The Business*

Barnes, Julian *England, England*

Barrie, J. M. *Peter Pan*

Beardsley, Aubrey *Yellow Book*

Berger, John *G*

Betjeman, John *Summoned by Bells*

Boswell, James *Life of Samuel Johnson*

Bowen, Elizabeth *The Heat of the Day*

Boyd, William *A Good Man in Africa; An Ice Cream War*

Bridges, Robert *London Snow*

Brighouse, Alfred *Hobson's Choice*

Burgess, Anthony *Little Wilson and Big God*

Burton, Richard *Kama Sutra;* (transl.) *Arabian Nights*

Byatt, A. S. *Possession*

Byron, Lord (George) *Childe Harold; Don Juan*

Celine, Louis-Ferdinand *Guignol's Band*

Chaucer, Geoffrey *The Canterbury Tales*

Chesterton, G. K. *Napoleon of Notting Hill*

Collins, Wilkie *The Woman in White* & Dickens, Charles *No Thoroughfare*

Conrad, Joseph *Almayer's Folly*

Dann, Colin *Animals of Farthing Wood*

Davies, W. H. *An Old House in London; The Autobiography of a Supertramp*

de Bernières, Louis *Captain Corelli's Mandolin*

de Quincey, Thomas *Confessions of an English Opium Eater*

Dickens, Charles *A Christmas Carol; A Tale of Two Cities; Bleak House; David Copperfield; Household Words; Little Dorrit; Martin Chuzzlewit; Nicholas Nickleby; Oliver Twist; Our Mutual Friend; Sketches by Boz; The Chimes; The Mystery of Edwin Drood; The Old Curiosity Shop; The Pickwick Papers*

Dickens, Charles & Collins, Wilkie *No Thoroughfare*

Doyle, Roddy *Paddy Clarke Ha Ha Ha*

Doyle, Sir Arthur Conan *The Hound of the Baskervilles*

du Maurier, George *Trilby*

Eidson, Thomas *St Agnes' Stand*

Eliot, George *The Mill on the Floss*

Eliot, T. S. *The Waste Land*

Empson, William *Seven Types of Ambiguity*

Farson, Daniel *Soho in theFifties*

Fielding, Henry *Tom Jones*

Fleming, Ian *Casino Royale*

Fletcher, Geoffrey *London's River; The London Nobody Knows*

Forster, E. M. *Howards End*

Fry, Stephen *The Liar*

Galsworthy, John *The Forsyte Saga*

Gibbon, Edward *The Decline and Fall of the Roman Empire*

Gibbons, Stella *Cold Comfort Farm*
Gissing, George *The Nether World*
Gosse, Edmund *Father and Son*
Grahame, Kenneth *The Wind in the Willows*
Graves, Robert *Goodbye to All That*
Gray, Thomas *Elegy Written in a Country Churchyard*
Greene, Graham *Brighton Rock*
Greenwood, Walter *Love on the Dole*
Hardy, Thomas *Far from the Madding Crowd; The Dynasts; The Return of the Native*
Hawthorne, Nathaniel *The Scarlet Letter*
Hijuelos, Oscar *The Mambo Kings Play Songs of Love*
Holmes, Richard *Coleridge: Darker Reflections*
Hope, Anthony *The Prisoner of Zenda*
Hughes, Richard *A High Wind in Jamaica*
Hughes, Ted *Birthday Letters*
Hughes, Thomas *Tom Brown's Schooldays*
Ibsen, Henrik *Hedda Gabler*
Jackson, Mick *The Underground Man*
Jerome, Jerome K. *Three Men in a Boat*
Johnson, Samuel *A Dictionary of the English Language*
Jonson, Ben *Bartholomew Fair*
Keats, John *Ode on a Grecian Urn; Ode to a Nightingale; Sleep and Poetry*
Kennedy, Douglas *Dead Heart; The Big Picture; The Job*
King, Stephen *Misery*
Lawrence, D. H. *Kangaroo*
Lawren ce, T. E. *Seven Pillars of Wisdom*
le Carré, John *Smiley's People*
Lejeune, Anthony *The Gentlemen's Clubs of London*
Lewis, Wyndham & Pound, Ezra *Blast*
Lively, Penelope *Moon Tiger*
Lowry, Malcolm *Under the Volcano*
MacInnes, Colin *City of Spades; Absolute Beginners*

Mackenzie, Compton *Whisky Galore*
Mansfield, Katherine *Journal*
Marber, Patrick *Closer*
McCann, Colum *This Side of Brightness*
McEwan, Ian *Amsterdam*
McInerney, Jay *Bright Lights, Big City; Model Behaviour*
Milne, A. A. *Winnie-the-Pooh*
Milton, John *Paradise Lost; Paradise Regained*
Mitford, Mary Russell *Our Life: Sketches of Rural Life*
Moravia, Alberto *The Conformist*
Mortimer, John *Clinging to the Wreckage*
Mortimer, John (ed.) *Oxford Book of Villains*
Munthe, Axel *The Story of St Michele*
Newby, Eric *Learning the Ropes; The Last Grain Race*
Norrie, Ian *Mumby's Publishing and Bookselling in the Twentieth Century*
Ondaatje, Michael *The English Patient*
Orton, Joe *Entertaining Mr Sloane; Loot*
Orwell, George *A Clergyman's Daughter; Nineteen Eighty-four; The Road to Wigan Pier*
Osborne, John *The Entertainer; Look Back in Anger*
Paine, Tom *The Rights of Man*
Pevsner, Nikolaus *The Buildings of England*
Picador (publisher) *Brief Lives*
Plath, Sylvia *The Colossus*
Polidori, John William *The Vampyre*
Pound, Ezra & Lewis, Wyndham *Blast*
Powell, Anthony *A Dance to the Music of Time*
Priestley, J. B. *The Good Companions*
Racine, Jean *Phedre* (adapted by Ted Hughes)
Radclyffe-Hall, Marguerite *The Well of Loneliness*
Richardson, Samuel *Clarissa; Pamela*
Rushdie, Salman *Shame; The Satanic Verses*

Russell, Willie *Shirley Valentine*
Sackville-West, Vita *All Passion Spent*
Scott, Paul *Staying On*
Shakespeare, William *Henry VIII*
Shaw, George Bernard *Pygmalion*
Shelley, Mary *Frankenstein*
Sheridan, Richard *The Rivals; The School for Scandal*
Simpson, Joe *Touching the Void*
Smart, Elizabeth *By Grand Central Station*
Smollett, Tobias *Humphrey Clinker*
Sobel, Dava *Longitude*
Spark, Muriel *The Prime of Miss Jean Brodie*
Sterne, Laurence *Tristram Shandy*
Stoker, Bram *Dracula*
Stopes, Marie *Married Love*
Stoppard, Tom *Shakespeare in Love*
Stow, John *Survey of London*
Strachey, Lytton *Eminent Victorians*
Swift, Jonathan *Gulliver's Travels*
Thackeray, William *Sketches and Travels in London*
Theroux, Paul *The Family Arsenal*

Thomas, Dylan *18 Poems; Under Milk Wood*
Thompson, Francis *Hound of Heaven*
Tolstoy, Leo *War and Peace*
Travers, P. L. *Mary Poppins*
Walpole, Horace *Castle of Otranto*
Waterhouse, Keith *Billy Liar; Jeffrey Bernard is Unwell*
Waugh, Evelyn *Put out More Flags; Scoop*
Wells, H. G. *The Time Machine; The War of the Worlds*
White, T. H. *The Goshawk; The Once and Future King*
Wilde, Oscar *The Importance of Being Earnest; The Picture of Dorian Gray*
Williams, Nigel *East of Wimbledon; They Came from SW19; The Wimbledon Poisoner*
Wilson, Colin *The Outsider*
Wolfe, Thomas *Look Homeward Angel*
Wollstonecraft, Mary *A Vindication of the Rights of Woman*
Woolf, Virginia *Kew Gardens* & Woolf, Leonard *Two Stories*

Bibliography

Ackroyd, Peter, *Dickens*, Sinclair-Stevenson, 1990

Ackroyd, Peter, *TS Eliot*, Penguin, 1993

Adams, Anna (compiler), *Thames: An Anthology of River Poems*, Enitharmon, 1999

Alset, Clive, *The Story of Greenwich*, Fourth Estate, 1999

Alvarez, A., *The Savage God: A Study of Suicide*, Weidenfeld & Nicolson, 1974

Bailey, Paul, *The Oxford Book of London*, Oxford University Press, 1995

Bebbington, Gillian, *Street Names of London*, Batsford, 1972

Birkin, Andrew, *J.M. Barrie & The Lost Boys*, Constable, 1979

Bohm, Dorothy and Norrie, Ian, *Hampstead: London Hill Town*, Wildwood House, 1981

Booker 30, *Booker PLC*, 1998

Burgess, Anthony, *Little Wilson and Big God: Being the First Part of the Confessions of Anthony Burgess*, Heineman, 1987

Clark, Roger George, *Chelsea Today*, Robert Hale, 1991

Cook, Judith, *J.B. Priestly*, Bloomsbury, 1997

Crick, Bernard, *George Orwell: A Life*, Penguin, 1992

Davies, Andrew, *Literary London*, Macmillan, 1988

Delaney, Frank, *Betjeman Country*, Hodder and Stoughton/John Murray, 1983

Denton, Pennie (Ed), *Betjeman's London*, John Murray, 1988

Eagle, Dorothy and Carnell, Hilary (Eds), *The Oxford Literary Guide to the British Isles*, Oxford University Press, 1977

Eisler, Benita, *Byron*, Hamish Hamilton, 1999

Ellmann, Richard, *Oscar Wilde*, Penguin, 1988

Farson, Daniel, *Never a Normal Man: An Autobiography*, HarperCollins, 1996

Farson, Daniel, *Soho in the Fifties*, Pimlico, 1993

Fifty Penguin Years, Penguin, 1985

Fletcher, Geoffrey, *London's River*, Hutchinson, 1966

Gerhold, Dorian, *Wandsworth Past*, Historical Publications, 1988

Hall, Martin, *The Blue Plaque Guide to London Homes*, Queen Ann Press, 1976

Hastings, Selina, *Evelyn Waugh: A Biography*, Sinclair Stevenson, 1994

The Highgate Literary and Scientific Institution 1839–1990, Heart of a Village, Historical Publications, 1991

Holland, Vyvyan, *Oscar Wilde*, Thames & Hudson, 1988

Holmes, Richard, *Coleridge, Darker Reflections*, HarperCollins, 1998

Holroyd, Michael, *Bernard Shaw*, Vintage, 1998

Hornak, Angelo, *London From the Thames*, Little Brown, 1999

Jacobs, Eric, *Kingsley Amis: A Biography*, Hodder, 1995

King, James, *Virginia Woolf*, Penguin, 1995

Kitchen, Paddy, *Poets' London*, Longman, 1980

Latham, R.C. & Matthews, W. (Eds), *The Diary of Samuel Pepys, Volume X Companion*, HarperCollins, 1995

Latham, Robert, *The Shorter Pepys*, HarperCollins, 1998

Leboff, David, *London Underground Stations*, Ian Allan, 1994

Levi, Peter, *Eden Renewed, The Public and Private Life of John Milton*, Macmillan, 1996

Lynch, Tony, *Dickens's England*, Batsford, 1986

Markus, Julia, *Dared and Done: The Marriage of Elizabeth Barrett and Robert Browning*, Bloomsbury, 1995

Meade, Dorothy and Wolff, Tatiana (compilers), *Lines on the Underground*, Cassell, 1994

Motion, Andrew, *Keats*, Faber, 1997

Neville, Richard, *Hippie Hippie Shake*, Bloomsbury, 1995

Norrie, Ian, *Mumby's Bookselling and Publishing in the Twentieth Century*, Bell & Hyman, 1984

Plath, Sylvia, *Letters Home*, Faber, 1976

Richardson, John, *Highgate Past*, Historical Publications, 1989

Ricketts, Harry, *The Unforgiving Minute: A Life of Rudyard Kipling*, Chatto & Windus, 1999

Sherry, Norman, *The Life of Graham Greene Volume 1: 1904–1939*, Penguin, 1990

Sherry, Norman, *The Life of Graham Greene Volume 2: 1939–1955*, Jonathan Cape, 1994

Southwark Heritage Association, *Southwark*, 1996

Stevenson, Anne, *Bitter Fame: A Life of Sylvia Plath*, Penguin, 1990

Summers, Judith, *Soho*, Bloomsbury, 1989

Tames, Richard, *Soho Past*, Historical Publications, 1994

Vansittart, Peter, *A Literary Companion, London*, John Murray 1992

Wagner Martin, Linda, *Sylvia Plath: A Biography*, Chatto & Windus, 1988

Weinreb, Ben and Hibbert, Christopher (Eds), *The London Encyclopaedia*, Papermac, 1987

Wientraub, Stanley, *The London Yankees*, W.H. Allen, 1979

Wright, Patrick, *The River, The Thames in Our Time*, BBC, 1999

Young, Geoffrey, *Walking London's Parks and Gardens*, New Holland, 1995

Indexes

Acknowledgements

Firstly, thanks to London's libraries, without whom this book could not have been written. I owe them a huge debt of gratitude (made up of some rather hefty fines, it has to be said). Secondly, I would like to thank *Publishing News* and *The Bookseller* for the use of their archives. Colin Randall at the latter was particularly helpful. Thanks also to fellow 'big London' enthusiast Louis Barfe, for his Internet skills, to Liz Thomson, for passing on an original letter, to Brigitte Bunnell of Hatchard's, and to my parents, in whose house some of this was written. But most important of all, thanks to Ann for a lot of patience.

SOURCES

J.M. Barrie and the Lost Boys by Andrew Birkin, reproduced by permission of the publishers, Constable Publishers Ltd. *Betjeman's London* edited by Pennie Denton, published by John Murray (Publishers) Ltd. *Chelsea Today* by Roger George Clark, published by Robert Hale. *Clinging to the Wreckage* by John Mortimer (Copyright © Advanpress 1982) reproduced by permission of PFD on behalf of John Mortimer. *Goodbye to All That* by Robert Graves reproduced by permission of the publisher, Carcanet Press Ltd. *Monody on the Death of Aldersgate Station* by John Betjeman, published by John Murray (Publishers) Ltd. *PG Wodehouse: The Authorised Biography* by Frances Donaldson, reproduced by permission of the publisher, Weidenfeld and Nicolson (UK and Commonwealth), and by permission of A.P. Watt on behalf of the Trustees of the Wodehouse Estate No. 3. *J.B. Priestly* by Judith Cook published by Bloomsbury 1997. *J.B. Priestly*, by Vincent Brome, published by Hamish Hamilton, reproduced by permission of Vincent Brome. *The Prince of Our Disorder: The Life of T. E. Lawrence* by John E. Mack, reproduced by permission of the publishers, Weidenfeld and Nicolson (UK) and Harvard University Press (US). *The Road to Wigan Pier* by George Orwell (Copyright © George Orwell 1937) reproduced by permission of A.M. Heath & Co. Ltd on behalf of William Hamilton as the Literary Executor of the Estate of the Late Sonia Brownell Orwell and Secker & Warburg Ltd (UK) and Harcourt Brace (US). *The Selected Letters of S.J. Perelman* by S.J. Perelman published by Perelman and Crowther, Viking; reprinted by permission of the Peters Fraser & Dunlop Group Ltd. *Summoned by Bells* by John Betjeman published by John Murray (Publishers) Ltd. Oscar Wilde, at Clapham Junction, and W. D. Morrison (quoted in *Oscar Wilde*, by Richard Ellmann, published by Penguin, 1988), reproduced by permission of the Controller of Her Majesty's Stationery Office.